WAVES OF DEMOCRACY

WAVES OF DEMOCRACY
SOCIAL MOVEMENTS AND POLITICAL CHANGE

SECOND EDITION

JOHN MARKOFF

Paradigm Publishers
Boulder • London

Copyright © 2015 Paradigm Publishers

Published in the United States by Paradigm Publishers, 5589 Arapahoe Avenue, Boulder, CO 80303 USA.

Paradigm Publishers is the trade name of Birkenkamp & Company, LLC, Dean Birkenkamp, President and Publisher.

Library of Congress Cataloging-in-Publication Data

Markoff, John, 1942–
   Waves of democracy : social movements and political change / John Markoff, University of Pittsburgh. — Second edition.
      pages cm
   Includes bibliographical references and index.
   ISBN 978-1-61205-292-2 (hardcover : alk. paper)
   1. Democracy—History.   2. Social movements—History.   I. Title.
JC421.M347 2014
321.809—dc23

                                                                    2014018907

Printed and bound in the United States of America on acid-free paper that meets the standards of the American National Standard for Permanence of Paper for Printed Library Materials.

19 18 17 16 15   1 2 3 4 5

For Małgosia, my sun, for what's most important.

Contents

PREFACE

Since the 1990s, more people than ever before in human history have been living in countries whose governments claim to be democracies. Yet the very idea of democracy faces severe challenges. Vast disparities in wealth and power challenge the notion of popular control over the activities of governments. New centers of power have developed alongside the world's nation-states. Claims that a place is "our" country and not "theirs" continue to form the basis for excluding many from political participation.

For more than two centuries, democracy has been the subject of debate and struggle. Powerholders have sometimes claimed that they ruled on behalf of the people, and that claim has sometimes been challenged by social movements. At various moments in the world history of democratization, particular movements have played special roles, and this book will call attention to some: the movement for the abolition of slavery, the labor movement, the movement for women's rights. At other moments, reforming powerholders in one country have attempted to emulate the practices of other countries. Such processes have continually redefined what democracy means.

Certain dramatic moments over these centuries stand out: moments when talk of democracy is in the air, governments seek reform, and social movements demand democracy. When such is the case in many countries simultaneously, we have a democratic wave. Our own historical moment follows the crest of one such wave—the greatest wave to date, in fact.

Yet the future of democracy is hardly secure. To understand why it is not secure and the possible ways we might fashion our future, we need to look back over the entire modern history of democracy. Democracy carries within it not only the conflicts of the present moment but also the legacy of past waves of democratization, which have shaped what we mean by democracy. On the way to the present, we need to take a look at the 1790s, at nineteenth-century struggles, at the teens and twenties of the twentieth century, and at the reconstruction of the world after World War II. And we need to take a look at many places. Democracy was not made just in the United States but also in England, France, Poland, New Zealand, Australia, Belgium, Holland, and many other locations. Democratic movements with varied outcomes have been important in the recent experience of Latin America, Asia, and Africa. The elements of democracy that were created in these places in the past were passed on to the future in which we now live, as illustrated by the set of maps in this book's appendix. If people try to write the history of democracy two hundred years from now, what will they say we passed on to them?

There is a vast and impressive literature dealing with democracy. More than two thousand years ago, ancient philosophers, observing how differently the city-states of Greece governed themselves, distinguished three basic patterns of government. One was called "rule by many people" and one of its forms was "democracy," literally "rule by the people." (The other basic patterns were "rule by a few" and "rule by a single person.") The eminent thinker Aristotle was very interested in the virtues and vices of different kinds of government and the ways that different basic patterns might be combined. Good government served the common interest; bad government ruled abusively. In fact, it was the bad version of "rule by many people" that Aristotle labeled "democracy," contributing to a long tradition of seeing that term in a very negative light. Other ancient thinkers, however, used the same word for the good version, helping us see that democracy has always been controversial.

In later centuries, educated Europeans tended to learn about these ideas. Thus, the word democracy continued to be well known in theoretical discussions of political systems. Yet until the late eighteenth century, the word was rarely applied to existing governments. A revolutionary upheaval at the end of the eighteenth century, however, not only brought the word democracy to the fore but also raised difficult questions. Was it inevitable that the few who ruled virtually everywhere were going to have to share power with the many who did not? And if some sort of democracy was coming, what would it be like? Would it be workable?

The brilliant French observer Alexis de Tocqueville visited the United States in the early nineteenth century. His book *Democracy in America* argued

that the new democracy functioned much more smoothly in this new country
than in his homeland, where the memory of the violence and turmoil of the
French Revolution of 1789 was still very much alive. The revolution in his
own country, as Tocqueville was painfully aware, had unleashed forces calling for democracy but had terminated with the establishment of an emperor:
Napoleon Bonaparte. Tocqueville's attempt to understand democracy in the
United States was only the first of many investigations into the conditions
that favor democratic rule and the conditions that allow democratic rule to
degenerate into new forms of tyranny.

More recent scholars have continued to elaborate on the frameworks of
their illustrious predecessors. A great deal of effort has gone into the Aris-
totelian task of classifying political systems and identifying the basic ways in
which political systems can vary. Probably the most important of these efforts
is Juan Linz's many discussions of what he calls "totalitarian," "authoritarian," and "democratic" regimes. But efforts to classify real, existing political
systems always generate considerable disagreement. Is Venezuela a democracy
today, to take an example my students argue about? Was the United States a
democracy in 1800? in 1830? in 1880? in 1950? In the twenty-first century
is it becoming more—or less—democratic? Scholars differ a good deal when
they start discussing such particulars.

Recent scholars have continued to grapple with the Tocquevillean questions of why some countries are democracies and why democracy sometimes
does (but sometimes does not) work out. Sociologists and political scientists
have tried to tackle these issues in many different ways. In the 1950s and
1960s, scholars paid much attention to the general level of economic development, and many were persuaded that a modern and prosperous economy
promotes democratic politics. Seymour Martin Lipset is probably the major
writer in this tradition. At about the same time, some scholars were arguing that democracy flourishes best if certain values are part of the national
culture. Tolerance of dissent, for instance, was often held to be an essential
background for democratic politics. Some researchers in this tradition, for
example, believed that Nazism had deep roots in an authoritarian German
culture; the failure of democracy in Germany was therefore in part due to
an "authoritarian personality." Writers dealing with such questions often addressed them comparatively. They might compare the political systems in rich
and poor countries, for example, or compare the political systems in countries
with different cultures.

A different approach was taken by some of the scholars who concentrated on analyzing why democratic regimes seemed viable in some places and short-lived in others. These scholars looked at democratic regimes that had collapsed and attempted to explain how such breakdowns had occurred. Rather than focus on broad economic or cultural patterns, these scholars looked at political crises, sometimes in minute detail. A great deal of research, for example, has been devoted to trying to explain how the Nazis came to power in the 1930s in a country with a democratic constitution. Much has also been written about why Latin American governments that claimed to be democratic were so often overthrown by their own armed forces. A good deal of writing in this vein was sparked by the overthrow of governments claiming to be democracies in the 1960s and into the 1970s.

More recently, as many more countries than ever before have been making democratic claims—sometimes for the first time—scholars have been trying to understand how democratic systems get started. One widely discussed notion is that elites, people of wealth and power, sometimes strike a deal among themselves to resolve their disagreements through electoral systems because they fear the consequences of not doing so. The threat of civil war, for example, may make the powerful fear that they will all be ruined if they don't come to some understanding to limit conflict. Some scholars have stressed the importance of an effective "civil society," meaning that associations of people are able to engage in vigorous public debate. Others have argued that successful economic growth lays a framework that more easily supports democratic politics. And others yet again have argued that there are emerging global norms that honor democratic government and delegitimate other kinds of political arrangements.

Still other scholars have pointed to the importance of democratic movements and have tried to understand why these movements form in certain times and places and why they succeed in certain times and places. This includes not only the study of when and where and why and how movements have sometimes sought to replace authoritarian political systems with democratic ones, but also when and where and why and how movements have sought to change the way already-established democracies work. In the early twenty-first century many countries have experienced democratic movements, and so a major goal of scholars is therefore to understand why this has happened in some places but not others and to consider how the movements of our time, like those of the past, may succeed or fail in changing our world.

The achievements of all this research and speculation are impressive and I will be drawing on these ideas here. But in this book I am looking at the subject from another vantage point. Instead of presenting democracy as an ideal political system that humans aspire to but only imperfectly realize, I look at democracy as something continually being reinvented. Instead of treating the political institutions and practices as largely a product of separate national histories and cultures, I focus on how social movements flow across national frontiers and the ways in which those in power in different countries influence one another. Instead of reducing democracy to well-defined and routine practices and institutions such as elections and parliaments, I show how political movements have repeatedly challenged and remade existing institutions. After reviewing more than two centuries of political conflict, I conclude with a discussion of what democracy means today and what its future might be. This implies four objectives.

First of all, I want to consider why broad notions of democracy exploded into political life late in the eighteenth century, how those notions have been argued about, and how those notions have changed. Democracy has been continually defined and redefined by the people challenging government in the streets and fields and by the powerholders writing new laws and constitutional documents. This makes it very difficult for scholars to agree on a best definition of democracy because the definition is not up to scholars.

Second, I want to consider how currents of democratization have crossed national boundaries. "Transnationalism" has occurred partly because democratizing social movements have themselves crossed those boundaries and partly because governing officials are sensitive to what governing officials in other countries do. The literatures of sociology and political science, with their overriding stress on why democratization has advanced in some places more than others, have sometimes obscured the profoundly transnational dimension of democratization. Twenty-first century scholars have been paying much more attention to transnational questions than many have in the past. It is an interesting enterprise for scholars to explain, for example, the different ways in which communist regimes were overthrown in 1989 in East Germany, Poland, Czechoslovakia, Hungary, Romania, and Bulgaria. But no one could understand why communism fell in any of those countries without paying attention to the fact that it happened in all of them. Scholars of western Europe have been very effective in explaining the great differences in the ways democracy emerged out of long-standing authoritarian regimes in Portugal and Spain in the 1970s. Scholars of Latin America have been equally effective in exploring the differences in how and why Argentina and Brazil returned to civilian rule in the following decade. And scholars of Africa have been just as effective in explaining why one African country democratized more than another the decade after that. In this book, however, I am more concerned with why all these countries have participated in the most recent multicontinental wave of democratization within just a few years of each other.

Third, I pay a lot of attention to the ways in which democracy has raised doubts and criticism from the democratic explosion of the late eighteenth century to the present day. Sometimes these complaints energized efforts to prevent, derail, contain, or overthrow democracy. But some of those disappointed in democracy's inadequacies sought to make it live up to its promises. Both kinds of complaint were already present in the late eighteenth century. Both are still with us today.

And fourth, I also pay attention to how surprising parts of the story have been. Because so many important things were happening in so many places, because both those in authority and the social movements that challenged them have been major players, because people have continued to rethink how democracy could work and should work, new institutions keep getting invented, new movements form when we haven't expected them, and new conflicts generate new solutions. When this happens, people are surprised, and this happens often. So the history of democracy is full of surprises. The future of democracy will be, too.

New to the Second Edition

Readers will find changes and updates throughout the text as well as two new chapters. Here are some of the highlights of the new edition:

- New research on both contemporary and historical social movements
- Discussion of the role of social media in new movements of the twenty-first century
- A new section, "Emerging Critiques of Democracy," in Chapter 3
- Coverage of the Occupy Movements and U.S. elections as well as recent international developments
- Spotlight on key regions including China, Africa, and the Middle East
- Two new chapters: "Beyond the Great Democratic Wave" and "Into the Twenty-First Century"

Some writers, especially the political scientists Robert Dahl and Samuel Huntington, have already looked at the ebb and flow of democratization. But in this book I want to look at this ebb and flow as inseparable from democratization itself. Democracy is not some fixed set of procedures that, once achieved, remains in place unaltered. As long as social movements and governments make democratic claims, democracy will continue to be re-created.

✳
ACKNOWLEDGMENTS

I'm still grateful to those generous souls who commented twenty years ago on the manuscript that became the first edition of this book: Larry Griffin, Habibul Haque Khondker, John Marx, Verónica Montecinos, Charles Tilly, Peter Bearman, Jeffrey Broadbent, and Gay Seidman. Steve Rutter of Pine Forge Press provided essential encouragement, and Rebecca Smith helped me unsnarl some convoluted prose. Peggy Sestak, who typed most of the multiple drafts of that first edition, was essential. Since that version appeared, disappointment with some of the results of the great democratic wave, exciting new movements for democracy, and the increasingly visible challenges of the new century suggested that more needed to be written. Jennifer Knerr of Paradigm Publishers provided vital encouragement for doing a new edition and Laura Esterman steered the text through production. Many ideas about just what needed to be written emerged out of conversation with friends and colleagues in Pittsburgh and elsewhere, especially Verónica Montecinos, Jackie Smith, Mohammed Bamyeh, Melanie Hughes, Lisa Brush, John Marx, Suzanne Staggenborg, Kathy Blee, Michael Goodhart, Aníbal Pérez-Liñán, Robert Hayden, and Antonio González Herrera de Molina. Gerardo Munck, Markus Kreuzer, and Miguel Carter commented on the proposal. But I haven't shown the final version to anyone, so for whatever errors it contains there is no one to blame but me.

Chapter 1
A Quick History of Modern Democracy

For many social scientists, the 1960s and 1970s were decades of considerable doubt about the future of democratic institutions. The Soviet Union and its communist clients and allies seemed remarkably successful in repressing dissent and controlling opinion through state-run institutions. Most of Latin America was under the sway of very different antidemocratic forces and even countries with long democratic histories were taken over by their armed forces. In Africa, postcolonial democracies crumbled and were replaced by military leaders and "Presidents for Life." In Asia, hopes for democratic evolution were dashed by martial law and mass violence. Even in the United States and western Europe, the democratic heartland, antigovernment protests were spinning off into the terrorist tactics of kidnapping and bombing.

Then, unexpectedly, from the mid-1970s into the 1980s and beyond, the antidemocratic wave was dramatically reversed. Antidemocratic countries in Europe, Latin America, Asia, the Middle East, and Africa suddenly embraced democratic principles. Most astounding of all, in 1989 one communist regime after another was replaced by an at least ostensibly democratic government.

But surprises didn't stop with this enormous wave of democratic transitions. In the early twenty-first century enormous protests were happening not only in nondemocratic countries but in places where people sometimes boasted of having a democratic society. In those countries social movements were challenging the kind of democracy in place. Why did movements for democratic change blossom so widely in so many different sorts of social settings? Why were new movements arising that were asking for something different, even in democratic countries? To answer these questions, we need to look at the history of democracy.

Democratic (and Antidemocratic) Waves

Described above is one cycle of what I call "waves": an "antidemocratic" wave from the late 1950s through the 1960s and into the mid-1970s and a "democratic" wave from the mid-1970s that has lasted at least into the early twenty-first century. Each wave is a group of political changes happening close together in time in different countries.

During a democratic wave, the organization of governments is altered—sometimes by peaceful reform, sometimes by dramatic overthrow—in ways that are widely held to be more democratic. During such a democratic wave, there is a great deal of discussion of the virtues of democracy, social movements often demand more democracy, and people in positions of authority proclaim their democratic intentions. During antidemocratic waves, governments are transformed in ways that are widely held to be antidemocratic, social movements proclaim their intention to do away with democracy, and government figures proudly express their hostility to democracy.

Of course, democratic and antidemocratic movements can coexist at the same moment in history, with some powerholders proud of democracy and others hostile to it. Often these powerholders denounce each other. Some governments may claim they are becoming more democratic at the same time that others claim to be less so. What defines a democratic or antidemocratic wave is that during a certain stretch of historical time (from the mid-1970s to the mid-1990s, for example), the changes in governments are preponderantly of one or the other kind.

Note that I have not said here what democracy is. This is a very important question indeed but not so much in the sense that social scientists require precise definitions. Rather, it is important because one of the things under contention during democratic and antidemocratic waves is the very meaning of democracy.

Democratic and antidemocratic waves did not just begin in the 1960s and 1970s but two hundred years earlier. If we take a much longer time perspective, we will see that there have been several such waves.

Eighteenth-Century Breakthrough, Nineteenth-Century Fallout

In the 1700s, the word *democracy* had already been known for a long time to political theorists, and more generally to the educated, as one of three types of political systems distinguished in ancient Greece (alongside aristocracy and monarchy). The term appeared often in abstract and learned discussions of idealized political systems and was often used negatively, as it had been by Aristotle. When people talked about ancient democracy they knew that decisions were taken by an assembly in which all citizens could participate. They also knew that important positions were generally selected by lot, not by election campaigns, and they knew that while all citizens equally could participate, others who lived in ancient cities might be excluded. Those with rights of participation in the best-known instance, Athens, were men, not women, adults, not children, the free, not the slaves, and Athenians, not foreigners. In the 1700s, it was commonly held that democracy would encourage the less well off to plunder the wealthier, that it would foster rebellions, and that it was not practical on a scale larger than a city. It was rare, therefore, for people to use the term to describe any actually existing political arrangements or any they might hope to bring about. People who fought in the American Revolution in the 1770s, therefore, did not claim to be fighting for democracy, but the new term started to spread in the next decade.

In the 1780s, people in the Low Countries—today's Belgium and Holland—made a major conceptual breakthrough. People began using *democratic* and *aristocratic* to describe two kinds of society and two rival social movements in discussing political arrangements that actually existed or that they hoped to bring into existence. Some people were seen as benefiting from or enlisting in the cause of a social order that was hierarchical, corporate, and ordered by God—that is, a social world in which people were regarded as inherently unequal, in which collectivities like village communities were seen as the central elements of society, and in which social arrangements followed a divine plan. These people were "aristocrats." By contrast, those who believed in contractual arrangements among free and equal individuals, arrangements that could be changed when people wished to change them, were "democrats." Eighteenth-century democrats held that governments should derive their powers from a contract with the governed or even—a more daring notion—a contract among the governed alone.

A series of revolutionary movements from North America to Poland appealed to such ideas in the late eighteenth century, but the United States and France played special roles in this first wave of modern democracy. The United States secured its independence from Britain, the greatest maritime power of the age, through a difficult war. The armies of France, a few years later, overcame the armies of Europe's kings and held Europe in a grip that, for a while at least, extended from Madrid to Moscow. From the moment that sacred monarchy was successfully challenged by force on both sides of the Atlantic, claims to base government on the people became an increasingly striking part of public life.

What, more precisely, were the institutions that constituted democracy? As used in western Europe and North America in the 1780s and 1790s, *democracy* did not at first refer to representative institutions such as a congress or a parliament but was more likely to suggest direct popular decision making in an as yet unspecified institutional form. At the time, *democracy* never meant competitive political parties, which were, in fact, seen in the fledgling United States and in Great Britain as corrupt betrayals of the search for the common good and in revolutionary France as virtual treason. Nor did *democracy* mean that all could vote in the new United States, where women and slaves were excluded, or in France, where the poor, women, and servants were excluded in the first elections. *Democracy* never referred to elections that satisfied the standards of honest counting and freedom of choice that we take for granted today; the general use of secret ballots was a later development.

In the long period from the 1780s to about 1910, very important battles were fought whose outcomes gradually came to specify what we understand as *democracy*:

- Struggles for the authority of elected parliaments over decision makers (the struggle for parliamentary control over ministers in Britain, for example)
- Struggles over the expansion of the suffrage (elimination of property qualifications, for example)
- Struggles to make powerholders subject to the will of electorates (as in Great Britain, where the unelected House of Lords exercised significant power until 1911)
- Struggles for honest electoral counts (as in France, where as late as 1913 politicians provided already-marked ballots to villagers, who, visible to all, placed them in ballot boxes, a practice still noted in some rural areas many decades later)

- Struggles for acceptance of organized political parties as legitimate social actors and contestants in elections
- Struggles to emancipate populations from ties of personal dependence that made a mockery of any claims that the entire people were freely choosing their government (as in the slave emancipations in the western hemisphere and the gradual ending of "feudal rights" over rural majorities in Europe)

Every one of these struggles has its own history, but without any one of them, the meaning of *democracy* in our time would be quite different. If none of these struggles had taken place, *democracy* would be vacuous.

According to the usages of the early twenty-first century, very few states in the world in 1910 even approximately fit notions of democracy. From two to perhaps eight states could have been called democracies, depending on how strict the definition. We can count as many as eight only if we are not very demanding about suffrage rules, for example, as only in New Zealand, Australia, and Finland did women have full voting rights.

Western Europe and some of its English-speaking offshoots seem the heartland of these nineteenth-century battles, but there were important developments in Latin America as well, with Chile in particular approximating a European timetable. And other places already were adopting democratic elements: weak representative institutions in Russia, a Japanese parliament modeled on Prussia's, and the like.

Twentieth-Century Oscillations

The history of democratization from about 1910 to the present gives a first impression of sudden, explosive changes of course. From about 1910 into the mid-1920s, there was a great spurt in democratic claims by governments: considerable parliamentary reform in western Europe, the extension of the suffrage to women in several countries, the formation of democracies in some of the new countries carved out of monarchies ruined by World War I, emulation by weaker countries of the constitutional forms of the victorious democratic powers. Then in the 1920s and 1930s, fascist movements, authoritarian monarchs, and antidemocratic militaries expelled democratic forces from the political stage in much of Europe and Latin America. German armies conquered most of the rest of democratic Europe during World War II.

The military defeat of the fascist powers brought in its wake, in the 1940s and 1950s, a diffusion of the political systems of the victors—either a democratic or communist model and sometimes both in contested succession. The United States helped restore democracies in western Europe in countries that had been conquered by the Germans (but were these democracies as they had been before, or were they changed?); the armies of the Soviet Union ensured the installation of compatible communist regimes in central and eastern Europe. The United States also presided over the attempt to plant the roots of democracy in the western part of Germany and in Japan, countries that were held to have previously proved infertile soil, and re-created democracies in Italy and Austria as well. Greece and South Korea, soon in armed struggle with proponents of the communism associated with the rival successful model, proved less enduring cases when anticommunist antidemocrats seized the polity.

Buoyed by their military success in World War II, the Americans and the British tended to promote democratic models as the way out of colonialism; after World War I, in contrast, the democratic victors had manufactured new monarchies. Malaysia, the Philippines, India, and various African countries achieved independence following World War II under democratic constitutions.

Latin America followed the multicontinental trends in the 1940s and 1950s, and several important countries shifted to democratic forms. The Brazilian military ended the authoritarian regime of Getúlio Vargas, who had ruled since 1930. Venezuela had the first genuine attempt at democratic government in its history in 1945 and its first peaceful presidential succession in the elections of 1958. It is symptomatic of the historical moment that in 1956–1957 Colombia terminated its extraordinary *Violencia*—a period of extensive and murderous violence between people associated with the major political parties—with a series of pacts that adhered to formal democracy.

The postwar wave of democratization was seconded by a wave of optimistic notions on the part of North American social scientists. Their hopes were buoyed by the military destruction of European fascism, the reestablishment of democracies in Nazi-held Europe, the implantation of democracy by the United States in such previously unpromising places as Germany and Japan, the new democratic constitutions of postcolonial Africa and Asia, the ouster of a nondemocratic regime in South America's largest country, Brazil, and the establishment of the first democratic government ever in previously chaotic Venezuela. Many social scientists, especially in the United States, argued that democracy was part and parcel of the modern world and would naturally accompany economic development.

Democracy in Trouble Again: The 1960s and Early 1970s

By the 1960s, however, social scientists' rosy view of democracy's prospects was beginning to look out of date. There was now considerable doubt about the future of the sort of democratic institutions characteristic of western Europe, North America, and a few far-flung offshoots of western colonization, such as Australia and New Zealand. The division of Europe that had followed World War II seemed frozen, and the communist East seemed remarkably successful in repressing dissent and controlling opinion through state-run mass media and well-thought-out domination of the educational system. Even without the direct backing of the Soviet army, forces allied with the Soviet Union were showing an impressive capacity to fight their way to power in poorer countries and to hold their own in the face of major challenges. Communist parties had come to power in the world's most populous country, China, and had managed to fight the United States and its allies to a standstill in Korea. They were in the process of defeating the large U.S. force in Indochina. And the Caribbean island of Cuba seemed to some to demonstrate that a determined revolutionary government of even a very small country could stand up to the wealth and power of the United States.

At the same time, most of Latin America was under the sway of very different kinds of antidemocratic forces. Mexico had long been ruled by the Institutional Revolutionary Party, whose official slogan of "effective suffrage" was contradicted by the reality of its elections. The application of force and fraud was so pervasive that no opposition party had ever been permitted to win a state governorship in Mexico, let alone seriously aspire to the presidency. Impoverished Central America was, for the most part, under murderous generals. Even the more economically developed countries of South America seemed to be falling into the hands of uniformed tyrants. The most shocking instance was Chile, with a long and deep tradition of democratic practice that came to an end in a coup in 1973. The violence of the military takeover was only a prologue to a long period of government-initiated terror. Uruguay, proud of a tradition of peace and democracy that had made it known as the Switzerland of Latin America, was also taken captive by its own armed forces, more gradually but with similar savagery.

In the 1960s and 1970s, economic growth seemed no protection for democracy. Such industrializing countries as Argentina and Brazil sustained military takeovers. In Brazil's case, the military ruled with a level of violence that violated Brazilians' beliefs about the ability of their elites to resolve problems with each other peacefully. By the mid-1970s only three Latin American countries (Costa Rica, Colombia, and Venezuela) still had serious claims to democratic politics.

In Africa, initial hopes for postcolonial democracy crumbled as one country after another threw out its initial democratic constitution, often derived in part from some European model. African governments variously declared that the rule of one party (no competition allowed) was more appropriate for their circumstances, that a great leader of the independence struggle should be "President for Life," or that military rule was essential for orderly progress. The army of the largest independent African state, Nigeria, overturned its democratic constitution in 1966. The European power with the most significant remaining African colonies, Portugal, was a nondemocratic state itself. Portugal did nothing to encourage democracy in Angola and Mozambique; moreover, it fought a protracted war against socialist revolutionaries who hardly looked themselves like sources of democracy. The most industrialized country of the continent, South Africa, rigidly insisted on the permanent exclusion of the great majority of its citizens from anything remotely resembling democratic participation, with voting rights restricted to its small white minority.

In western Asia, the Turkish military staged coups in 1960 and 1971. In most other Middle Eastern countries, claims of democratic procedures were weaker still. Turkey's western neighbor, Greece, was seized by its military in the mid-1960s. And western Europe's authoritarian states, Portugal and Spain, were looking remarkably long-lived. Spain showed few signs of moving into the democratic camp as the agents of its durable leader, Francisco Franco, planned carefully to assure an authoritarian future after his death.

East of Turkey, in Asia, democracy's prospects also looked bleak. Many saw Japan as a success for U.S.-sponsored democratization. But in many places in Asia, democratic processes were upended in the postcolonial era. In the Philippines, an elected president declared martial law. Antidemocratic systems in Burma, Thailand, Indonesia, South Korea, and Pakistan became even more thoroughly closed. Even India, the country generally regarded as the best-established democracy on the Asian mainland—the world's largest democracy, in fact—was ominously shut down when its prime minister proclaimed a state of emergency in 1975. Many would have said that India's multitude of regional, religious, and linguistic conflicts and incredible poverty made a democratic future a long shot even before the "emergency." Another Asian country, Malaysia, had seemed a fairly happy example of democratic practice in a postcolonial society. Its Muslim Malays, Chinese, and Indians elected representatives who managed to peacefully negotiate their differences. Violence among these communities in the late 1960s, however, precipitated a considerable contraction of Malaysia's political process and moved the political system into a gray area that was more or less authoritarian.

Democracy seemed on the run and perhaps on the ropes. The incapacity of democratic states to prevail on the battlefield against determined opponents had been demonstrated several times before (by the French in Algeria, for example), but the U.S. defeat in Indochina seemed to many a sign of fundamental weakness in democracy itself.

Beginning in the 1960s, a wave of protest engulfed the West, in the United States, France, Germany, Italy, and elsewhere. Demonstrations and other forms of mass action in the streets and in the classrooms challenged the central economic, political, and cultural practices of those societies so deeply that those who identified with established democratic patterns feared the movements as antidemocratic. Such fears hardly evaporated when, in the early 1970s, clandestine offshoots of these movements espoused (and to some extent practiced) the violent tactics of kidnapping and bombing, especially in Italy and Germany.

Social scientists were enormously creative in explaining the fragile character of democracy during the 1960s and early 1970s. The political scientist Samuel Huntington lectured to the Central Intelligence Agency on the poor prospects for democracy in the Third World. A group of scholars of Latin America showed how deep were the roots of an antidemocratic culture derived from medieval Spain and Portugal. Some of them argued that democracy depended on unusual cultural characteristics and that places like Asia and Latin America were infertile soil for democratic trees. Others saw the patterns of economic development in the most recently industrializing countries as inimical to democracy and debated the previous wisdom of social scientists who saw development as a spur to democratization.

The most influential of the era's books in this vein was the brilliant essay by the Argentine Guillermo O'Donnell, *Modernization and Bureaucratic*

Authoritarianism. It drew on the seizure of power by the Brazilian military in 1964 and the Argentine military in 1966 to argue that industrial development in Latin America had generated powerful antidemocratic forces. The book appeared in Spanish in 1972, in English one year later. It was almost at once confirmed by the violent Chilean coup of 1973 and was reinforced by the concurrent militarization of Uruguayan politics. The withdrawal from power by the Argentine military in 1973 defied O'Donnell's thesis. But when a turbulent period in Argentina gave way to a new and far more violent military period beginning in 1976, it was as if democracy's unsuitability for the region had been decisively demonstrated.

During the 1970s, the O'Donnell thesis had great influence among scholars in and out of Latin America. They debated how to extend the thesis to the antidemocratic practices of Latin American countries other than those originally considered; some even thought about extending it to other continents as well. At the same time, other scholars continued to develop cultural explanations for national differences in political practices. If eastern Asia or the Middle East or Latin America seemed unable to create democracies or frequently overthrew those that existed, perhaps some aspects of democratic practice ran against deeply held values in those places.

Democracy Triumphant: The Mid-1970s to Mid-1990s

In retrospect, the entire debate between those who favored economic explanations and those who favored cultural ones was profoundly ironic, for the Chilean and Argentine coups were among the last major advances of the antidemocratic wave of the mid-twentieth century. In the mid-1970s, democracy once again began to gain strength while the scholars, not yet noticing, continued to elaborate and debate their cultural and structural accounts of the antidemocratic character of many countries. Events called many of their conclusions into question.

In the mid-1970s the three remaining nondemocratic regimes of western Europe—Spain, Portugal, and Greece—embraced democracy. The immediate precipitants differed considerably and the course of events was quite different in each case, yet democratic change occurred.

Also in the mid-1970s, the Brazilian military began negotiating a relaxation of its authoritarian style. Its coup in 1964 had become the paradigmatic case of antidemocratic rule for industrial Latin America. The left scoffed at the generals' overtures. Nevertheless, the generals' efforts led to the selection of a civilian president a decade later. By the 1980s, indeed, military governments throughout South America had left the scene. Some fell precipitously, as in Argentina after Great Britain defeated a military attempt to occupy some disputed islands; other governments negotiated a return to civilian rule, as in Brazil and Uruguay. Even the more old-fashioned tyranny of General Stroessner in Paraguay, a holdover from an earlier era, went under. Chile became the last country in South America to democratize, when the first civilian president since 1973 was elected in 1989.

In Central America, civilian control over militaries remained dubious (except in Costa Rica), and civil war raged in El Salvador, Nicaragua, and Guatemala for much of the 1980s. Yet elected civilian authority resumed everywhere. The Nicaraguan Sandinistas, a revolutionary socialist party, startled some by first holding an election and then accepting electoral defeat. The United States startled others by removing Panama's authoritarian president by force. El Salvador and Guatemala made peace. By the early 1990s every state south of Mexico was at least nominally democratic, a state of affairs unprecedented since the independence wars of the early nineteenth century.

The only significant Latin American holdouts in the mid-1990s were Cuba and Mexico. But the Mexican political system opened up, and for the first time, publicly announced election results showed victories for candidates from opposition parties. In 2000 the longtime dominant party was defeated in a presidential election.

If the 1980s were not already startling enough, the year 1989 was positively stupefying. One communist regime after another was replaced by an at least ostensibly democratic government. The bipolar confrontation of the Soviet Union and the United States evaporated. Undefended by Soviet arms, not one regime in central and eastern Europe had any staying power in the face of rising protest. Only one regime, in Romania, even put up a fight. When the Soviet Union itself collapsed and fragmented into fifteen self-governing states, many of those fragments claimed to be struggling to establish democracy. Some postcommunist regimes quickly democratized and others developed authoritarian rule. But even in some of the latter cases, democratic movements developed and sometimes succeeded.

Although southern and eastern Europe and Latin America were the broadest regions transformed, talk of democracy was also much farther afield. In the Philippines, the government of authoritarian Ferdinand Marcos fell apart in 1986 in the face of massive opposition. The South Korean military regime gave way to electoral politics in 1987. Democratic movements in Taiwan made headway in significantly liberalizing a once unyielding regime. Less successful was the Chinese democracy movement of 1989, suppressed by armed force, and the Burmese movement, whose electoral success of 1990 was unrecognized by the military regime. A leader of the Burmese democracy movement, awarded the Nobel Peace Prize in 1991, was barred from travel and often under house arrest, but was finally able to accept the award in 2012 as some observers thought they saw movement toward democracy. The 1990s saw other democratic movements in some of the poorest countries on earth. For example, the first president chosen through credible elections in the history of Haiti took office. Although he was ousted by the Haitian military, he was later returned to office by the U.S. military.

In the Middle East and northern Africa, Islamist movements in the 1990s embraced democratic procedures as the route to power. They achieved such successes in the first contested national elections in the history of Algeria that the military quashed the elections by coup in 1992. A violent struggle between the military rulers and their Islamist enemies followed. Attacked by Islamists in 2001, the United States and allies occupied first Afghanistan and then Iraq, claiming to be bringing those countries democracy. A decade later, enormous movements for democracy overturned authoritarian rulers in Tunisia and Egypt, launching what has become known as the Arab Spring, and movements spread to other Middle Eastern countries.

Further to the south, in Africa, there has been talk of democracy as well. There have been democratic movements in Kenya, for example, and elites proposed democracy as an alternative to civil war in Mozambique. And no such discussion would be complete without mentioning the long process by which South Africans in the early 1990s painfully negotiated a formula for bringing political rights to all. The first election in which all adult South Africans could vote took place in 1994.

As you can see, the most recent democratic waves have been truly multicontinental. During the 1960s and early 1970s, in many different countries, regimes believed to be more democratic were replaced by others believed to be less so; the central institutions of the remaining democratic states underwent challenges; and many different kinds of nondemocratic political systems—from Paraguay to Poland, from South America to South Africa—seemed secure.

But during the later 1970s, the 1980s, and continuing into the 1990s, in many different countries, regimes believed to be less democratic were replaced by others believed to be more so and in the early twenty-first century most of the countries that had become more democratic remained so. The central institutions of some of the remaining nondemocratic political systems faced serious challenges from movements for democracy, in places as different in culture as Burma and Egypt, as different in size as Nepal and China. These waves were genuinely multicontinental.

What, culturally, do South Korea, Czechoslovakia, and Paraguay have in common that allowed them all to change? What structures—economic, political, or otherwise—join Haiti, Burma, South Africa, and Taiwan? And why were social scientists so poor at foreseeing these changes in the countries they studied? Few scholars of eastern Europe, for example, guessed at the coming end of communism. Chilean scholars often expected that democracy would eventually return, but by the 1980s, after economic problems had failed to dislodge the regime, those scholars were often quite pessimistic. Many thought redemocratization was impossible while General Pinochet continued to hold the reins. Democratic movements do not always succeed and when they do so it is sometimes a surprise. They also sometimes raise new issues that redefine democracy itself.

A Look Ahead

How are we to understand the wavelike character of democratization outlined in this chapter? How are we to understand the ways that democracy has been redefined during the past two hundred years? These questions seem quite different, but both refer to the dynamic character of democratization.

In the next chapter, I sketch a number of concepts that help in explaining the ebb and flow of democratization. In subsequent chapters I use these concepts to explore several periods in the world history of democratization briefly sketched here. In Chapter 3 I look more closely at the democratic explosion at the end of the eighteenth century and the long fallout from that explosion through the nineteenth century. In Chapter 4, I examine the democratic and antidemocratic waves of the twentieth century, including the greatest of all democratic waves, which began in the mid-1970s and continued into the early 1990s. In Chapter 5 I step back from this rough chronological treatment to reflect on how the coexistence of democratic and nondemocratic elements has shaped the actions of social movements and powerholders alike. In Chapter 6 I ask what has happened to the great democratic wave since the 1990s. And in the final chapter, I consider the challenges facing democracy in the early twenty-first century and speculate on the future.

CHAPTER 2
STATES, SOCIAL MOVEMENT CHALLENGERS, AND ELITE REFORMERS

Why are political systems more democratic in certain countries at certain times and less so in other countries at other times? We may think of this very big question as containing a group of somewhat smaller, though still substantial, questions: Why do movements for democracy arise at certain times and places? Why do regimes sometimes claim to be making "democratic" changes? Why do some of these democratic regimes endure for relatively long periods while other experiences of democracy prove to be fleeting? And why do multicontinental waves of democratization (and waves of antidemocracy) arise? When we look at the pattern of democracy in the world, the timing of democratic waves, and the durability of the democratic transformations in different places, we will find that many social processes play a role.

In this chapter I introduce some fundamental sociological ideas that help in understanding democratic waves. First, we need to look at the power of states and the way power is organized. Notions of democracy, however varied they have been, have always involved claims about what sorts of powers governments have and should have, as well as claims about who has a say (and what sort of say) in the making of decisions—including such very important decisions as who is to occupy positions of authority and how the government is to be organized.

We also need to look at the activities of two different sorts of people. One group consists of those who hold official positions in government and those who have ready access to those powerholders, both of whom have sometimes promoted democratizing change. I will speak therefore of democratic reforms and democratic reformers. But others outside the presidential palaces and sometimes very far away have also played important roles, especially when they have been able to engage in concerted action in the form of social movements. Movements that claim to speak for the weak, poor, suffering, or silent and invisible members of society are often threatening to the more powerful, richer, more comfortable, and more influential members. Thus the actions of social movements often challenge the interests of particular social groups, previous government policies, the fortunes of particular government officials, and sometimes the very organization of power. So we will also look at social movement challenges and challengers.

Both elite reformers and social movement challengers have tugged and pulled in many directions over the past two centuries. They have sometimes created new kinds of antidemocratic political systems. At other times, however, movements and reformers have converged on democratization—not just in individual states but in transnational democratizing waves.

The role of this chapter, then, is to sketch some ideas about state power, about elite reformers, and about social movement challengers—ideas that we will be using in subsequent chapters as well.

Power and Myths about Power

We will be studying state power from two rather different perspectives. First we will consider the ability of states both to make and to carry out policies—that is, states' power capacities. Second we will consider the claims that are made as to why people should obey powerholders. Are the powerholders claimed to be agents of God, for example, or are they held to have received a mandate from the people? Or do they merely have control over weapons and lack such justifications? When we find a claim that justifies the exercise of power, we are dealing with legitimation. States often make legitimating claims, among them the claim to democratic practice.

State Power

Those who occupy certain positions have the capacity to make decisions that affect the distribution of resources among the population of a territory.

Powerholders may decide who will pay taxes and at what rates, who will receive payments from the state, who will be employed by the state, or where roads will be built. The power capacity of a state is its ability to make and enforce such decisions. Many of these decisions benefit some people but injure others.

To what extent does the state exercise control over social resources? Over the past several centuries that concern us, states have come to make many more decisions than they used to and to affect the lives of their citizens in many more ways. For example, compared to the past, there is now more detailed regulation of economic life, greatly expanded capacity for law enforcement, a great expansion of "social" policy aimed at affecting the distribution of resources among various sectors of the population, and an astronomical leap in the ability to inflict violence. One could measure the changes between the 1780s and the present by comparing the sheer quantity of laws and regulations issued by central authorities, by comparing the number of police who enforce government rules, by calculating the proportion of national wealth spent by governments, or by counting the total number of people who earn a living in government service. Whichever measure we favored, we would have to conclude that far more is done by states today than was done two centuries ago, on a virtually worldwide basis. In general, then, we may say that the *power capacity* of states has grown considerably.

The power capacity of states needs to be carefully distinguished from how decisions are made about how that capacity is to be used. We can imagine arrangements under which power is divided among several clusters of powerholders, who must come to some negotiated agreement if state capacity to tax, to use violence, and so on is to be exercised in a concerted fashion. And we can imagine arrangements under which powerholders are accountable to others—perhaps, as in contemporary democracies, to an electorate. The relationships among powerholders, then, are an important matter. With whom, if with anyone, must a powerholder negotiate? To whom, if to anyone, is a powerholder responsible? Thus powerholders differ in the constraints and opportunities under which they act.

If we are tracing the increasing scale of state taxation or the growth of state policy, we are concerned with state power capacities. If we are concerned with the degree to which those outside the state apparatus can affect the identity of powerholders or the policies they follow, we are dealing with *decisional constraints*. Almost all states in the early twenty-first century have vastly greater capacities than almost all states two centuries ago, but political figures today operate under constraints in decision making at least as severe as in the past. One of the distinctive constraints in today's democracies is that many powerholders are directly responsible to electorates. An even larger number are indirectly responsible by virtue of being under the authority of those who must stand for election.

Legitimating Myths

In addition to considering state decisions that affect resource distributions, we will be considering a second aspect of power: claims about the ultimate sources of power and the ultimate justifications for decisions. Prior to the 1780s, when our story begins, the ultimate source of power was often held to be God or some other principle beyond the control of human action. The ultimate justification for a decision was that it accorded with immutable principles: divine will, sacred law, ageless tradition.

A distinguishing feature of the past two centuries is the claim that power is exercised on behalf of the people; often the claim is even made that power is exercised by the people. Abraham Lincoln's brief formulation at the Gettysburg battlefield—"of the people, by the people, and for the people"—concisely embodies this image. Most of the world's states now have written constitutions, and a written constitution is very close to being an implicit claim that human beings have set the rules under which authority is exercised. That claim is quite explicit, however, in the preamble to the U.S. Constitution, which invokes "we the people." But most constitutions also claim that power derives ultimately from God (or some other principle that transcends a specific human action). Thus both a divine and a human source of or justification for the exercise of power may coexist. The constitution of Argentina, for example, identifies God as "the source of all reason and justice." The German constitution claims to be a statement of the German people "conscious of its responsibility before God and men." One finds parallels in such other constitutions as those of Indonesia, Colombia, Ireland, and Greece.[1]

Ambiguity about whether the ultimate source of authority resides in human assemblies or in God was embodied in one of the founding documents of modern democracy, the Declaration of the Rights of Man and Citizen, adopted by the revolutionary National Assembly in France in 1789. According to its third article, "The principle of all sovereignty rests essentially in the nation. No body and no individual may exercise authority which does not emanate from the nation expressly." But is "the nation" really the ultimate authority behind all other merely delegated authority? The National Assembly stated that it was enacting this very Declaration itself "in the presence and under the auspices of the Supreme Being."[2]

Political systems involve specific capacities of states to extract and expend resources and, therefore, to allocate costs and benefits. Political systems also involve specifiable relations among powerholders and between powerholders and others. The "rules of the political game" consist of empirically verifiable statements about who can tell whom to do what and with whom one must come to an agreement before telling someone else what to do. These rules may be embodied in formal, written statements, such as those in the U.S. Constitution that allocate particular powers to the president and other powers to Congress. Often they are unwritten but equally real by virtue of being known to all significant participants—for example, which senators need to be persuaded if a particular piece of legislation is to have any chance of being passed.

These aspects of power are visible: Either they are embodied in formal rules or can be discovered in conversation with knowledgeable and talkative insiders. But we may also speak of the *mythic constitution of society,* of claims about on whose behalf decisions are made and about what principle allows powerholders to make decisions at all. The broadest of these claims are claims that power rests on some immutable principle (God, tradition, history) or that it rests on "the people." These claims are not empirically observable. We cannot see God or the people making policy, only powerholders allocating resources and (sometimes) electorates choosing powerholders (or occasionally making a choice in a referendum drawn up by powerholders). But the study of public discourse can reveal something of a society's mythic constitution, namely the sorts of claims made about the basis of power.

Discovering what people really consider to be the basis of authority is more difficult than discovering how and by whom decisions are made. The reason is that some public discourse about the principles on which power rests is uttered in bad faith. One observer, for example, characterized the socialist rhetoric of the 1980s in eastern Europe as emanating from officials who did not believe their own words. Furthermore, those officials addressed publics who did not believe the words, who did not believe the officials believed them either, and who were not even thought by those officials to believe.[3]

One of the central questions for the history of democracy is how mythic claims about rule for and by the people became conflated with particular decisional structures: parliamentary bodies, elections, competitive parties, certain civil liberties, certain suffrage rules, and so on. That is, when and where and why and how did claims of popular rule come to be seen as carried out by such institutions and practices? When people spoke of democracy in the 1780s, they rarely spoke of parliamentary bodies; if they thought of elections, they rarely thought of women's suffrage; if they thought of electoral technology, they were more likely to have in mind open ballots than secret ballots; if they pictured organized political parties at all, they probably did so with horror.

The identification of the mythic constitution of a democratic society (for example, "The people exercise power") with a set of empirically observable institutions is one of the great processes of *political creativity*. Where and when did people first speak of elected representative bodies as the embodiment of democratic principles rather than aristocratic principles? Where and when did people first speak of political parties competing in elections as representing the voice of the people rather than defying it? Where and when did people begin to deliberately enact constitutions? Where and when did they decide that voting was to be secret? That suffrage was to be independent of property ownership? Or of gender? (I will attempt in Chapter 5 to sketch the times and places where these questions were answered.) We can speak, then, of the history of what has been meant by democracy in practice. We may even speak of the social invention of democracy as a continual process; we may speak, that is, of the modification over time of what democracy means. And we may try to identify the times and places that democracy was "invented."

Notice that this line of inquiry is different from the more usual attempt to identify particular political systems as democratic or nondemocratic, a type of activity with which this book will not be very much concerned. Indeed, social scientists often disagree on whether or not particular countries are democratic. For example, Mexico has long held elections at regular intervals for president, state governors, and national legislators, and several rival parties run campaigns. Some social scientists, therefore, spoke of Mexico as a democracy. Yet others point to the fact that, until recently, only the candidates of one party won. Not only had all presidents since the 1920s been from a single party, but until the 1980s, so had all governors and most of those in the legislature. Outright electoral fraud has been one very conspicuous mechanism to bring about this result. Similarly, Japan is usually called a democracy, but some scholars have occasionally questioned this label. Japan's Liberal Democratic Party, like Mexico's Institutional Revolutionary Party, had until recently never lost a presidential election. Major decisions were made not by open debate but by consensus, achieved behind closed doors, largely among Liberal Democratic Party leaders. (By the mid-1990s the dominant parties of Japan and Mexico had both clearly slipped, and other parties came to the fore in the first decade of the twenty-first century; in 2012, however, both were returned to power.)

So it is sometimes difficult to say whether a country is to be regarded as democratic or not. What is more, even the most democratic of countries have undemocratic aspects. In the United States, for example, blacks in the southern states were generally not able to vote until the 1960s. One might therefore contend that the United States ought not to be called a democracy until that point, a contention that would no doubt be startling to many of its citizens. In fact, one comparative history of democracy dates its establishment in the United States from about 1970.[4] Similarly, most people think of Great Britain as democratic, but critics point to the absence of codified statements of rights (like the U.S. Bill of Rights) and the British government's capacity under the Official Secrets Act to suppress press reporting of embarrassing news. Such critics of British government in practice sometimes question, therefore, the democratic label.

If governments that we usually call democratic have some antidemocratic features, the reverse is also the case. By the late twentieth century few countries failed to have at least some democratic aspects, even governments that few who call themselves democrats would accept. Iran under the ayatollahs has had competitive elections, although one could be imprisoned for supporting the wrong positions. The former Soviet Union probably held more elections for more positions than any other country on this planet ever did, although the elections were rarely competitive. South Africa had a parliament chosen by competitive elections, although the great majority of South Africans did not have the right to vote.

The attempt to decide which states "really" are or are not democratic will continue to be difficult. I will not, therefore, try to classify particular political systems as democratic in this book. Nor will I undertake an abstract definition of democracy here (a definition on which, we may be sure, others will not agree). I will take democracy to be first and foremost an actor's concept, not a detached observer's analytical tool. By this I mean that the term democracy has been used since the 1780s by those engaged in political struggles to praise some ideas, governments, political figures, and social movements and to condemn others. The "democrats" may be the good guys or the embodiment of evil, depending on one's position. (For conservatives in the late eighteenth and early nineteenth centuries "democratic" was more often than not a term of condemnation.) Rather than decide in the classroom what the proper use of democracy is, we will consider how its meaning has evolved in the course of political struggles over two centuries. (This is a much understudied subject, by the way.) I will also pose the question of how democratic and nondemocratic elements combine in particular times and places.

This book is both comparative and historical. It is comparative in that I point up common elements in many countries at given moments, as well as pointing up differences among those countries and seeking to explain the differences. For example, we will consider possible explanations for why democratic movements occurred in the 1790s in some parts of the world and not in others. In exploring why, say, western Europe evolved in different ways than Latin America, we will be studying what may be called comparative history.

Although we will look at instances from many times and places, however, this book is not primarily that sort of comparative history. It is more precisely a world history of democracy, exploring how the institutions that are held to embody the mythic democratic power structure have changed on a world scale, as democratic waves have come and gone. In other words, rather than being primarily concerned with why some countries have more democratic features than others, we will pay more attention to the interconnections among countries, to the ways that democratic or antidemocratic developments in one place affect democratic or antidemocratic developments someplace else.

The Transnational Dimension

In trying to understand waves of democratization, we will be considering several sociological processes. We will pay special attention to the role of social movements in making demands on governing elites and the role of governing elites in attempting to secure popular compliance. When we study democratization processes within a single country, in fact, we can often see a sort of dialogue between social movements (sometimes on behalf of people with relatively little power) and those who occupy the formal positions of government.

A great deal of the story, however, is a transnational one, for the dialogue in a particular country is taking place at the same time as other dialogues are taking place elsewhere. It is important to realize that these dialogues are not taking place in sealed compartments but on something like a telephone party line or a gigantic online computer forum; both social movements and governing elites pay attention to what other social movements and governing elites are doing elsewhere. The result is sometimes a transnational convergence of political transformations driven in some places by movements, in others by elite reformers, in still others by both.

An Example: The Abolition of Slavery in the Americas

One example of a major historical process shaped by both social movements and the pressures of states on one another is the antislavery movement. By the late eighteenth century, black slaves performed a great deal of the work in the western hemisphere. The European colonial powers and their fortune-seeking settlers had come to depend on slaves from Africa to provide the labor for the profitable economic enterprises established in the New World. In the first centuries of European control of the Americas, in fact, more of those who crossed the Atlantic were Africans in chains than whites seeking opportunities.[5] It would be hard to imagine a place like the island of Barbados in the Caribbean providing such lucrative returns to those who invested in its sugar production without the slaves who grew and cut the cane and then extracted the sugar. Indeed, few Europeans before the late eighteenth century imagined that slavery would ever end. Yet it was ended. By the late nineteenth century the European slave-holding countries (including England, France, Spain, Portugal, Denmark, and Holland) had abolished slavery in their colonies, as had the independent countries of North and South America.

How did this change come about? Slave resistance, including sabotage, flight, and rebellion, had long troubled colonial slavery. Resistance began on the slave ship and continued on land. In some places, escaped slaves set up countersocieties, as in Brazil, and in others rebelled, as in Jamaica and Haiti. In Haiti, they won their freedom after a terrible struggle with French armed forces. White elites generally feared slave revolt, but when such elites themselves revolted against Spanish rule in early nineteenth-century South America, some white leaders encouraged blacks to support the independence cause by promising them freedom. In 1816 Simón Bolívar, at the northern end of the continent, promised to free slaves who would fight the Spanish, in return for which the new government of Haiti sent him arms. Far to the south, José de San Martín made the same offer to slaves who enlisted in his campaign to drive the Spanish from Chile. However, others among the local elites feared that their leaders were encouraging a slave insurrection, and Bolívar himself came to have second thoughts.

In England and the United States, powerful social movements were working to abolish slavery. The English movement, for example, rounded up vast numbers of signatures on petitions and forwarded the petitions to Parliament. Boycotts of colonial exports produced with slave labor, public meetings, pamphlets, local committees to organize activity, and a national coordinating body were all established features of the British antislavery movement by the 1790s. Early in the nineteenth century, this movement did succeed in ending British slavery. The movement in the United States was equally active but less successful; the new constitution protected the existence of slavery. U.S. slavery was not actually abolished without an extremely bloody war several decades later.

American and English antislavery activists were in such close touch that one historian speaks of "The Antislavery International." In 1783, for example, antislavery Quakers in London and Philadelphia coordinated simultaneous petitions to the British Parliament and the American Continental Congress. When French abolitionists founded their Society of the Friends of Black People, their model was the London Society of Friends.[6]

Most other countries had no antislavery social movement of comparable strength, but reformers among the ruling elites had a growing sense of what was proper for a civilized country. Although Napoleon Bonaparte had sent a large military force to France's Caribbean possessions in 1801 to combat insurgent blacks fighting for their freedom, in 1814 he decreed the end of the slave trade. He was probably trying to avoid new troubles with a British navy that was solidly backed by a huge public petition drive that associated the French enemy with slavery.[7]

The British navy, in fact, had become a significant force in the international antislavery scene. Although Britain had abandoned slavery, it wished to keep its now slaveless colonies economically competitive. Thus the British government promoted the ending of the international slave trade, and the British navy backed up that proposal with force. Once the African slave trade was abolished, slavery became a much more costly enterprise because of the difficulty of replacing slaves. As a result, elite antislavery reformers had an easier argument, even without a mass movement.

These different paths to the abolition of slavery cumulatively redefined people's expectations. As one country after another ended it, slavery seemed less and less the expected state of affairs. After France's Revolution of 1848, for example, the new government's reforming elites showed their adherence to the emerging international definition of a civilized country by moving to end colonial slavery. By the time the U.S. Civil War had ended, such places as Brazil and Cuba, where slavery still existed, had a sense that world opinion was running against them. Ultimately, the elites of the last holdout, Brazil, organized a peaceful abolition of their own.

In this brief summary, we see the role of antislavery social movements (among slaves in various places, most dramatically in Haiti, and among whites and free blacks in England and North America); of reforming elites (in France after the Revolution of 1848); and of the combined actions of elites and movements (as in the emancipations in the rebel countries in South America). We also see, very forcefully, the transnational character of the whole process. American antislavery activists learned from the English movement; later on, elite reformers took note of the rising costs of slavery; and still later, the governments of the few remaining slave powers became aware of their growing isolation.

Social Movements in National and Transnational Contexts

Let's take a closer look at social movements and their role in democratization, at the part played by elite reformers, and at how the two processes may sometimes interact. In doing so, we will keep in mind the important transnational dimension.

From Popular Resistance to Social Movements

The capacity of ordinary people to challenge the powerful, of those with less to threaten those with more and of those with uncomfortable lives to disrupt the routines of the comfortable, has always been considerable. Well before the modern era of democratization, peasants challenged the claims of local lords and royal tax collectors, urban artisans and shopkeepers demanded favorable government regulations on food prices, urbanites and country people alike enlisted under the banner of dissenting religious ideas, and everyone resisted the recruiting sergeant.

In seventeenth-century France, for example, the forests and marshes of the southwest were known for their hot-blooded ferocity in fighting tax collection. Beginning in the 1690s, French administrators also knew that major roads and rivers could become the scene of collective attempts by local people to stop the shipment of grain to distant markets, thereby keeping the grain available where it was grown.

Beyond such open, explicit, and collective challenges lay a whole world of concealed, disguised, and individual resistance. Open challenge to authority was extremely dangerous, so resistance was often disguised: Tax evasion was pervasive, tax rebellion intermittent; concealing a pig or a weapon from the lord was widespread, burning the lord's records unusual; falsifying the measurement of one's harvest when it was time to pay a portion to the church was common, seizing the bishop's property rare.

But rarer still was what we would recognize today as a social movement, an open, collective, sustained challenge to prevailing ways of doing things. A social movement is open in that there is an explicit statement calling for change; it is collective in that there is a group of people who are together doing the calling; and it is sustained in that it is more than a single event or a small number of events.

A social movement might challenge the way in which powerholders are chosen, as the women's suffrage movement in England did when it organized demonstrations in the early twentieth century to obtain the right to vote. It might challenge the relationship of different powerholders to one another, as when Parisians rallied in 1789 to support the revolutionary National Assembly against the threat of military action by the king. (The relative strength of local and distant authority is a perennial issue; for example, Massachusetts farmers organized militia companies in the 1770s to have the capacity to resist the British army.) Finally, a social movement might challenge particular policies of those in power. A rather spectacular example was a movement of shipyard workers in Gdańsk, Poland, in the summer of 1980 that rapidly came to embrace millions of participants. The central demand was the right of workers to form their own unions and to engage in strikes, although many other demands were also at issue, ranging from prices to freedom of the press. The critical element in recognizing a social movement is not the specific challenge, nor the strategies and tactics employed, but the capacity for sustained, collective, and open action, which permits an ongoing dialogue between the movement and powerholders.

A specific movement organization may emerge that can coordinate actions of participants, articulate demands, and strike explicit deals with governing elites. In the Polish example, such an overall coordinating organization—called Solidarity—soon emerged. Several or even many such organizations may form, sometimes cooperating to pressure the authorities and sometimes competing with one another for resources (even, perhaps, competing violently). To take another Polish instance, resistance to the murderous Nazi occupation of Poland during World War II was organized by a Home Army, a People's Army, the National Armed Forces, the Peasants' Battalions, and other groups as well, whose relations with one another could be extremely hostile. Sometimes, however, there may be no national organization at all. During the French Revolution, for example, for over half a dozen years villagers staged thousands of dramatic disruptions of the activities of local elites, urban inhabitants, and government officials. These villagers won considerable attention and concessions by the revolutionary legislature, but they had no national coordination (and hardly any organization at all beyond the village level).

The capacity for sustained social action has contributed to democratization in a wide variety of ways. For one thing, governing elites have sometimes met popular demands for participation. For example, after a protracted struggle, in 1992 the South African government shifted from totally resisting effective voting rights for the black majority and took part in negotiations for a new constitution. But concessions to social movements have only been one element in the role of elites in democratization. Elites have sometimes acted preemptively, out of fear of social movements. In this fear, the knowledge of what social movements have accomplished elsewhere often plays an important role. In the waves of political turmoil that swept Europe in 1830 and again in 1848, both the conservative governments trying to avert change and the new, liberal governments trying to promote limited change often emancipated their peasantries from the many oppressive claims of local lords. Both liberals and conservatives knew what a mobilized peasantry had been able to do in France during the 1790s, when people in thousands of rural communities defied the new revolutionary authorities until they got legislation that ended the lords' rights.

In addition to making concessions or trying to preempt social movements, elites have also attempted to actively engage the support of their populations. Polish nobles in the 1790s tried to recruit peasants to fight the combined armies of Russia, Prussia, and Austria by promising to end the rights of lords over peasants. They lost the war, however, and the victors carved up a Poland whose peasants still were under the lords' dominion. In the early nineteenth century, South American patricians, trying to recruit an army to fight for independence from Spain, promised to free slaves who joined up. They won, and slaves were emancipated in independent Spanish-speaking America.

Sometimes one elite faction has sought popular support in struggles with other elite factions. One tactic for doing so is to develop democratic rights of one sort or another. In nineteenth-century England, some of the support for initial expansion of the very limited right to vote came from those elites who thought the newly eligible voters would favor their party. In nineteenth-century Chile, the right to vote was extended to poor country people. A significant element in the expanded franchise was the correct perception that the newly enfranchised would support the candidates preferred by very conservative landowners.[8] In subsequent chapters, you will see all these mechanisms at work. Democratic institutions grow out of such movement-government dialogues.

But why were social movements of all sorts flourishing from the eighteenth century and onward as never before? One important part of the answer, as suggested by the political scientist Sidney Tarrow, appears to lie in the expansion of transportation and communication.[9] The growth of literacy increased awareness of the actions of distant people, permitted long-term and long-distance coordination of the activities of many people who had never met, and encouraged those reading the same newspapers and pamphlets, even at a great distance from one another, to experience themselves as members of a community—a movement—engaged in a common purpose. This is very much the same cluster of circumstances that scholar Benedict Anderson sees as the seedbed of modern nationalisms,[10] and it is not at all surprising that nationalism has been one major theme carried by social movements. But social movement participants have felt themselves engaged in other common causes as well, including struggles for altering power relationships within existing states. We will look a bit more closely at the growth of communication and transportation (as well as at other important trends that nurtured social movements) in Chapter 3.

Democratic movements, from the 1780s on, have been remarkably transnational, with some participants readily traveling from one movement to another. Let's note just two of many possible examples, chosen from the late eighteenth century. A former English sailor, corset maker and schoolteacher, Thomas Paine, served as an effective promoter of the American rebels through his writing while attached to George Washington's army in 1776. Back in England, he championed local democratic causes and published a major defense of the French Revolution against conservative attack. He then crossed the English Channel and, having been given French citizenship, was elected as a deputy to the French Revolutionary Convention, where he was an important participant in debates on the fate of the king. In his statement of his views in that debate, he drew on his American experience. Ultimately, weary of the European struggles of the 1790s, he returned to the more securely republican America.

Tadeusz Kościuszko, a liberal Polish aristocrat and military engineer, also joined the American rebel forces as one of a small but significant group of European officers. Later, in Poland, he participated in defending his country against its conservative neighbors, who were frightened by the Polish Constitution of 1791, the first European constitution produced in the wake of the U.S. model that had been ratified in 1789. (The Polish events that so frightened neighboring monarchies had led Paine, whose concerns defied national boundaries, to think about becoming a Polish citizen.) As Poland fell prey to the armies of Prussia, Austria, and Russia, Kościuszko took up residence in revolutionary France, whose legislature granted him citizenship. There he observed the radical democratization that accompanied France's military mobilization against the invading European monarchies. Returning to Poland, he organized a similar broad, popular mobilization, similarly accompanied by democratic promises, and led the stubborn but failing defense of Warsaw against the Russian army. Following the collapse of Poland's democratic forces, he passed several years in America before returning again to France.

It is noteworthy that Paine and Kościuszko were able to find democratic causes in America, England, France, and Poland at the same historical moment. Paine and Kościuszko lived not so much in a country as in a social movement. Paine even referred to himself as a citizen of the world. How do social movements take on a transnational character? Several different aspects of social movements may cross national frontiers, and they have several possible ways to travel.

What Can Social Movements Borrow from Each Other?

Social movements of many different types have proved extremely mobile, often crossing national frontiers with ease. At least four aspects of social movements are sometimes imitated by social movements elsewhere: broad ideas, forms of public action, organizational vehicles, and symbols or slogans.

Broad ideas. A social movement may draw on broad ideas developed elsewhere about the nature of social injustice and the structure of a better social order, sometimes adding a local elaboration to those ideas. The socialist movements that developed in many countries in the nineteenth century, for example, drew on a common body of general ideas but were elaborated with many national variations. Late nineteenth-century Russia nurtured a number of groups that claimed to be Russian branches of Marxian socialism. In the early twentieth century, one of these groups coalesced into a highly disciplined party of full-time revolutionaries and became known as the Bolsheviks.[11] The Chinese variant that developed a bit later emphasized the role of disadvantaged nations rather than continuing the usual focus on the industrial working class.[12] Yet the common elements in these and other socialist movements were strong enough that adherents could move from country to country, participating in turn in each country's political life. In the first part of the twentieth century, for example, Rosa Luxemburg was an important figure in socialist parties in Russia as well as in Germany.

Forms of public action. A second element of social movements that is capable of diffusion from one national setting to another is a specific form of public action. The sit-in was developed by a small number of black Americans who insisted on being served at a lunch counter in the southern United States. Within a few years, student groups all over western Europe were staging sit-ins of one sort or another for diverse purposes. In this case, television played a major role in the rapid diffusion of the new model of protest. Similarly, Soviet miners staging a hunger strike at the Hotel Rossiya in Moscow in 1991 claimed to have gotten the idea from TV footage about the Irish Republican Army.[13]

It is sometimes possible to identify a particular event that has provided models for social action. The sit-in model, for example, can be very precisely placed at a lunch counter in Greensboro, North Carolina, on February 1, 1960. But that event itself borrowed from predecessors. One scholar of the sit-in has found that in the late 1950s similar actions had been organized by blacks in no fewer than fifteen cities, but it was the Greensboro event that dramatically caught wide attention.[14]

Even further back, some detect another layer of transnational borrowing and adaptation. The power of nonviolent disruption had been explored by an

Indian lawyer working with Indian immigrant laborers in South Africa in the early twentieth century. These laborers were attempting to resist new legislation denying them voting rights while subjecting them to new taxes. Later on, Mahatma Gandhi brought that experience home to India. He organized astounding, massive refusals of compliance with British regulations in the 1920s and 1930s. The Gandhian model suggested a variety of nonviolent disruptive tactics to others in other countries, for example, the Defiance Campaign in South Africa in the 1950s, shortly before the U.S. sit-ins.

The sociologist Aldon Morris has traced the role of the pacifist organization The Fellowship of Reconciliation in carrying the tactics of nonviolent protest into the American civil rights movement in the 1950s. Members of that group were active in introducing the leaders of the Montgomery bus boycott to Gandhian ideas, speaking at churches, organizing workshops, and disseminating literature. A particularly influential book circulating in these early days of the civil rights movement explained that the author was interpreting the Indian experience in American terms.[15] So although it is possible to say that the Greensboro event caught many an imagination, it is not possible to really fix a single moment as the precise point that the sit-in was put together for the first time.

Organizational vehicles. The organizational vehicles of social struggles may also be copied. In the nineteenth century, labor unions, political parties, and clandestine, underground cells all proliferated worldwide. In 1989, to choose a more recent example, many eastern European countries experienced the development of an oppositional voice that avoided calling itself a party, the word *party* having been discredited by the Communist Party: Civic Forum (Czechoslovakia), New Forum (East Germany), Democratic Forum (Hungary). In the early twenty-first century, a wide array of countries has experienced huge mobilizations brought together by overlapping networks of people connected through the new electronic technology of social media without any overall organization at all.

Symbols or slogans. Finally, social movements often seem to appropriate (and sometimes to domesticate) symbols or slogans from elsewhere. The Goddess of Democracy, put up by Chinese demonstrators in Beijing's Tiananmen Square in 1989, looked much like a daughter of the U.S. Statue of Liberty. The Statue of Liberty, itself a nineteenth-century French present to a sister republic, revived an image from the French Revolution of the previous century. Chinese students in France at the time of the Beijing demonstrations, which coincided with the French Revolution's bicentennial, underlined the connection by wearing buttons showing the Goddess above the caption "1789–1989."

Such appropriations, however, are often creative adaptations rather than simple copyings. Let's take another look at China's Goddess of Democracy. It wasn't named "Liberty" after the late eighteenth-century European slogan; its visage was taken to be Asian by onlookers; its bearing suggested a Chinese goddess of mercy; its color and location recalled (ironically) a well-known statue of Mao.[16] And although foreign observers of Chinese events in 1989 might reflect on the 200th anniversary of the French Revolution, some Chinese might well have thought of the 70th anniversary of the May 4 Movement of 1919, an important moment in China's own revolutionary history.

Symbolic borrowings need to be locally meaningful. One might add that organizational forms need to be locally viable (western models of socialist parties were most definitely not viable in repressive nineteenth-century Russia); general notions of justice and social good need to be locally interpretable. A great deal of what is creative in social movements lies in forging the amalgam that is both transnationally and nationally meaningful. The history of democracy involves a great deal of such creativity.

How Do Social Movements Cross National Frontiers?

Quite distinct aspects of movements can travel far. But how do they travel? A variety of routes produce such transnational diffusions, including replication of structural circumstances, transmission of a cultural model, and movements of people across frontiers.

Replication of structural circumstances. Certain features of social structure may powerfully constrain the goals, symbolisms, or tactics of social movements. If such structural features migrate transnationally, the concomitant elements of social movements should similarly migrate. Giovanni Arrighi and Beverly Silver have explained this mechanism using the example of the sit-down strike.[17] The occupation of a factory by workers is an obvious tactic when very expensive machinery that is central to production processes (such as an assembly line) is lodged in a confined and defensible space. The sit-down strike flourished in Michigan in the 1930s and then followed the world movement of the auto industry everywhere. It reemerged in western Europe in the 1960s, in Argentina in the 1970s, and in Poland and Brazil in the 1980s.

Ironically, one important reason that automobile production moved to new locations is that investors became anxious to avoid the places where labor conflict was taking place and sought new locations. But similar production technologies generated similar vulnerabilities to disruption, which were simply rediscovered in the new locations.

Transmission of a cultural model. Symbols or tactics sometimes strike responsive chords across a wide variety of issues and social circumstances, as in the rapid spread of the idea of two broad forces, democracy and aristocracy, in the 1780s and 1790s or in the diffusion of the demonstration in the nineteenth century. Movement themes and tactics can both migrate across social boundaries to the extent that people are linked through communication networks. The histories of printing and of literacy are of central importance here, not to mention the electronic media of the twentieth century—or the nonelectronic media, for that matter. Once the technology for putting words and images on T-shirts was developed, the idea of putting social movement slogans on this inexpensive item became widespread within a very few years. Tourists might have readily observed local people wearing such slogans as "Corsica—Liberty or Death" in the 1970s. In 2002, when a storm caused a tanker to dump twenty million gallons of oil off the coast of Galicia in northwest Spain, a large movement for environmental defense mobilized around the slogan "Never Again." A decade later, local merchants were selling T-shirts with that phrase to tourists shopping for souvenirs. Photojournalists diffused such images even more widely. By the mid-twentieth century, sounds and images of protest were carried to living rooms by TV. In the early twenty-first century, people could get the latest protest news with sound and images on their smartphones that some activist or curious bystander had uploaded on the other side of the world.

Sidney Tarrow has made the very interesting suggestion that certain forms of action are far more transmissible than others because they can be used for a wide variety of purposes and by a wide variety of groups. He calls such forms of collective action "modular," because they can be combined with a wide range of ideas and organizations.[18] The *demonstration,* beginning in the nineteenth century, became the great all-purpose form of action. Many ideas of justice could be expressed in demonstrations; many symbols could be carried on signs or chanted; many kinds of organizations could stage them.

Movements of people across frontiers. As people migrate, they carry with them their experience of particular models of conflict. It is often alleged, for example, that late nineteenth-century and early twentieth-century immigrants to the western hemisphere from Spain and Italy carried European anarchist traditions with them (in broad orientations, specific tactics, and symbolizations) and imparted thereby an anarchist component into labor movements from Canada to Argentina.

Perhaps certain social roles are inherently fruitful carriers of models of social action. Peter Linebaugh and Marcus Rediker have explored the role of sailors in the early modern Atlantic world in carrying models of social conflict from port to port. The sailors' world was almost quintessentially multinational and multicultural, as people jumped ship in one place and later signed on another vessel. The English word *strike*, incidentally, seems to derive from defiant sailors announcing their refusal to obey by striking the sails—that is, by hauling down the sails so the ship could not leave port.[19] The subsequent use of the word to describe actions by other groups of workers—who might similarly announce their intention by putting down their tools or stopping their machines—is an example of the diffusion of a concept beyond its original social location.

A World of States

Social institutions have sometimes been shaped in similar ways in different countries, we have just seen, by social movements pushing in similar directions. There is a second way that institutions have been similarly shaped in different places: the tendency of states to imitate each other. Sociologists have come to recognize that organizations, far from solving their own problems in isolation from one another, are profoundly influenced by one another. John Meyer and Brian Rowan, for example, speak of organizational structures as having an important ceremonial component: The purpose of a particular way of organizing certain tasks may be to give a proper appearance. Some organizations may innovate to solve a problem; other organizations, later on, may then mimic that innovation to look like the successful pioneers.[20] I will take a brief look at the theory of organizational mimicry that sociologists have been developing and then apply that theory to the particular kind of organization that is important for us—namely, the state.

Why do organizations come to resemble one another? Why, for example, do universities look much alike? Or hospitals? Or libraries? Paul DiMaggio and Walter Powell suggest several ways in which such mutual resemblances are produced:

- If organizations depend on external resources, they tend to try to look like organizations that already have succeeded in obtaining those resources. If universities all depend on government grants, for example, they will all come to look alike. Those giving the grants have some ideas of what a proper university should look like, and universities seeking such grants will try to fit those ideas.
- To the extent that one organization can actually make demands on another, the weaker organization may come to resemble the dominant one. This proposition presumes that decision makers in the stronger organization desire that the weaker one be similarly organized. This condition is not always the case, however, as you will see when I apply these ideas to the system of states.
- If it is difficult to understand how to solve problems, weaker organizations will try to ape the easily visible characteristics of those that appear to have solved them. If organizations that have done well have accounting departments, soon all will, even if no one is sure that accounting departments made the leaders do well. Uncertainty about problem solving may occur when people are unsure of how to arrive at some desirable goal, but it also characterizes a situation in which there is no consensus about what the goals are.
- To the extent that there is a common culture among organizational personnel, then similar ideas permeate organizations. This common culture might be achieved by exposure to common sources of training or by the development of professional networks that cut across organizational lines.[21]

These propositions apply to national states as well as to other types of organizations. Poor countries that need to borrow from foreign sources of credit may attempt to model themselves on countries that have already succeeded in obtaining loans. Weak states depend on stronger ones and may bid for favor by mimicking their political structures. Conquering armies often try to dictate a new political system. Young people are often trained in foreign schools and sometimes by foreign militaries. An increasingly interconnected world sees a blossoming of professional contacts that cross the boundaries of the nations within which those professionals are employed.

We would therefore expect many resemblances among states. In fact, there is a remarkable convergence of much about modern nation-states. For example, states resemble one another in their national flags; all states have them, and most flags are similar in size and shape.[22] National constitutions are also similar. They may or may not actually be enforced, but increasingly they resemble one another in claims of fundamental citizen rights and government responsibilities.[23]

Among the elements of government subject to these imitative processes are those that indicate the existence of democratic or authoritarian regimes:

- *Direct imposition*: States have sometimes been able to directly impose their forms on one another. In the 1790s the armies of the revolutionary French Republic imposed constitutions very much like its own on a wide variety of "satellite republics," including Holland, Switzerland, and several states in Germany and Italy. After 1945 the United States and the Soviet Union each remade the lands held by its troops in its own image.
- *Models of success*: At other moments, one or another structure has seemed to carry the stamp of success. When the Spanish-American colonies threw off Spanish rule, they could follow the striking North American model of republican constitution writing. But they could also follow the recent Spanish constitution of 1812. When Japan produced a constitution in the late nineteenth century, it had a Prussian model. When the early twentieth-century Russian Empire considered constitutional rule, it had the Japanese model. Constitutions written following the victory of the western democracies in World War I embodied many democratic elements, as in Mexico and Turkey. Some states that achieved national independence at that time, like Ireland and Iceland, were set up as and have remained democracies. But states that achieved national independence in the wake of World War II, when two impressive but rival political models joined to defeat fascism, often started with a democratic constitution that was later torn up in the name of socialism. Antidemocratic models exist as well. The military coup staged by Brazilian generals in 1964, for example, helped inspire similar coups in nearby countries.

- *Resource dependence*: It is more difficult to demonstrate the impact on political institutions of depending on another state for loans, weapons, or defense. It is probably the case that such resource dependence is conducive to imitation, but powerful states sometimes do not wish to be imitated, and their clients in weaker states may realize that they do not. In the wake of World War I, the victorious western democracies supported some democratic elements in the Balkans, although they strongly promoted monarchies over republicanism. In the dismembered Arab provinces of the defeated Ottoman Empire, however, the western democracies sometimes promoted princely regimes with no democratic features whatsoever. Nazi Germany sometimes seemed to prefer local authoritarian regimes among its allies rather than having to deal with dynamic fascist ones. The Soviet Union sometimes (but not always) was skittish about revolutionary socialist movements that might not be under its control. And the United States has hardly always been a friend to democracy in Latin America. During the Cold War the United States supported military regimes that claimed to be joining it in its global struggle against communism and became more clearly supportive of democracy with the Cold War's end. But in the early twenty-first century it funded authoritarian Middle Eastern regimes to help control Islamicist terrorism and defend what it defines as its strategic interests.
- *Cultural ambience*: Finally, the general intellectual culture of an age, which leads problems and their solutions to be conceived in certain terms, also leads powerful states to publicize their cultures abroad and praise their own institutions. The United States in the 1990s, for example, was actively promoting the notions of a dual transition to democracy and the free market, virtually worldwide. States may offer fellowships to foreign students from weaker states and send training missions abroad to socialize foreign professionals, from economists and engineers to physicians and military officers. During the Cold War, the United States brought many military officers from other countries to train with American officers; the Soviet Union created Patrice Lumumba University in Moscow for students from poorer countries. Since the 1990s, the economics departments of leading U.S. universities have actively recruited foreign graduate students and have thereby been training many of those who will shape economic policy in other countries.

By virtue of such mechanisms, there are usually a small number of political models that are widely followed. This fact is one important key to the wavelike character of democratization. At certain historical moments, countries identified with democracy have been conspicuously successful models of power or wealth or both, and they have had considerable influence on reforming elites elsewhere. In the 1790s, the United States and France seemed models of dynamic new possibilities; in the wake of World War I, the western democracies were the clear (if wounded) victors; in the wake of World War II, the fruits of victory were divided between two models of social and political organization; and since the late 1980s, some of the major contenders for global influence have made democratic claims, but an increasingly powerful China seemed an alternate model, one that combined successful economic growth and wealth accumulation with the suppression of democratic movements. In 2014, an increasingly authoritarian Russia was organizing a Eurasian Union of authoritarian states.

Reforming Insiders and the Challenge of Social Movements

The ideas in this chapter will help us explore, in the coming chapters, how social movements and elite reformers have shaped democracy. But social movements or elite reformers often do not act alone but instead confront one another. Thus we need some notion of how they interact.

Those in positions of authority may respond to democratizing forces in a wide variety of ways:

- They may ignore them, especially if they seem weak and unthreatening.
- They may attempt to suppress them.
- They may be pushed into democratizing changes by social movements.
- They may attempt to undercut potential movements by making changes quickly.
- They may even be led to encourage democratization in their own interests.

You will see all these mechanisms at work in subsequent chapters.

Powerful elites may have other reasons for espousing democracy, apart from being challenged by movements, and here other states may be very influential. Those in power may feel a need to please foreign sponsors by appearing democratic, may even have been placed in power by external democratic forces, may find foreign democratic models appealing when at a loss for what to do, or may participate with other states in a culture that shares democratic values.

Now let's consider how these two sorts of processes—a dialogue between governing elites and social movements on the one hand and the pressures of the international order on governing elites on the other—can occur jointly.

One extremely favorable circumstance for the mobilization of social movements is elite action that provides resources and encouragement. The interstate processes that I have discussed sometimes have such a consequence. To the extent that governing elites experience a need to present a proper appearance to powerful foreign interests, they may provide opportunities for the mobilization of movements attempting to gain some access to power. In Chapter 4, we will look at how commitments to notions of "human rights" provided an important opportunity for democratizing movements in the 1980s.

A second favorable circumstance is an elite divided between reformers committed to change and traditionalists who are opposed. The reformers may point to the threat from a more challenging movement to gain the assent of their conservative fellows. At other times the reformers may even attempt to mobilize popular support themselves. In a number of nineteenth-century European countries with very restricted voting rights, elite reformers were often able to neutralize the opposition of more conservative elite factions by pointing to the threat of social movements taking a potentially revolutionary form. In such situations, it is often very difficult to figure out whether we are looking at a social movement that has successfully intimidated an elite or at a portion of the elite that has made use of a social movement (or both).

Whether elite factions have democratic commitments because they have been educated in a democratic country, because they see democratic states as successfully solving problems, or because they depend on foreign democratic states for funds, the elite may provide opportunities for democratic movements. External pressure for a democratic appearance may also enable a social movement to challenge the existing arrangements.

Conclusions

The exercise of power is often a major focus of conflict. We have suggested that ideas about power have been a central aspect of such conflicts. Both social movements and reforming elites have played significant roles in the history of democratization. The actions of both movements and elites have been profoundly shaped by transnational social processes.

In the chapters that follow, we will find movements, often involving transnational components, demanding democratization; we will also find important antidemocratic movements. We will find elites advocating democratizing reforms, often in response to the initiatives of other states; we will find antidemocratic actions by elites as well. And we will see movements and elites interact: movements pushing elites and elites opening opportunities for movements. When these processes come together in a great multinational convergence, the result is a wave of democratization (or a wave of antidemocracy).

CHAPTER 3
EIGHTEENTH-CENTURY REVOLUTION, NINETEENTH-CENTURY EDDIES

Around 1770, most governments of large territorial states were headed by monarchs, whose position was inherited and whose authority was held to derive from God and to be a part of the cosmic order. Most people were not "citizens" of any state, with clearly defined rights to engage in political life. In most countries people were regarded as belonging to groups that differed in their rights and privileges. A special class of people was often regarded as having specialized knowledge of the will of God (or the gods). They claimed considerable power, because royal authority, at bottom, came from sacred roots.

For many centuries, political life in most places had had such features. Yet less than a century and a half later, on the eve of World War I, a great deal had changed. By the early twentieth century, in many parts of the world, rulers claimed that they ruled by the will of "the people." Even monarchs often (but not always) claimed that they ruled in the name of the people as well as God. Some large states had elected bodies with considerable power. In others, elected officials shared authority with hereditary officials. A handful of countries even approximated our current notions of democracy.

Democratic Breakthrough

How did this breakthrough into democratic politics come about? And how did democratic ideas and institutions spread? It is exceedingly difficult to pinpoint the place and time of this breakthrough, but its center was certainly western Europe and the Atlantic colonies. Why did it take place in this part of the world and at this moment in history? Scholars suggest three different places to look for an answer.

The first approach suggests that we direct our attention to unique features of western culture. Western culture, so this line of argument goes, was a uniquely favorable environment for the development of ideas about limiting government power, making those in authority responsible to other human beings, and holding individual human beings responsible for their actions and equal before God.

Scholars taking the second approach suggest that we look for unique features of the economic and political arrangements that developed in the West in the Middle Ages. During the era of western European feudalism, political power was widely dispersed among numerous barons, counts, dukes, and kings. Political and religious authority were separated, and popes and kings disputed who had the authority to appoint bishops. And new kinds of economic power were developed by merchants and bankers, who flourished in the towns. The merchants and bankers managed to acquire and protect their considerable autonomy from counts, kings, and bishops, often by playing them off against each other. Scholars who take this approach often disagree on the prime agents of democratization. Was it those who held the wealth, struggling to assert their rights against kings, counts, and bishops? Or was it movements of the people who worked in the fields and urban workshops, who were able to extract concessions from the complex and divided western elites?

The third approach finds the explanation in neither some European cultural distinctiveness nor Europe's economic and political institutions. Rather, this third approach looks to the economic, political, and cultural interplay of Europe and the non-European world. The outward expansion of European power—down and eventually around the African coast, across the Atlantic, into the Indian Ocean—brought new products, new wealth, and new knowledge into Europe during the fifteenth, sixteenth, and seventeenth centuries. And it brought an awareness of peoples, previously unknown, some of whom had (or appeared to have) profoundly different social institutions. Europeans not only had new medicines to understand, new maps to draw, and new tastes to savor but also had a suddenly wider array of human practices to consider. Europeans found in the New World unknown religions; unexpected ways of agriculture; alien patterns of kinship, property, child rearing, warfare, and sexuality; and hardly the least of such novelties, new forms of government. Some Europeans found the settled knowledge of the past inadequate. These contacts fueled by economic gain and political conquest brought a new cultural awareness and profoundly opened up Europeans' discussions of their own institutions.

Some writers of the era described the cultures and institutions of Africa, Asia, and the New World more or less accurately. Other observers, like Thomas More in 1516, began to imagine "utopias," societies with improved economic, social, and political institutions. (Symptomatically, More set his pioneering utopia in the New World.)[1] If one of the roots of the democratic breakthrough was the capacity to imagine that genuinely new institutions could be created, this particular root was very likely nurtured in European reflection on the diversity of non-European practices and the consequent creation and contemplation of fictional social arrangements.

The absence of some of the constraints of European societies led these observers to find among the peoples of the western hemisphere both the absence of recognized social hierarchies and the presence of "liberty." Here is a Spanish account from the 1580s:

> A number of the peoples and nations of the Indies have never suffered Kings nor Lords of an absolute and sovereign sort. They live in common and create or ordain certain Captains and Princes for certain occasions only, during which time they obey their rule. Afterward, their leaders return to their ordinary status. The greatest part of the New World governs itself in this fashion.[2]

In the centuries that followed the voyages of Columbus, European discussion of political institutions sometimes showed significant awareness of the non-European world. When Europeans wrote favorable accounts of political institutions in the New World or Asia, were they simply projecting the hopes and concerns that they already had onto foreign institutions? Or did new knowledge arouse new hopes and new concerns? These are very difficult questions. It is certain, however, that some were quite fascinated by, say, the

Indians of North America (as were Thomas Jefferson and Benjamin Franklin, for the latter of whom the world's outstanding model of decentralized federalism was the Iroquois).[3]

This debate on the origins of modern democracy is extremely important. If unique characteristics of western culture favored the emergence of democratic concepts, perhaps, some might argue, this uniqueness persists and we therefore cannot expect democratic institutions to take root elsewhere. But if democracy was rooted in the interplay of western political and economic institutions, then the development of similar political and economic institutions elsewhere could foster the development of democracy. And if the initial burst of democratization was energized by awareness of others' institutions and cultures, then perhaps subsequent democratizations have retained a transnational character. Finally, perhaps the power of democratic notions is so great that, once created, they can implant themselves in a wide variety of places. In this latter line of argument, understanding the origins of democracy will not help us guess its future.

In this book I wish only to raise these large questions. But whether or not we see western culture as uniquely favoring democracy, western culture did provide the language with which emerging democratic notions were usually expressed in the late eighteenth century—and beyond. Political theorists trying to explain what was happening around them were likely to refer to the European past, however powerful an impact the world outside Europe was actually having.

In the next few sections, I will explore how the commercializing and increasingly literate late eighteenth-century world of the North Atlantic was beginning to talk about government just as the modern era of social movements was beginning. Social movement activists and powerholding elites alike responded to the changing world around them in a language rooted in a Christian and feudal past by launching the modern debate over democracy.

Negative Ideas about Democracy before the Democratic Breakthrough

Before the late eighteenth century, *democracy* was a term that generally carried a strong negative resonance. For example, when a learned French writer's dictionary was published in 1690, a reader could find democracy defined as a "form of government in which the people have all authority," but this is taken as both impractical and undesirable. Impractical because only a long time ago and on the scale of a single city had it ever existed ("democracy only flourished in the republics of Rome and Athens"). Undesirable because "seditions and turmoil happen often in Democracies."[4] Democracy was not possible in a large, modern state, which was just as well because, as the critics of ancient democracy realized, it would encourage the less well off to plunder the better off, it would bring disorder, and it would yield undesirable policies since the less well educated know neither what is in their own interest nor what is in the interest of the larger community.

Some writers, however, saw all forms of rule recognized by ancient writers as having their own distinctive deficiencies and advocated a "mixed government" in which a bit of each could balance the vices of the others. These writers imagined that an ideal structure might combine a monarch, an aristocracy dominating a judiciary or an upper house of a legislature, and, for balance, a lower house where representatives of a broader stratum could sit. But even for them, democracy in itself was viewed very negatively. For such reasons few people called themselves "democrats" before the 1780s and indeed the word was not commonly used before then. This is why those who sat in the U.S. constitutional convention did not describe the political system they were constructing by this negative term and only later, but not much later, did people begin to think that the new country was a new kind of democracy.

Western Traditions and English Upheavals

When people in the late eighteenth century began to call themselves democrats and to seek words to describe the new political institutions they were advocating, they could draw on western culture in at least two important ways. First, it was easy for them to think of those with power as having responsibilities to ordinary people; this notion arose from the culture of feudalism that characterized western Europe in the Middle Ages. Second, it was easy for them to see current social arrangements as violating the highest ideals of justice; this notion was a vital part of Christian culture.

The feudal concept of a contract. Feudalism dictated that a man owed various services (payments, labor, military service) to his lord. But it was understood that the lord in turn owed services to those below him. Furthermore, lords could freely enter into contracts to exchange services; for example, a king and a count might swear their mutual support. However much those with power might avoid any real reciprocity, those down below always had rights in principle.

In addition, feudal authority tended to be spoken of as limited. Even when they were most powerful, the kings of England and France were held to be under God's law, bound by the traditions of their own kingdoms and subject to the dictates of common sense. Outside of the West, monarchs' authority was not always seen as so limited: Russian tsars, for example, were regarded as being filled with God's spirit, and some Asian monarchs were held to actually be gods. The notion that aristocrats had rights that even monarchs could not abuse was very important in western conflicts but harder to sustain in some other parts of the world. In western Europe, as elsewhere, the notion that ordinary people had such rights was far harder to sustain. Nevertheless, the language of reciprocal rights and obligations that characterized the feudal elites may well have made it easier to think about the rights of every person.

At the level of the local rural communities, in which most people lived around 1770, some experience of collective discussion and decision making was probably widespread. Villagers in China, India, and Africa, as well as France and England, had considerable experience of this sort.[5] Thus the experience of autonomous decision making was unlikely to have been more characteristic of western Europe than of other places. The breakthrough into modern democracy in the countries around the North Atlantic probably had more to do with the ways in which the powerful, the wealthy, and the educated interacted with the urban lower classes and the great majority in the countryside than with any differences in the daily political experiences of most people. But it must be said that the ways in which the political practices of the less powerful may have shaped the early history of modern democracy as it unfolded in different countries is a subject about which scholars still have a great deal to learn.

It is clear, however, that in western Europe and its American offshoots, educated people easily got into the habit of regarding governments as if these were created by contracts in which all had rights and duties. Indeed, several important western political philosophers, such as the English Thomas Hobbes and the French Jean-Jacques Rousseau, wrote about what such fictitious contracts might have been like, as if such contracts had been real, historical events in which people had voluntarily created the social and political institutions under which they were to live. From writing about fictitious contracts it was a relatively short step to writing a real one. This short step is where modern constitutions come from. (Indeed, modern constitutions themselves in some ways continue the tradition of fictitious contracts, because most people who live under those constitutions have never had any opportunity to give or withhold assent, let alone participate in writing them.)

The Christian conceptions of equality. In addition to the contractual notions of European feudalism, Christian traditions were drawn on in the development of democracy. Christians had developed a distinctive way of speaking of "the people." From the Gospels on, one side of Christianity challenged the claim that one person was above another in the eyes of God. The only person specifically named as achieving salvation was a thief crucified with Jesus. We also read of Jesus showing compassion to such scorned persons as a prostitute and a tax collector while criticizing the rich and rejecting the temptation when Satan offers to make him a king on earth. Again and again in the Middle Ages, various groups embraced this side of Christian teaching (often against the opposition of the ecclesiastical hierarchy) and found nobility in the common people rather than a narrow upper class.

In the sixteenth and seventeenth centuries, Europe was devastated by very bitter warfare between different kinds of Christians, who have come to be known as Catholics and Protestants. In the course of that conflict, theologians on one side or the other sometimes justified the assassination of monarchs of the opposing group. They endorsed the idea succinctly conveyed by an old Latin phrase, "Vox populi, vox Dei," meaning "The voice of the people is the voice of God"—in other words, maybe God sometimes speaks directly through ordinary people and even empowers the assassins of evil kings. Thus apologists for particular acts of regicide in France's religious wars of the sixteenth and seventeenth centuries helped undermine the priestly legitimation of monarchical authority. If God's will was manifest in an assassin's act, perhaps it was manifest in less murderous forms of protest as well; and if God could speak through someone other than a priest in deciding the future of a kingdom, perhaps one could look elsewhere than priests' wisdom in other matters as well.

In England in the seventeenth century, the Parliament and the king actually went to war against each other, in part over differing ideas of true Christianity. The supporters of Parliament eventually gave up on kings altogether. After capturing the king, they tried and executed their royal prisoner. On what basis was Parliament now to rule? They found that rather than needing a king as God's agent, England needed a parliament as the people's agent.

While Parliament attempted to mobilize support on behalf of its religious vision, others claimed that God could reveal himself directly to ordinary people. They did not need a specialized class of priests to interpret God's will for them. Some found the right of Parliament to rule as questionable as the right of kings.

Parliamentary armies managed to defeat royal forces on the battlefield and to reassert control over a tumultuous country swept by radical religious doctrines—for a time. Kings eventually came back to England, but they never again had the fully divine authorization of the past. And some found in Christianity radically egalitarian principles. Said one participant as he awaited execution for involvement in a regicidal plot after the parliamentary forces were finally defeated, "I am sure there was no Man born marked of God above another."[6] Moreover, the habit of speaking of "the people" as the ultimate bedrock of politics had been strongly implanted in England's colonies across the Atlantic, where king and parliament alike were quite remote. Colonial governors, appointed in England, had to contend with locally elected town councils and colonial assemblies in Massachusetts, Pennsylvania, Virginia, and the other North American colonies.

The Late Eighteenth Century in Europe

European polities were generally imagined as a collection of juridically un-equal persons, often organized as some collection of corporate structures, and headed by a sacred monarch whose powers derived from the divine scheme of things. The ways of God being esoteric, those with specialized knowledge of those ways carried great weight; and monarchs entered into a variety of mu-tually supportive arrangements with such masters of knowledge. Established churches, therefore, were of great political significance.

The various social strata composed three or four "estates," classes of people with distinct privileges and obligations. A "noble," for example, could be tried in distinctive courts, was exempt from certain taxes, and might have tremendous advantage in careers that carried authority, as in the church or the military. Other estates typically included the clergy and a "third estate" consisting of everyone else, from impoverished peasants to wealthy merchants. Sometimes this last category was divided in two, with peasants in Sweden, for example, having their own estate.

Society, instead of being made up of individuals with identical rights, consisted of collectivities. People belonging to these collectivities—whether estates, provinces, towns, villages, or guilds—had distinctive rights. Just as the estates differed in their rights, so might one town or one province differ from another town or province. This structure is often referred to as a "corporate" conception of society. In a society consisting of so many different and distinct components, nobody other than the king could reasonably claim to speak for the whole. Thus we find in Shakespeare's plays that a French king may be referred to as "France," as if he were the whole country.

Of course, European states had differences. Some of the smaller political systems did without a monarch, as in the city-states of northern Italy or in the Swiss Confederation, but they still conformed to the hierarchical and corporate pattern.

In the East, on the other hand, the corporate rights of groups against claims of the monarch were quite weak. The Russian tsar was literally, as the Russian formula had it, an "autocrat"—a person who rules by himself—in a way without western parallel. The independence of the interpreters of the divine (in Europe, the clergy) also varied a good deal, with that independence being far greater in France or England than in Russia. In most large states outside Europe, recognized inequalities and divinely connected monarchy were the norm as well. Farther from Europe, indeed, monarchs sometimes were believed to be so remote from the common run of humanity as to be not merely divinely sanctioned (as in France or England) or imbued with the divine spirit (as in the Byzantine conception that passed to Russia) but divinely connected (as in Japan).

One distinction of the European world and its offshoots in the western hemisphere was the development of a rival social conception. In this view, government was a contract, freely entered into by juridically identical individuals. Collectivities were held to arise from contracts, and the divine sanction applied to the sacred rights of individuals and not to the authority of states, custom, or tradition. Those who challenged existing social arrangements could point to the absence of a proper contract—and call for one. So powerful did this contractual view become that even the most profoundly hierarchical relations were subject to reinterpretation, to try to fit them into contractual terms. By the late eighteenth century, for example, centuries-old feudal contracts in France were defended as if they were freely consented agreements. Some of those who defended the right of lords to demand payments from their peasants would claim that at some time in the past, peasant communities had voluntarily agreed to pay the lords in return for such services as protection from marauders. In other words, not only did critics of existing arrangements speak of the need for a new contract, but even those who sought to defend the existing social hierarchy on the eve of the democratic breakthrough were often justifying it as the will of sovereign individuals rather than the will of God.

Those who defended the existing order were also very likely, however, to speak of a divine plan that put people in their proper station in life. It was God, in this view, who made kings to rule over peoples; it was part of the divine plan that a lord held a higher station than a peasant. But others were beginning to talk of God's plan in a different way, by stressing the sacred rights of all people.

Most countries in 1770, including western Europe, still had monarchs who claimed to rule by the grace of God and whose monarchies were unalterable components of the divinely sanctioned cosmic order. But many people in the countries bordering the northern Atlantic Ocean found it possible to imagine a "people" who could write a contract (called a constitution) and set up a form of government in which they themselves were the ultimate authority.

The Rise of Public Participation in Politics: Governments Grow, People Protest, Social Movements Are Invented

If the countries bordering the Atlantic were the place of the democratic breakthrough, why was the late eighteenth century the moment? This is another very big question, but a large part of the answer probably is to be found in the increasing capacities of ordinary people to develop and sustain social movements.

Social movements as we know them today were beginning to flourish in England by the late eighteenth century and during the nineteenth century took root in Europe, North America, and elsewhere. To understand why, we need to consider many linked changes: a strengthened government but a weakened king; people organizing themselves to assert claims on that government; a political elite prone to claim that it ruled in the name of the people; transportation improvements and commercial relations linking distant people; the beginnings of widespread literacy and new communications media leading people separated in space to feel themselves moving to a common rhythm.

Social conflict has existed as long as human societies have. But sustained social movements emerged in relatively recent times, partly the result of changes in state power capacities and partly the result of changes in the way people could mobilize. By the eighteenth century in western Europe, separate communities were increasingly connected to one another through the marketplace. Large numbers of people in the countryside were involved in domestic manufacturing, especially of textiles, and buying the food they needed in local markets; others worked as artisans and shopkeepers in the growing cities. A great deal of commercial exchange linked the port cities of the whole Atlantic world, and ships carried goods as well as people and books.

At the same time, European states were growing in power. As states used some of the wealth in their territories for making war on one another, they also acquired the capacity to defeat internal rivals. European governments were subduing independent aristocracies. And the growing numbers who passed part of their lives in military service got to see distant parts of their own country and often other countries as well.

In larger states, the growing central power was usually wielded by a monarch and those close to him; institutions through which townspeople, aristocrats, or others could be represented were usually weak. England was unusual in the degree to which central power was shared by a king and a parliament. People with complaints no longer found it fruitful to take their problems to a local lord, whose own capacity to solve anything had been eroded by the advance of state power. So governments levied taxes to pay for their activities and then became the focus of complaints about taxes; governments organized food supplies to make sure that their capital cities were provisioned and then faced riots from those who felt shortchanged when food was scarce; governments raised permanent armies to wage war and pacify their own kingdoms and then faced resistance from those subject to conscription. Government, in a nutshell, came to be seen as both the source of problems and as the place where problems are solved.

As governments grew, people in villages, in mining communities, in the great ports, and in administrative centers were discovering how to get the attention of governments in a sustained and systematic fashion. In hard times there could be waves of riots over food, as in England in the 1750s or France in the 1770s. But something more than occasional, separate incidents of violent conflict was emerging.

The development of literacy and cheaper printing meant several important things. People could formulate programs for themselves, find their own voice, and petition the authorities. And other people, far off, could read about those events as newspapers began to develop. A reader might sometimes feel a kinship with those in conflict elsewhere; a reader might also feel a kinship with other readers elsewhere.

We may ask about the experience of reading. A lone reader, making up his or her mind about an argument appearing on paper, might be unaffected by whether the author was the son or daughter of a count or the son or daughter of a knife grinder and might indeed not even know the author's status. Yet a reader could feel that the emotions or ideas evoked by the printed page were emotions and ideas shared by other readers. Benedict Anderson speaks of reading creating "imagined communities."[7] Reading was a quintessential experience of belonging to a community made up of individuals, thinking for themselves, and not bound by ties of social dependence.

The English experience. In such circumstances, ways of confronting authorities could spread quickly from place to place, and waves of disturbances could traverse England or France or even cross national frontiers. But England was the leading European country for social movements before the nineteenth century, in part because of an unusually literate population and the early development of journalism. Travelers to England from other countries noted with surprise English people sitting in coffeehouses, leafing through newspapers, and talking about public affairs.

Another important element in the English lead in creating social movements was the linkage of popular concerns and national politics. People were increasingly likely to take their issues to the central government because, increasingly, that was the seat of real power. Local magistrates were more controlled from the center than in the past. The central power in England since the 1640s had been, to a large extent, Parliament, but reasons other than the sheer power of Parliament played a role: England had been early to develop an electoral politics and to begin to legitimate the actions of central government by reference to the popular will.

In the 1640s, as mentioned previously, Parliament and king had fought a great civil war, in the course of which Parliament came to claim that it represented "the people." Although such claims were made much less often in the eighteenth century, when parliaments and kings were no longer competing on the battlefield, the habit of claiming that the people ultimately ruled was a very powerful notion, especially when mechanisms existed by which the will of "the people" could be determined. Petitions of the people were one very old way; elections were another.

Traditionally, a small group of English people would deliver a petition and only a thin layer of the wealthy would vote. But both petitioning and parliamentary elections provided opportunities to mobilize large numbers in a regular way. The petition was considered a legitimate form of political action when a few people peacefully delivered it. Increasingly in the eighteenth century, however, large crowds began to converge on public officials—not with guns but with their wishes in written form. These gatherings stretched the traditional act of petitioning to the point that the authorities sometimes reacted with violence. But such petitions eventually came to be commonplace and had become a regular and accepted part of political life by the early nineteenth century.

Now imagine that this petition-bearing crowd begins to march through the streets, accompanied by a few speakers and some signs or chanted slogans. The result would be what we today recognize as a demonstration. This scenario is probably how the demonstration was born.

As for elections, even though only a very small number of well-to-do English men (no women; no poor; no one who worked in factories, fields, or mines) could actually vote, parliamentary elections became occasions to air opposing viewpoints and mobilize people. Sometimes the elections had a carnival flavor, sometimes a violent one. As enterprising people saw the opportunities in these forms of action, they sometimes organized national petition campaigns, which produced something clearly recognizable as a social movement. But elites could also see the value of claiming a popular demand for positions they favored. Sometimes the petition campaigns were initiated by members of Parliament themselves, in an attempt to show a groundswell of support from "the people." At about the same time, the contenders for political office began to join forces for mutual support in getting bills passed in Parliament and winning elections—and the political party was born. Social movements and political parties, petitions and elections, all developed together. The practice of organizing a collective effort by ordinary people to bring pressure to bear on the political elite was developing—and so was the practice of elite promotion of such collective efforts to generate the appearance of a popular movement.

An example of the way these elements could come together occurred in the 1760s, when the British Parliament would not recognize the election of John Wilkes, a critic of government policies. Crowds proclaiming "Wilkes and Liberty" took to the streets, and an enormous petition campaign was launched. The continuing struggle of Wilkes's supporters and the government involved court battles and election campaigns as well. By the time this dispute quieted down, many ordinary people and many powerholders had gained the experience of a protracted campaign for popular support pursued in the legislative, judicial, and electoral arenas, as well as through mass mobilization and pamphleteering. This early model for future social movements was permeated with questions about Parliament's rules, and it cemented the connection between popular mobilization and elite politics. The Wilkes affair was a prototype for many later struggles.[8] The prototype already showed that social movements would be intertwined with electoral, judicial, and legislative processes.

Some variations. Similar processes were happening elsewhere, but they always had distinctive elements. In England's thirteen North American colonies that were soon to revolt, for example, elected bodies had developed alongside colonial governors. The special twist was the colonies' lack of representation in the English Parliament, as well as the colonies' great distance from England. By the middle of the eighteenth century, many in the colonies were thinking of themselves as a separate people. Parliament's claim to represent "the people," an important claim since the 1640s, often rang hollow enough in England, but it was especially easy to challenge on the western edge of the Atlantic.

In France, until the Revolution of 1789, ordinary people were less likely to form social movements than people were in England. France lacked a regularly meeting parliament and associated election campaigns, had very little by way of journalism, and had lower levels of literacy. With the collapse of France's old social order, however, large numbers of people joined political clubs, and a large number of elections were organized. People began to see themselves as capable of influencing government, and powerholders claimed to act on behalf of the people. As had happened earlier in England, however, a revolutionary government that claimed to rule in the name of the people had persistent difficulty in dealing with organized groups that claimed they actually were the people. Finally, a new breed of revolutionary journalist found an audience among French people wanting to know the fast-breaking news of the day. The breakdown of the Old Regime's police controls encouraged the launching of a vast number of journals aimed at this new audience. The Revolution's journalists espoused a diversity of viewpoints, and many of them claimed a close affinity to "the people" rather than to the political elite, any political elite. Some radical journalists, indeed, encouraged fears that even elected representatives were but a step away from becoming new tyrants unless carefully watched by an ever-vigilant people, highly organized and as capable of rising against the new national leadership as they had proved to be against the Old Regime. These journalists, by the way, were defining a new role for themselves as the watchdogs of the people.

At war with the rest of Europe since 1792, the French government carried ideas of democracy abroad by supporting local democrats as well as by succeeding militarily. The French armies expanded enormously by proclaiming that all French citizens had a duty to defend the fatherland. It took the European monarchies more than twenty years of warfare to finally defeat the French. By then, with the cooperation of those in neighboring countries who wanted change, the French had supported the writing of constitutions in Belgium, Holland, Switzerland, western Germany, and northern Italy. French armies actually penetrated farther and, for a while, dominated Europe from Spain to Russia. Divine-right monarchy was profoundly shaken.

Throughout Europe over the next century, the conditions favoring social movements and those weakening the sacred claims of kings evolved together. The more that social movements pressed successful claims, the more governments tried to appear as embodiments of the will of the people. The more governments claimed to rule by the will of the people, the easier it was for social movements, claiming to be the people speaking directly, to feel comfortable in taking action. Much popular agitation was focused on questions of food availability and price and, later in the nineteenth century, with industrial advance, on wages. But essential questions of electoral rules and citizenship rights were also a part of social movements from their very beginnings in eighteenth-century England. Governments making democratic claims encouraged social movements and social movements struggled to define how democracy would work.

How the Institutions and Ideas of Democracy Spread

In the 1780s people in Belgium and Holland began to speak of "democrats" as opposed to "aristocrats," and for the first time such terms came to be widely used. All over the European world, people recognized sufficiently similar conflicts about the nature of society that similar terminology was taken up.

Before the end of the century, the future Pope Pius VII, in his Christmas talk, was saying that "democratic government" was compatible with the Gospel.[9] Such developments were to a significant degree stimulated by French events. But even after the French defeat, countries that had experienced French rule could not restore the previous divine-right hierarchy. To match the French achievement, France's enemies had to build enormous armies. To do so, many of them needed to court the ordinary people who would fill the ranks and supply the troops. Even governments with no wish to give real power to those below were beginning to find it essential to claim to be doing so.

The American and French Revolutions together demonstrated the viability and power of democratic states. The American success was especially significant as a demonstration of the viability of rule by the people. The new nation did not collapse, as conservatives might have expected, but clearly flourished. The French did not demonstrate the same sort of success; their revolution led to continual changes of regime, internally murderous politics, military coups, and ultimate defeat. For the next century, conservative forces could point to France to demonstrate that the attempt to construct a more democratic order must lead to chaos and violence. But if the French experience failed to reinforce the American example that a government of the people could be stable, it certainly demonstrated that a government of the people could be powerful. The professional and aristocratic armies of monarchical Europe went down to defeat until they themselves managed, like the French, to mobilize the masses.

For many Europeans, the staying power of French armies was a sign of a new form of society. The German poet Johann Wolfgang von Goethe, observing the battle of Valmy, in which French forces held their own against the Prussian army (which was the most impressive of the monarchical forces), claims to have commented, "Here and today a new era of world history is beginning."[10] In the nineteenth century, then, in Europe and well beyond, governments came to claim that they, too, ruled on behalf of the people.

We can see some of the ways such claims began to spread. In Spain, for example, the invading French forces caused a major crisis that led the Spanish government to convene an old representative body, in order to involve "the people" in the anti-French struggle. This development triggered elections in the Spanish colonies. In Mexico these elections, which seem to have had a very wide suffrage, began a process of talking about "the people" there. By the time Spanish America achieved independence early in the nineteenth century, the leaders of the triumphant revolutionary forces, like those before them in the new United States, were so profoundly committed to the repudiation of sacred monarchy that almost all the new Spanish-speaking states set themselves up as republics—that is, as states without hereditary monarchs at their head. Even the major Spanish-speaking attempt at a new monarchy, by a man who called himself emperor in Mexico (Agustín de Iturbide), was itself an interesting sign of the general trend. He announced that he ruled "by the grace of God and the Mexican people," joining the new democratic formula to the older sacred one.[11] Brazil's new emperor similarly acknowledged "the grace of God and the unanimous vote of the people."[12] Perhaps an established monarchy could still maintain the older model of rule by divine authority alone, but by the early nineteenth century a new royal line in the western hemisphere probably could not.

Great Britain: Social Movements and the Established Order

This general trend continued slowly in country after country throughout the nineteenth century and into the twentieth. Consider Great Britain. At the end of the great military struggle against France, the British Parliament, rather than the king, had the upper hand. It held the power to initiate legislation, approve budgets, and somewhat less securely, remove ministers. Yet the House of Commons, elected by less than a tenth of the adult male population,[13] could still easily be swayed by royal favors, payoffs, and support in elections. Thus ministers were not really fully responsible to Parliament and Parliament alone. One of the great matters at issue in many nineteenth-century European countries was whether unelected kings would continue to have the power to appoint ministers and discharge them or whether that power would pass to elected parliaments. On this question, parliamentary power was far more secure at the beginning of the nineteenth century in Britain than elsewhere in Europe, but it was not all that secure even in Britain. Britain's elected House of Commons, moreover, shared power with a hereditary House of Lords. As for parliamentary elections, they were not by secret ballot, and voters could be intimidated or bought.

Increasing ferment around a multiplicity of social movements led to an expansion of the suffrage (by about half) in 1832 and a significant decrease in royal capacity to control election results. Thus the ministerial need for parliamentary support increased, thereby increasing parliamentary control over government policies. In the extremely intense debate over defining those who would have the right to vote, Britain's powerholders largely claimed to be trying to defend, rather than alter, the existing patterns of wealth and power. Those who opposed the extension of the suffrage, of course, claimed themselves to be the party of tradition, order, and good sense. But even those who favored extension of the suffrage spoke of the necessity of giving a few of the excluded the right to vote in order to defuse the threat of popular mobilization. As stated clearly by one member of Parliament, the historian T. B. Macaulay, the limited extension of suffrage was an antidote to the threat of a democratic revolution:

> I hold it to be clearly expedient, that in a country like this, the right of suffrage should depend on a pecuniary qualification. Every argument, Sir, which would induce me to oppose Universal Suffrage, induces me to support the measure which is now before us. I oppose Universal Suffrage, because I think it would produce a destructive revolution. I support this measure, because I am sure that it is our best security against a revolution.[14]

Some of those working to mobilize a mass movement on behalf of a radically expanded right to vote had grave reservations about parliamentary support for limited reform. In fact, those parliamentary reformers vehemently denied an accusation they took to be a malicious slander, the charge by the conservative forces that the reformers were "democrats." Listen to the radical Henry Hunt explain to a crowd in Manchester in 1831 how the conservative Sir Robert Peel was attacking the reformers and what the reformers had to say in response:

> When Sir Robert Peel charged them [the reformers] with going to make a democratical House of Commons ... they said "No, we are going to keep power out of the hands of the rabble."[15]

The expansion of voting rights was therefore the work of a divided elite trying to retain its authority by one means or another while under pressure from organizations like the National Union of the Working Classes, which declared that it would not settle for "any future measure for improving the representation which does not recognize the just right of every man to the elective franchise."[16] But expanded voting rights opened the way (just as the conservative members of the elite predicted it would) to further social movement challenges and ultimately a very much expanded franchise.

One struggle led to another. Within a few years a huge social movement formed around the People's Charter, a proposal for universal male suffrage and secret ballots. Over time, prestigious intellectuals came to embrace the notion of popular participation in national life. In a long series of slow steps, the right to vote expanded. By 1867, the essayist Walter Bagehot thought the monarchy had been reduced to a pleasing and reassuring decoration.[17] But the conflicts we have been examining were not over. As late as the beginning of the twentieth century, British women could not vote, some men had extra votes, and the hereditary House of Lords could still block legislation passed by the House of Commons. On the other hand, ministers depended exclusively on Parliament, and the secret ballot was in force in parliamentary elections. The British case shows how many different issues are part of democratization. Parliamentary control over ministers, voting rights for poorer men, and voting rights for women raised different questions and developed on different timetables. What we now are likely to call democracy, as if it is a single thing, was often experienced in the nineteenth century as a large number of separate questions.

The United States: Rule by "the People"

The new United States had many of the same sorts of conditions that favored the early development of social movements. Unusually high levels of literacy by eighteenth-century European standards, a lively press, extensive exposure of intellectuals to European developments, and a tremendous maritime vitality on that enormous Atlantic coast all guaranteed considerable interchange of ideas from near and far, for ordinary people as well as for an educated elite. Moreover, social movements in the late eighteenth century arguing for the right to participate in the government of the new United States were in the fortunate position of having the language of popular rule already in place. In throwing off a king, the new state (like almost all the western hemisphere's states that soon followed it into independence from Europe) did not create a new monarchical order.

In searching for a nonmonarchical principle to justify some authority over the thirteen former colonies, the elite authors of the U.S. Constitution began with the famous words "We the people." Those who participated at the Constitutional Convention in the late 1780s were from the well-off sectors of the newly independent colonies; most of them were delegates from the established elites of the ex-colonies, chosen by the new state governments. Yet the constitution adopted by these elites does not begin with "We the agents of the state establishments."

Over the next several decades, new state constitutions and federal laws clarified who "the people" were and eliminated definitions of the right to vote that were tied to possession of property or payment of taxes. It is useful to look at this very important shift in two different ways: the general conceptions of social order that people held and the specific and sometimes conflicting interests involved.

Responsible people and other people. The first question is more difficult, the tentative answer more speculative. Residents of the British colonies in North America, like many other peoples, had traditionally tended to speak of political authority as conferred by God. In such a conception, there is a proper order beyond the will of human beings to which those with power may appeal in order to justify their acts to themselves and others. Now imagine that we are in the seventeenth century and questioning this conception. We may be speaking of society as governed by the will of the people, as many were in England in the 1640s. But if God is no longer the source of authority, we may ask anxiously, how is responsible behavior to be assured? If political life depends on the desires and decisions of living human beings, who are not angels, how are stupid, crazed, immoral, or nasty actions to be avoided?

The claim that some people are inherently more responsible than others is a partial resolution to this dilemma. One can trust those with a "stake" in the social order not to be too short-sighted or demented to destroy society, even with God now playing a reduced role. Property holders, so the argument ran, by virtue of having something to lose, are more likely to be public spirited, wise, moderate, and reasonable. This doctrine of the responsible minority was a new way for the few to claim power over the many without having to depend on the claim that the political order is divinely sanctioned.

By the time of the American War of Independence, the way in which such things were discussed on the western edge of the Atlantic Ocean was often no longer tied to property. Responsible behavior was widely held to be lodged in a rather more broadly defined group—namely, those who were materially well-off, whether the source of their well-being was property, commerce, or a profession. Rather than claiming that property made owners responsible, people now often claimed that being well-off gave one the education to know the public good and the independence to stand up for one's convictions. As one participant in the American debate about proper government put it in the 1770s, "There must be some restriction as to the right of voting: otherwise the lowest and most ignorant of mankind must associate in this important business with those who it is to be presumed, from their property and other circumstances, are free from influence."[18]

So although the notion that society should have a government based on "the people" was widely acknowledged even before the birth of the new United States, who was to actually choose those to occupy positions of power was very much in question. Very different notions of who was to speak for the people, and how, coexisted. But then mobilization for the War of Independence advanced the notion that all the people were to actively participate in peace as in war. To invite the less-well-off into the hardships of military campaigns and the risks of rebellion against the greatest maritime power of the age was easier if those who signed on could see themselves as among those who were to rule.

If powerful democratizing currents ran deep in the new country, so did powerful concerns with exclusion. The western hemisphere was a place of settlement not merely for adventurous Europeans but also for the Africans they shipped there in chains and for the indigenous peoples they subdued. Ideas of self-rule coexisted with the enslavement of large numbers of people and the uprooting, displacement, and marginalization of others. Notions of divinely ordained social hierarchies were disappearing, only to be replaced by the elaboration of new measures to exclude many. The question of just who were the American people became, and has remained, a central question in American life.

When the United States emerged from the war, the stage was set for an expansion of voting rights. Historians write of the boisterous, exuberant character of elections in early nineteenth-century America, which were celebrations of the sovereignty of "the people" as much as times of decision. The tradition of local elections as a sort of carnival goes back before the Revolution. Echoes of this carnival still are visible in the hoopla of national party conventions in the United States today.

As in England, however, expansion of the suffrage was not all fun; it took place amid considerable debate and some violence. At one dramatic moment in 1841, to take a particularly striking example, several thousand adherents of the Rhode Island Suffrage Association armed themselves, called a People's Convention, wrote a new state constitution, and elected a governor. For a moment, Rhode Island had two governors, one elected with a broader franchise than the other. Each denounced the other as illegal. Both sides claimed to be defending a "free government" against tyranny.[19] This is a characteristic of struggles over democratization: The defenders of the existing order denounce the rebels as enemies of the freedoms already established, and the rebels claim to represent a democratic advance and denounce the establishment as a sham. Although those favoring an expanded suffrage lost the battle of Rhode Island, some other state governments decided to avoid similar popular mobilizations by expanding voting rights.

What was "universal" suffrage? Efforts to round up a large vote, a language of popular sovereignty embodied in the founding document, a long electoral tradition, and the general ease of mobilization may help explain the achievement in many states of what was called universal suffrage. But some were excluded from the political universe. For one thing, most states restricted voting by free blacks or barred them from voting altogether. Indeed, when the new state constitutions were written, free blacks in some of the northern states actually lost voting rights they had previously enjoyed. New York State's new constitution of 1821, for example, specified no property qualifications for white men, but blacks could not vote unless they were property owners. About thirty thousand free black men who previously had had the right to vote were thereby denied.[20] Similar limits were enacted in most states. Even without legal restrictions, as the French traveler Alexis de Tocqueville noted in the 1830s, "If they come forward to vote, their lives are in danger."[21] Terror could complete the work of legislators.

Women, too, were more profoundly denied the vote by the middle of the nineteenth century than they had been right after the Revolution. Prior to nineteenth-century systematizing and standardizing, small numbers of women seem to have succeeded in casting votes locally. In New Jersey, property-owning unmarried women could vote; married women were regarded as nonowners on the grounds that the property was all their husband's. But the systematizing spirit undid these anomalies (as in New Jersey in 1807).[22] So the "universal suffrage" that Americans were so proud of and that astonished Europeans, at the middle of the nineteenth century, was merely extensive voting rights for white men.

What social conceptions were concordant with such exclusions from universal suffrage? The simplest were arguments that members of excluded groups were, in some essential sense, inappropriate participants. Women were sometimes held to be, by their very nature as women, more suited to private, harmonious, nurturing, and domestic activities than to the public, contentious, tough-minded activities demanded by politics. A more complex thesis argued that women's social circumstances made their full participation a poor idea. Women (or the poor or children or those employed as servants) were sometimes held to be "dependent," unlikely to form a detached and independent intellectual judgment because they lived in the shadow of, in the service of, or under the thumb of others. Such a conception might be coupled with laws that acknowledged such a dependent status—and that also created or perpetuated it. If women were dependents, for example, was it not appropriate that married women own no property in their own name? All property was, therefore, properly administered by their husbands. Such a law, common in the United States in the early nineteenth century, guaranteed that women remained dependent. And if they were not even capable of administering property, how could women be expected to vote on public affairs?

Later in the nineteenth century, it was held that many Native Americans, as "wards" of the United States following their subjugation and consequent impoverishment, were dependent on government handouts and beneficence and therefore were not suitable as citizens. In nineteenth-century America, it was possible for a white man to see himself as benevolent toward Indians (or women), shielding them from the dangers and responsibilities that would go along with losing the protections afforded to the dependent.

The denial of voting rights to free blacks before the Civil War could also rest on a social theory: that black participation in a fundamentally alien culture made it difficult for them to join with whites in pursuing the public good. Even whites who could write of slavery as a crime committed against Africans and their descendants in the New World could contend, as Thomas Jefferson did, that freed slaves must constitute a distinct people with a state of their own rather than be voting participants in the new United States.[23] Later on, some of those who objected to slavery also favored "colonization," the resettlement of freed blacks in Africa, a view initially shared by Abraham Lincoln. Thus American democracy could excite and astonish many observers for its egalitarian aspects while holding millions in bondage and denying the vote to many others, although not on the grounds of lacking property.

In the twenty-first century, people are sometimes surprised to learn that nineteenth-century ideas about democracy were compatible with such extensive exclusions and, for some, compatible with human slavery. It is less surprising when we recall that those who associated the very idea of democracy with some of the city-states of ancient Greece understood that Greek democracy was for free men, not women or slaves. It was the social conflicts of the nineteenth and twentieth centuries that redefined what democracy means.

Old doubts continue and new ones emerge. Although some were embracing the democratic label in the era of the American and French Revolutions, others continued to use the term in a very negative way and to embrace the common critiques of the past. In 1793, the Prussian government justified sending its army into neighboring Poland to combat "the spirit of French democratism" and "to subdue the malevolent who are stirring up troubles and insurrection."[24] Equating democracy with disorder continued. Many still held that the less well educated do not know their own interests, let alone the general interest, and so favored restricting the right to vote to people with significant property, wealth, or education, as commonly argued in Great Britain in the early nineteenth century. In other places, advocates of a democratic order in the abstract came to favor severely limiting democracy in practice for such reasons. Simón Bolívar, a leader of South America's independence struggles who was appalled by the prospect of voting by indigenous communities, recommended that the new country Bolivia, named in his honor, adopt a lifetime president who would name his own successor.[25]

But new worries, unanticipated before the democratic breakthrough, were soon to emerge with even a little experience of democratic realities. Some of those who participated in designing the U.S. Constitution, for example, found that the new country they had helped launch did not live up to their expectations. Many had hoped that democratic processes would generate leadership by a disinterested, enlightened elite that looks out for the general welfare. In the view of some, the new United States in actual practice was producing a political class using public office for private gain, and rather than accepting the wise rule of the educated was developing a far more egalitarian culture in which people were not acknowledging that some knew more than others.[26]

Alexis de Tocqueville visited in the 1830s and wrote admiringly of how much better democracy was working out in the United States than in it had in his native France, yet he saw some new dangers emerging. Democracy in the United States, he held, threatened to lead to mass conformity in ideas and behavior and to replace intellectual distinction with mediocrity, since all were held equal. As for his own country, democracy was tied to centralized government that was grinding locally distinctive traditions into uniformity. But Tocqueville was also of the view that democracy was the inexorable wave of the future, so the task for modern statesmen was to mitigate its drawbacks. Like it or not, it was coming, everywhere.

Movements of the excluded as allies and opponents. Movements on behalf of excluded groups often cooperated and learned from each other. Many people in the movement on behalf of women's rights before the American Civil War had experience in the abolitionist movement, for example, just as the British antislavery movement was a major source of many forms of social activism in that country. Participants in one movement gained valuable experience in organizing, dealing with government, raising funds, and planning actions, which they could then take to other causes. Sometimes participants exchanged ideas. Women working against slavery in England and the United States in the early nineteenth century started thinking about how women, too, were in bondage, what female emancipation might mean, and how to go about achieving it. In the period before the American Civil War, the newer movement for women's rights often joined forces with the older movement for the abolition of slavery.

At other times, however, democratizing movements acted at cross-purposes. In the early nineteenth-century United States, some held that the first and foremost principle of the Declaration of Independence—"all men are created equal"—demanded not only that all white men should vote but also that slavery was unacceptable and that emancipated blacks should vote. As campaigns to expand the right to vote to poorer male citizens gathered steam in state after state, however, many champions of the rights of poorer whites abandoned the cause of blacks. They did not want the many enemies of black voting to join forces with those opposed to votes for poorer white people. In Rhode Island in 1829, for example, a committee of the state legislature opposed extending the right to vote in order to avoid voting rights for blacks and Native Americans.[27] Indeed, some of those who campaigned to extend the vote to all white men vigorously championed rewriting state laws and state constitutions so as to explicitly take the vote away from those free blacks who had it. And some advocated extending the vote to poor whites precisely to exclude blacks even more powerfully than before. In 1829 a Virginia senator said, "We ought to spread wide the foundation of our government, that all white men have a direct interest in its protection."[28]

For some who participated in these debates the choice must have been painful: Should we struggle equally on behalf of poorer whites and free blacks, or should we abandon the rights of one group to secure the rights of others? This was a hotly debated issue, for example, among participants in Rhode Island's movement for suffrage extension in the early 1840s. When the movement decided to limit itself to the cause of white men who had not met the franchise qualification, its opponents bid for black support by proposing to enfranchise propertied blacks.[29]

This sort of dilemma has frequently arisen in the history of democracy in the United States and elsewhere. At the conclusion of the U.S. Civil War, Congress set about amending the Constitution to end slavery and redefine the status of blacks. Many in Congress supported a constitutional amendment extending voting rights to the former slaves. For those in the movement for women's rights, this appeared to be a very favorable moment to advance their own cause as well. The women's movement had been quite close to the antislavery movement; many participants in the women's movement had first gained political experience in the antislavery cause. As pointed out earlier, many ideas about women's "bondage" and "emancipation" were deeply influenced by the ideas and language of the antislavery movement. But now the abolitionists saw that attainment of their own goal was threatened by opposition to women's voting. Some within the antislavery movement feared that linking the causes of women's and black's rights would doom both. Those against extending voting rights to either would oppose extending voting rights to both. Thus, some leading champions of voting rights for freed slaves distanced themselves from the cause of female emancipation. For example, Frederick Douglass, one of the major figures in the movement for abolition and a strong supporter of women's rights, held that voting rights for black men, at this moment, needed to take priority.[30] Others, like Elizabeth Cady Stanton, disagreed:

> No, no, this is the hour to press woman's claims; we have stood with the black man in the Constitution for over half a century, and it is fitting now that the constitutional door is open that we should enter with him into the political kingdom of equality.[31]

The Fourteenth and Fifteenth Amendments, adopted after the Civil War, extended voting rights to black men. This was, in fact, the very first time the Constitution openly distinguished the rights of men and women. As these events unfolded, some advocates of women's voting rights dropped out of the struggle for the political rights of former slaves. Elizabeth Cady Stanton said, "I protest against the enfranchisement of another man of any race or clime until the daughters of Jefferson, Hancock, and Adams are crowned with all their rights."[32] (The logic of this position was to lead some champions of women's suffrage to oppose voting rights for foreign-born immigrants later in the nineteenth century.) Former participants in the antislavery American Equal Rights Association established the National Women's Suffrage Association.[33] For some of those who had participated in both the abolitionist movement and the women's movement, repudiating former allies was a painful experience.

By the early twentieth century, the situation was reversed. Late in the nineteenth century, the southern states had managed to largely undo the effects of the post–Civil War laws. State after state restricted the voting rights of blacks by requiring all sorts of impossible tests. When legal means proved inadequate, opponents of blacks' voting rights threatened economic ruin: Blacks attempting to vote could lose their jobs or have their businesses shut down. When economic pressures failed, violence came into play. All blacks were aware of the waves of lynchings.

For many in the women's movement, once again, the struggle for women's rights was part of a larger struggle for the excluded generally, including blacks. But some thought it was increasingly clear that getting voting rights for women would be easier if that issue could be separated from the plight of black southerners. Southern chapters of women's rights organizations, for example, tended to embrace the "whites only" policies of their state governments. Faced with the difficult choice of losing their southern adherents or distancing their cause from the causes of others, the women's movement on the whole opted for restricting their concern to their own central issue. Once again, participants in democratizing movements felt they had to choose to promote one aspect of democracy and abandon others.

Ultimately the cause of women's suffrage won in the United States. Indeed, one of the reasons it was able to gather support from conservative forces was that enfranchising white women seemed a way of counterbalancing the feared votes of radical immigrants as well as further subordinating the blacks in the South.

As you can see, movements for excluded groups often cooperated, sometimes acted as though they were a single movement, and sometimes competed.

And movements for the excluded sometimes found allies among conservative forces more fearful of other excluded groups.

There is another important lesson here. Many great struggles over democracy in the first half of the nineteenth century had in some important ways profoundly left many people out. In the early nineteenth century, people could talk about universal suffrage, but the universe comprised only white men. One of the most important achievements of abolitionist groups and women's movements was their ability to redefine that universe. What was once almost literally unthinkable eventually became part and parcel of the very idea of democracy—and not only in the United States. Foreign visitors to the United States in the early nineteenth century called it a democracy, although non-whites and women had no votes (and very limited rights). But in the 1970s and 1980s, although South Africa had multiparty competition, very few would have called that country a democracy because only its white minority could vote. A great change in the meaning of democracy had occurred.

Western and Central Europe: Democratic Appearances and Realities

On the European continent, the same story was playing out with variations. Generally speaking, by the mid-nineteenth century most states in western and central Europe had some sort of constitution providing for some sort of elections for a parliament with some sort of powers. However, monarchs still had considerable control over ministers at the turn of the twentieth century, and parliaments had not achieved even the full control over budgets that they had in Britain.

The case of Prussia is a particularly significant instance, for this powerful state became the nucleus of the German unification process that came to fruition in 1871. Prussia's growing economic power in the nineteenth century and eventual military renown (especially after decisive and devastating defeats of Austria and France in 1866 and 1870) made it an inspiring model for states outside of western Europe and North America. The Prussian parliament could not name or remove the king's ministers, nor could it refuse to grant a budget; but it could refuse to increase appropriations. That right gave the parliament significant bargaining power with the ministers, but it still was far short of having control over government and further still from ensuring a government controlled by "the people."

Although the realities of power in much of western and central Europe still limited suffrage and left hereditary monarchs in a very strong position, the claim of representing the people was coming to be seen as essential, especially after a wave of social upheavals shook many European states in 1848 (including Italy, France, Switzerland, much of Germany, and Hungary). In 1851, the president of France, Louis Napoleon Bonaparte, overthrew the new French constitution and ruled largely by decree for more than two decades. Yet he held plebiscites in which the French people were asked to approve his rule. Bonaparte had initially been elected under rules that gave all adult men the vote, making him the only ruler of a major European power who had this particular claim to be the embodiment of democracy.

Of course, many democratizing institutions did not actually aim to alter power relations but rather to provide a new way of justifying the rule of the few over the many. Nonetheless, these changes are important, for they provided many opportunities for social movements aiming at a more genuine democratization.

An evolution similar to western Europe's and North America's took place elsewhere from early in the nineteenth century. By the late nineteenth century, social movements were pressing for rights even where such rights had never existed; governing elites saw western European and North American institutions as models of respectable modernity, as sources of power, or as necessary concessions to social movement challenges. In Germany in 1890, for example, a new king legalized the socialist party, which had been outlawed for a dozen years, in part out of a sense that a respectable modern country had to have such a party. Germany also became famous for its very early commitment to major social welfare programs (which has been generally interpreted by historians as a move to preempt a major issue of parties on the left). This case illustrates how emerging transnational norms (a modern country permits socialist parties) and fears of mobilization by the lower classes (who favored welfare rights) can generate democratic measures from conservative elites.

Beyond the North Atlantic World

By the end of the nineteenth century, the combination of social movements aware of successes elsewhere and governing elites trying to solve problems, appear respectable, and cope with actual and potential movements in their own countries was beginning to bring elements of democratization to states far from western Europe. In Latin America, Chile had begun electing its presidents in 1830. Members of parliament were also elected, and people ran for office as members of organized parties. Parliament continued to expand its own powers, and the president's became weaker. Although this conflict led to a civil war late in the nineteenth century, by the early twentieth century, Chile's parliament controlled budgets and ministerial appointments. The electorate, as in Europe, was quite restricted for much of the nineteenth century. No women and no men without a certain level of property could vote. Nor was voting secret. In 1874, however, the electorate was expanded to include all men, and the secret ballot was adopted.[34] Some of these features were developed in Chile before they were developed in parts of western Europe.

More generally, with independence from Spain and Portugal, Latin American countries quickly drafted constitutions, carried out elections—sometimes with very broad suffrage rights—brought slavery to an end—early in Spanish-speaking countries and late in Brazil—and, with few exceptions, generally avoided hereditary aristocracies and monarchies. But more or less democratic periods alternated with civil wars and constitutions were upended by coups. Latin American elites became skilled at maintaining their domination, sometimes by keeping democracy within limits or overthrowing constitutional governments. And other leaders became skilled at mobilizing the excluded, sometimes opening the way to greater democratization and sometimes establishing new forms of undemocratic rule.[35]

By the latter part of the nineteenth century and the early part of the twentieth, democratizing currents had spread much further afield. Elite reformers, spurred by European models of modernity, often incorporated democratic elements into their reforms. Japan presents a striking case. Although eminently successful for centuries in keeping out the West, the Japanese political system was overthrown in 1867–1868 by a movement claiming simultaneously to modernize the country, better defend Japan, and restore tradition. In particular, the triumphant rebels claimed that they acted on behalf of an emperor held to be divine. In the turbulent period that followed, a new social movement called for a western-style parliament. The movement formed itself on the model of the political parties emerging in the West and adopted some of the western language of rights. In spite of a long period of Japanese isolation, a small number of participants knew of western parliamentary institutions from visiting Europe as political tourists, and others had read of these institutions.[36]

The new Japanese government at first attempted to control the new parties that were springing up, then agreed to draw up a formal constitution. Some Japanese were interested in American or French notions of popular sovereignty; others were impressed by British ideas of parliamentary rule. But the Japanese elite were particularly taken with the Prussian constitution, perhaps because Prussia had just inflicted devastating military defeat upon France, perhaps because of Prussia's economic dynamism, perhaps because Prussia seemed to have "modern" institutions like constitutions and parliaments without having the sort of popular control over government that Japanese elites feared. Japan's constitution of 1889 established a weak parliament with a hereditary upper house, no right to name or remove ministers, and only limited control over the budget. No budget item could be cut, but parliament could refuse to increase the previous year's appropriation. Sovereignty was held to reside in a divine emperor. The suffrage was limited to men with a high tax assessment—only a little more than 1 percent qualified in the election of 1890.

Scholars of Japan differ about the degree to which this structure grew out of the desire to appease Japanese social movements, to modernize by copying the West, or to achieve international respectability by displaying the democratic trappings of other successful states without actually sharing power. Despite differences, resemblances to Prussian institutions were striking. But, as in Prussia, even the limited budgetary authority turned into a weapon for the parliament to extract concessions from the ministers. Even though the conservative rulers were upset, they did not close the parliament, out of fear that the West would not treat Japan as an equal unless it had the sort of constitutional rule that signified a modern state.

In Japan the claim of a divine monarch was largely a claim made by others who ruled in that monarch's name. But in the Russian case, the tsar was a very active ruler and one whose decisions were regarded as divinely inspired. In the tsar's coronation ceremony, for example, the phrase "The tsar's heart is in God's hands" was taken to mean that the will of the tsar, through which God spoke, was above all human law.[37] Yet by the early twentieth century, even in Russia some elements of evolving democratic structures were deployed.

The Russian case parallels Japan's. Following Russia's defeat in the Crimean War in the 1850s, the drive to overcome a sense of backwardness and consequent military vulnerability became very powerful. Among the reforms generated at this time was the installation of elected councils in the rural districts of three-quarters of Russia's provinces. These councils had the power to tax and to administer roads, sanitation, and famine relief. Elected town governments were also created, but they had only limited powers and were elected by very restricted suffrage. Although the poor had no voting rights and the central government whittled away at the autonomous authority initially granted the local governments, social movements pressed to extend the power of such councils as well as to extend suffrage beyond the rich.

Under the combined pressure of defeat in war with Japan and quasi-revolutionary upheaval in 1905, Russia's rulers allowed the establishment of a national parliament, the Duma. Borrowing from the Prussian constitution and, even more heavily, the Japanese constitution, Russia's elite only gave the Duma the power to refuse a new budget (leaving the old in force). The Duma had no authority in defense or foreign policy, no supervision over ministers, no power to pass legislation over the tsar's wishes, and the Duma had to share its very limited powers with an appointed upper house. Even with regard to the budget, many items were not within the Duma's authority at all. At no point did the tsar recognize, even in principle, any limit to his own authority, sticking to the claim of divine inspiration. Nonetheless, in its brief history the Duma managed to have greater influence than its original powers would suggest. Its capacities to openly debate, to question ministers, and to make limited trouble over budgets allowed it to negotiate laws and policies (even on defense matters) beyond the letter of its very weak formal position. By the eve of World War I, the tsar still ruled alone in principle, but social movements were debating whether to push for expanding the Duma's authority (and to conforming more to models further west) or for overthrowing the whole social order.

An Example: The Multicontinental Women's Movement

The principal movements for democratization shaped one another. Antislavery campaigns in England and the United States, for example, were a school in organizing. Those who participated, especially working-class people and women, went on to establish other organizations and other campaigns. These movements, moreover, traveled from one country to the next. People in one country read of antislavery actions, changes in the social role of women, or the formation of worker's parties that were taking place in other countries. And people traveled—sometimes fleeing in exile, sometimes forming transnational organizations, sometimes just moving on—and brought ideas with them: general ideas about social justice, familiarity with particular tactics, knowledge about how to organize.

Let's pause to look at the movement for women's rights as an example. The classic statement of the nineteenth-century movement was John Stuart Mill's *The Subjection of Women*. It was published in Mill's England, the United States, Australia, and New Zealand in 1869 and within a year appeared in French, German, Swedish, and Danish; the next year it appeared in Polish and Italian.[38]

Later on, the American women's movement functioned as a sort of template for women's movements in many other countries. Sometimes American activists brought their ideas or organizational models with them. Among the major organizations in the very successful movements in New Zealand and Australia—the first and second countries to enfranchise women in national elections—were branches of the Women's Christian Temperance Union, set up by an American organizer from the parent organization in 1885. Other women activists discovered their commitment to the cause and found organizational models while visiting the United States. Immigrants from England also sometimes carried sympathies for women's rights to Australia and New Zealand. The tactics of Irish nationalists were taken up by a part of the British women's movement; their own tactics in turn were later partially borrowed by Americans. And women's rights activists in many countries organized numerous international congresses and international organizations where they could meet, exchange ideas, and provide support.

Political Creativity in the Eighteenth and Nineteenth Centuries

The German, Japanese, and Russian cases reveal two important lessons: first, that elites can be very creative in using democratic mechanisms in ways that weaken those mechanisms or even completely destroy their efficacy; and second, that oppositions can be equally creative in using even very limited opportunities to make more opportunities for themselves. This dialogue has redefined and continues to redefine political life, including the meaning of democracy. Let's look a bit more closely at elite efforts in the eighteenth and nineteenth centuries to rule through democratic appearances and at the efforts of social movements to seize opportunities.

Elites: Adapting to Democracy

In the late eighteenth century, some governments in western Europe and North America began to claim that their authority derived from the people. In the nineteenth century, many other states made similar claims. In the terms introduced in Chapter 2, we may speak of a dramatic shift in the mythical constitution of society, away from a belief in an unchanging, hierarchical social order headed by a monarch claiming a special and sacred status. By the nineteenth century, governments claimed to rule by virtue of popular will; even monarchical governments were beginning to borrow such claims. In some places, elected bodies were evolving, and where they took root, questions of their powers in relation to hereditary monarchs and questions of who would have the right to vote became very important.

Sometimes these changes were promoted by the new social movements coming into existence, which were significantly encouraged by the general claim that government derived its powers from the governed. But sometimes these changes were instituted by elite powerholders themselves, in an attempt to emulate the forms of dynamic and successful states while avoiding being swept away altogether by the reality or the threat of mass mobilizations.

Decade after decade, for example, an increasing number of states adopted written constitutions, thereby creating the appearance that their powers were assented to by "the people" rather than or in addition to being conferred by God. But the constitutions did not necessarily constrain hereditary monarchs in practice or overturn traditional social hierarchies. The new parliamentary bodies often had sharply limited powers, the right to vote for elected representatives often remained severely limited, and the ability of people to form organized parties to contest elections was often slight. The claim to rule by the will of the people was becoming quite widespread, but the actual structure of power depended on continual challenges by those demanding change and the often successful attempts at containment by the powerful.

Rather than saying that democracy emerged in the nineteenth century, then, we should talk about the emergence of a contest over what democracy means in practice. In the nineteenth century, those who liked the status quo were increasingly likely to say, in the new climate of democratic legitimation, that the current state of affairs already embodied the will of the people. Therefore, they could claim that challenges represented small minorities or were mounted by those who did not accept the popular will. But challengers, too, could use the new language of politics to claim that the current state of affairs flouted the will of the people, violated their rights, and did not grant their proper share of influence to the people or to particular excluded groups.

Social Movements: Seizing Opportunities

Just as elites adapted to democratizing currents by ruling through new institutions and by justifying their acts in new language, ordinary people used the limited possibilities available to them to open up political systems. Consider the U.S. Constitution. Those who crafted it aimed in part to contain democratizing forces within bounds. However, the historian Gordon Wood has shown that, in their later years, those who had adopted that document at the Constitutional Convention were bitterly disappointed at the United States they had helped to create. The wrong sorts of people were getting elected, they felt, and the social movements forming around the turn of the nineteenth century had quite a different flavor than the elite thought proper.[39] For one thing, the people of the new United States were far more prone to form religious movements than the authors of the Constitution, who were deeply committed to notions of reason and science, found congenial. For another, a new kind of political figure was quickly becoming noticeable, the elected figure who advances his constituents' interests by cutting deals with other, similarly oriented representatives; politics as an open negotiation among different interests seemed quite different from the enlightened search for a common truth of which many among the revolutionary elite had dreamed.

Another example of the opportunism of social movements revolves around the cluster of instances in which autocratic rulers set up parliaments with extremely limited powers. In Germany, Russia, and Japan, as you have seen, parliamentary control over budgets was limited to rejecting increases in spending. Nonetheless, by the early twentieth century, these parliaments had forced governments to negotiate a broader range of issues than indicated in their written constitutions. And in spite of efforts to use restrictive suffrage rules so that only the upper strata would be included in this limited negotiation process, parties claiming to represent the interests of working-class people emerged. For example, in spite of all the restrictions in parliamentary powers and electoral representation, the socialist party in Germany eventually became a force to be reckoned with. An important element in the history of social movements in such countries is their sense of the limited possibilities permitted by the prevailing rules. A significant part of the history of the socialist movement in Germany and Russia down to World War I, for example, came from a sense of just how narrow the possibilities were. With the rules stacked against them, including the outlawing of their party at one point, it is not surprising that a key goal for German socialists was political change, which some identified with a more genuine democracy and others with social revolution (and for some, those two goals were the same thing).

Emerging Critiques of Democracy

We have seen that social groups left out of full participation on equal terms repeatedly developed movements to demand inclusion. We have particularly stressed those on behalf of women, workers, and nonwhites. Sometimes these attacks were framed in extremely strong language. At an event marking American Independence Day in 1852, abolitionist leader and former slave Frederick Douglass famously asked, "What, to the American slave, is your 4th of July?"[40] Two years later, abolitionist publisher William Lloyd Garrison marked the same anniversary by describing the U.S. Constitution as "a covenant with death," a view that led to a refusal to participate in electoral politics.[41] As we see, movements on behalf of those profoundly excluded could generate considerable anger—on both sides, since their opponents might not only reject their vision of change but find them a threat to their idea of the nation. Garrison, for example, frequently got death threats and once was nearly lynched by an infuriated crowd. Such movements might find themselves debating whether what was needed was improving the democracy that already existed or replacing it with something very different. To continue with our present example, Douglass thought the U.S. Constitution could be used to combat slavery and Garrison did not. So movements might find themselves debating whether the path to a better future lay in following the legal procedures, including getting favorable candidates elected and campaigning for better rules, or whether a dramatic rupture with current notions of procedure was needed. As industrialization and concentrations of workers in large cities sparked movements on behalf of their rights, socialist parties formed and within those parties there was often considerable debate about whether a better future could be obtained through democratic means or whether what was necessary was revolution.

A new critique of democracy as actually experienced was emerging. We have seen how in the past some people feared democracy because they thought it would allow the poor to plunder the rich. But now, some were arguing, through unfair electoral rules, through control of the police, the courts and the educational institutions, through their greater influence with the government (regardless of who won elections), democracy was permitting the rich to dominate the poor. In this view democracy was holding out to poorer people the prospect of participating in voting that did not actually make any great difference in the actual distribution of wealth and power. In socialist circles, many were persuaded that even where legal equality was achieved, the great range of wealth and income would mean that the wealthy would dominate. Socialists were dividing into those favoring more or less revolutionary strategies and those favoring more or less legal and gradual reform. In some countries, socialists were competing with anarchists, who argued that the very existence of increasingly powerful central states that could impose their laws on local communities made a mockery of claims of democracy. While socialist labor organizations tended to be closely linked to socialist parties that competed in elections, anarchist organizations tended to see parties as wasted energy. The mix was quite different in different countries. In the highly repressive climate of Russia, advocates of working people found a revolutionary strategy attractive. Within a liberal parliamentary system like Spain's, in which local bosses and national powerbrokers generally determined election results in advance, anarchist strategies of steering clear of electoral politics had many adherents in its growing factories. In Britain, at the center of a great empire that seemed worth participating in, many workers' organizations favored the path of reforming democracy for greater inclusiveness.

By the late nineteenth century broad doubts about how democracy was working in practice were emerging in many countries, not just among excluded groups and not just among socialists and anarchists. Political parties were frequently seen as highly corrupt organizations that traded favors for votes, as party bosses cultivated relationships with poorer people. In a U.S., or Argentine, or German city a party boss got to know a neighborhood, helped kids get jobs, helped people in trouble with the law find lawyers, helped immigrants fill out forms, and got the streets swept from time to time—and in return they wanted votes. An English student of the world's democracies in the late nineteenth century, James Bryce, thought that the only thing the major U.S. parties actually stood for was getting jobs and contracts for their followers and the power to give out jobs and contracts for their leaders: "[Their] interests are in the main the interests of getting or keeping the patronage of the government."[42]

Others, like the German socialist Robert Michels early in the twentieth century, argued that when even a party committed to democracy actually got into power, once in power its leaders developed their own interests that had little in common with those who voted for them and a lot in common with the leaderships of other parties. For that reason, Michels argued that one day the German socialist party might come to power but that wouldn't mean that socialism would come to power. The early twentieth-century German sociologist Max Weber thought that the large, powerful bureaucracies of all modern governments made democracy a hollow illusion. It was possible, Weber argued, that a minister might be accountable to a democratically elected parliament. But that minister would hardly be fully in charge of the ministry. Career bureaucrats, who knew how things were done, who were there before the minister came in and would be there after the minister was replaced, who had a sense of solidarity with each other and had gotten good at concealing things from ministers and parliament, were a world of their own and not really accountable to the voting citizens. And finally, democracies, it was increasingly said by many, were too slow, prone to endless debate and to ignore pressing concerns.

These diverse critiques could energize movements to replace democracy with something else—or to deepen it. Although American poet Walt Whitman regarded the choice in the presidential election of 1884 with little enthusiasm, he made it the occasion of some excited lines, declaring that "the powerfullest scene and show" known in America was the act by which this huge country chose its leaders.[43] The specific choice might be dreary, but the act of a people choosing its leaders was extraordinary and exhilarating. While some scorned democracy for its failures, others, at least from time to time, found it moving.

Conclusions

By the turn of the twentieth century, organizers of social movements had much experience in many countries to draw from in considering issues, tactics, and organization. Elite reformers had many examples of borrowing and adapting the practices of other states. Russian efforts at government reform, indeed, used as models not merely Japanese institutions but also Japan's adaptation of Prusso-German practices, which were themselves reworkings of practices farther west. Social movements and elite reform often moved in tandem in several countries. Thus one can find considerable similarities in constitutional ideas emerging in Russia's revolution of 1905, Persia's revolution of 1906, and Turkey's revolution of 1908 (although one can see differences as well).[44] The same sort of convergence took place in the twentieth century. In several great waves, many countries at once headed toward democracy—or away from it.

CHAPTER 4
TWENTIETH-CENTURY PENDULUM SWINGS

The world of the early twentieth century differed profoundly from our starting point on the brink of the American and French Revolutions. For one thing, it was much more of a single world. The telegraph had radically decreased the time needed to communicate with distant places; radio was beginning the even more radical change of making distant voices audible to many listeners at once. Railroads, steamships (aided enormously by the Suez and Panama Canals), and, later, automobiles radically decreased the time required for people to move from one place to another. Nineteenth-century colonial conquest had connected the lives of people in Africa and much of Asia with people in western Europe. Extraordinary migrations brought communities of Europeans and Asians to the western hemisphere, Indians to Africa and the Caribbean, Chinese to southeastern Asia. A developing industrial technology underlay an equally dramatic shift to a new urbanized way of life in the wealthier countries of the world; the many poorer countries, some of them colonies, stood in striking contrast. The new industrial technology not only transformed daily life but also created possibilities for warfare of a destructiveness that would previously have defied imagination.

The scene at the start of the twentieth century—growing wealth, dramatic contrasts in access to that wealth, and equally marked contrasts in national power, radically increasing life expectancies and extraordinary violence—provided many issues for powerholders to cope with and many issues to galvanize social movements. Questions about how states were to be governed continued to be salient. Struggles over the meaning of democratic practice continued, building on the nineteenth-century experience discussed in Chapter 3. Although traditional patterns of rule had been eroded, claimants to democracy by no means had the political arena to themselves. Antidemocratic social movements and powerholders were as creative as democratizing forces and developed new forms of nondemocratic rule. The twentieth century was to be marked by the ebb and flow of multicontinental democratic and antidemocratic currents.

The Eve of the Great War

In 1910, only a small proportion of the world's population lived under governments with a claim to democracy. Much of Africa and large areas of Asia were held as colonies by European powers. Thus many Africans and Asians were governed by Europeans they had no hand in choosing and subject to policies over which they had no control. They could often not even protest without risking considerable violence at the hands of colonial authorities. In other Asian countries as well as in central and eastern Europe, people lived in one sort of empire or another, under monarchs who still often claimed to have a divine connection.

By 1910 some of these regimes had experienced some of the elements of democracy. The German parliament was a significant part of that country's political life, although it lacked the powers of its counterparts to the west. Late in the nineteenth century, Japan and the Ottoman Empire had taken on constitutions that defined the powers of various bodies, and there were attempts to follow suit in Persia and Russia early in the twentieth. In Thailand, women were enfranchised on the same terms as men in local elections in 1897.[1]

The countries of the western hemisphere, for the most part, were neither colonies nor claiming to be the heirs to ancient empires. Spanish America had long gone without a monarch, since attaining independence through violent warfare early in the nineteenth century. Portuguese-speaking Brazil joined in this tradition with the removal of that country's emperor in 1889. Latin America generally, along with Italy and Spain, had considerable experience with elections, although suffrage was limited, vote counts were often fraudulent, and violent intimidation was far from rare. In Spain, for example, ministers were officially named following parliamentary elections and from 1890 there was universal manhood suffrage. But in reality, powerbrokers, including the king, decided who should occupy the formal positions of authority and which party should have a parliamentary majority to ensure that result. The powerbrokers then negotiated with local bosses (called *caciques*) to deliver enough votes to bring this about. The local power of those bosses was based on their ability to give benefits (like jobs or access to lawyers) as well as outright coercion. So the way a Spanish national election worked in practice was that those powerbrokers first decided on the results, then organized the election to get the results they wanted. Parties opposed to this system had some success in large cities but the basic system remained in place for decades.

In western Europe, elected parliaments had acquired considerable power, and hereditary monarchs had been correspondingly weakened. But monarchs still named cabinets in Sweden, a nonelected House of Lords shared power with the House of Commons in Britain, secret ballots were not fully developed in France, and restrictions on the right to vote were widespread. In some countries, the votes of wealthier citizens were more heavily weighted. In Belgium, for example, all adult men had the right to vote, although a significant minority of more privileged citizens each got two or even three votes.[2] In no European country except Finland could women vote regularly in national elections; and in Finland, part of the Russian Empire, the tsar held impressive power.

The restriction on women's suffrage also characterized the United States (although women had obtained the vote in some states). In the United States as well, citizens of African ancestry in the South, where many lived, faced an interlocking set of restrictions on their capacity to vote, including legal barriers to registration, threats of such forms of economic retaliation as being fired or thrown off the land they worked should they try to vote, and violence. The states where Native Americans lived in large numbers limited their right to vote. Minnesota, North Dakota, California, Oklahoma, and Wisconsin, for example, required voters to be "civilized" and had various mechanisms for denying Native Americans that status.[3]

Besides Finland, only in Australia and New Zealand could women vote in national elections, although both countries were British dominions in 1910 and not fully sovereign states. In Australia, the descendants of the original inhabitants ("aborigines") could not vote.

A Democratic Surge: 1910–1925

Over the next decade and a half, democratic institutions increased substantially. One student of the subject would call as many as twenty-two countries democratic in 1922.[4] Even if there are reasons to be dubious about the precision which with such a classification can be made, it is impossible to deny that some very important developments were taking place. In 1911 most of the remaining powers of the British House of Lords were ended; in 1912 Italy eliminated earlier restrictions on male voting; the following year Norway went considerably further by enfranchising propertyless women as well as men. This was more than a strictly European phenomenon: Argentina instituted universal male suffrage and the secret ballot in 1912, and in 1913 the United States instituted direct election of senators by the voters (replacing the previous system of indirect election by state legislatures).

In Europe, World War I (1914–1918) provided a favorable opportunity for women and for those with little property to mobilize. Tens of millions of men were away from home and work, and many millions never came back. Labor peace became a vital national interest in wartime; at the same time, many more of those workers were women, replacing the men who were fighting (or already killed or crippled). Under these circumstances, not only did union membership jump, but pressures for expanding the suffrage were more likely than earlier to be successful. Indeed, Canada extended the suffrage in 1917, and Britain adopted universal male suffrage (although not quite with equal votes) in 1918.

Consider Belgium, which entered the war with a voting system in which older men owning property had three votes. Large numbers of workers had engaged in strikes over the previous thirty years (in 1886, 1888, 1891, 1893, 1902, and 1913), demanding universal suffrage with an equal vote for all but getting mostly violent reactions. To obtain labor movement compliance in the war, the Socialist Party, which had been demanding universal suffrage for decades, was given a ministry in the government. By war's end, Belgium had equal male suffrage.

Direct wartime pressures were not solely responsible for advancing democracy, for important suffrage extensions were happening in noncombatant states as well, as in Denmark in 1915 and Sweden in 1918. Appeals for democratic government leaped. President Woodrow Wilson of the United States famously spoke of making the world safe for democracy, for example, and described the Great War, especially after the fall of the tsar in Russia in 1917, as a great struggle between democracy and autocracy. A study of major newspapers in the United States, Great Britain, France, Germany, and Russia shows a jump in the occurrence of the word democracy during this decade.[5]

The war ultimately led to the collapse of Europe's major nondemocratic monarchies in Germany, Austro-Hungary, and Russia as well as the monarchical Ottoman Empire, which still had a toehold in southeastern Europe. Borders changed, the Austro-Hungarian Empire disintegrated, new states broke loose from a Russia in the turmoil of revolution, and the Ottoman Empire lost its Arab provinces as it contracted into the new Turkey. The clear winners of the war were the western democracies, which now stood alone in appearing to maintain political continuity. The power and prestige associated with democratic institutions were greatly enhanced.

Many of the new governments that succeeded the overthrown European monarchies wrote themselves democratic constitutions: Germany, Austria, Poland, Czechoslovakia. The same happened in the Balkan states that lay between the now defeated and crippled former Austrian, Russian, and Ottoman Empires: A newly created country, Yugoslavia, convened an elected Constituent Assembly in 1920; Romania adopted a constitution in 1923 that called for a lower house elected by universal male suffrage; and other neighboring countries introduced other democratic elements. Finland had been a part of the Russian Empire, but before the war it had developed autonomous democratic institutions. After the war it broke away from Russia. Iceland and Ireland also achieved independence from colonial rule at this time and adopted the democratic constitutions in fashion in Europe.

Outside of Europe, a number of states in political upheaval wrote new constitutions with significant democratic elements, such as Mexico in 1917 and Turkey in 1924. The Turkish constitution of 1924, for example, declared that a parliament would be elected every four years by all male citizens. In the mid-1920s, Japan adopted universal suffrage for men. While maintaining the constitution of 1889, in which ministers did not have to be named by their parliament, Japan was in practice forming governments with parliamentary support. Some hoped Japan was experiencing democratization. (The era is known to historians as "Taisho democracy," named for the current emperor.)

On the other hand, when the major western democracies had an opportunity to directly influence political structures outside of Europe, they did not always attempt to initiate democratic structures. The end of World War I found British armies dominating the Arab lands that had formed part of the now disintegrated Ottoman Empire. Thus Britain played a major role in organizing the new governments of the regions, but it supported profoundly undemocratic monarchies. Similarly the U.S. military, which was active in Mexico in 1914 and 1916 and seized Haiti in 1915 and the Dominican Republic in 1916, hardly advanced democratic institutions in the three states. Historians continue to debate what President Woodrow Wilson, who repeatedly claimed devotion to democratic principles as the ideal of national self-determination, was trying to accomplish.

Some scholars would answer such a question by pointing to American culture. In this interpretation, the very idea of America from colonial times has involved a mission to show the rest of the world the proper path. President Wilson claimed (as have other presidents) that U.S. actions in the world were unlike the self-interested actions of European colonial powers; the United States was genuinely devoted to doing good. On the other hand, some scholars would point to the significant interests of U.S. companies in Central America and the Caribbean and the desire of those companies to have sympathetic governments in the region. For evidence, these scholars look at the scale of the profits that U.S. investors could make and the degree to which U.S. actions rewarded governments favorable to those investors and punished or even overthrew governments that were unfavorable.

We must remember that the meaning of democracy itself was continually debated. President Wilson himself expressed unhappiness about universal suffrage, quite specifically suffrage for African Americans voting in the U.S. South and suffrage for women; he was also concerned that American traditions might be swamped by new waves of immigration and was convinced that the Philippines (acquired by the United States in the Spanish-American War at the turn of the century) must be governed by Americans rather than supported in governing themselves. Wilson argued that there were multiple, rival conceptions of democracy and that he was an advocate of a particular one (and a foe of others). And he sometimes changed his mind—for example, coming around eventually to favoring the enfranchisement of women.

Alternating Currents

By the middle of the 1920s, many states had significant democratic claims, particularly in western Europe and North America; but some elements of democratization were found elsewhere. By that time, political movements often were taking explicit positions on "democracy." Social movements aiming to transform authoritarian political systems were claiming to be democratic. Other social movements openly rejected democracy, sometimes demanding a return to the values of the past and sometimes heralding the new values of a superior future. (One Brazilian political theorist in the 1920s, for example, felt that new kinds of rule were needed for the new times and that democracy ought to be consigned to "the museum of political antiquities."[6]) Still other movements proclaimed themselves to embody a truer democracy than was currently institutionalized in western governments; this has been a frequent characteristic of socialist movements. At moments democratic systems seemed to be losing ground, and at others they seemed to be advancing. All the while, the meaning of democracy continued to evolve and to be debated by existing states and social movement challengers seeking to bolster their positions.

We have seen how by the late nineteenth century a significant range of complaints about how democracy worked was often heard. Here are some of them as sometimes amplified in twentieth-century conflicts:

- It is slow to make decisions, there is too much talk and debate, it can get paralyzed by disagreement.
- It doesn't really express the will of the people but merely of the party leaderships.
- It often seems not to actually stand for anything; it's just a set of procedures rather than a big idea, and can't really mobilize people to fight for it. A firm leadership, guided by a set of big principles, will be far more likely to succeed on the battlefield.
- It may work in some rich countries, but in poorer countries where there is a shortage of resources, where social conflicts are acute, and especially where there are extensive systems of patronage, democratic procedures mean the rule of backward, out-of-touch, corrupt elites who give out favors in return for votes and selfishly keep the country from advancing.

Some of these complaints helped fuel fascist movements and others movements of the revolutionary left, some were more persuasive in some countries than others. Some seemed especially persuasive when democratic institutions were failing to produce solutions to great crises of human suffering, an important reason for the appeal of alternatives to democracy in the 1930s when much of the world was in the grips of the Great Depression and many democratic governments seemed unable to solve its terrible problems. But complaints about democracy have also often fueled movements to fix democracy.

Reactions between Two Wars

I will first briefly sketch the broad movements of political systems since that first twentieth-century surge of democratization during the World War I era. I will then explore the very big question of why the democratic tide has ebbed and flowed. The democratic impulse, already advancing around the time of the Great War, accelerated with the victory of the western democracies. But by the mid-1920s a wave of reaction set in, overturning many of the democratic achievements of the past decade and a half.

The suffering of World War I soon generated an ultranationalist reaction in Italy in the form of fascism. In short order the Italian Fascist party came to power, and similar movements took root throughout Europe and to some extent even beyond Europe. The new fascist movements denounced the competitive parties and parliamentary debates that were established components of most notions of democracy. Competitive parties were condemned as divisive; true nationalists sought national unity. And parliamentary debate was contrary to fascist notions of swift action against enemies. As with other social movements, fascist organizational patterns, symbols, and conceptions crossed national frontiers. The Italian fascists, for example, had uniformed militias wearing distinctive black shirts. Others followed suit with variations: The German storm troopers wore brown, the British fascists blue, the Brazilians green. Romanian fascists adopted the Nazi swastikas they noted in Germany. Spain's *falangistas* adopted the straight-armed salute they saw in Italy.

The advances of democratization in Germany and Spain, as well as Italy, were overturned completely. The electoral triumphs of Germany's Nazis in the early 1930s showed that fascists could win within the legal rules of a democratic system. The victory of Francisco Franco's forces (backed by Italian and German support) in the Spanish Civil War showed that fascists could win on the battlefield. For many people, democracy did not seem up to the dynamic new challenge.

Elites felt much less pressure to conform to democratic rules than they had at war's end, even when they did not embrace fascism. In Europe's newly democratized states, antidemocratic elites managed to gain power. Military forces were instrumental in promoting authoritarian rule in Poland in 1926, Bulgaria in 1934, and Greece in 1936, to take a few examples. Elsewhere, monarchs gathered the strength to undo constitutional limitations on their power, as in Yugoslavia in 1929 and Romania in the 1930s. By the late 1930s, almost every European political system with democratic claims of recent vintage had been overthrown. Outside of Europe, antidemocratic forces followed suit, at least when there was a democratic or semidemocratic regime to overturn: In 1930 Argentina and Brazil were seized by antidemocrats. During the next decade, the Japanese military eliminated the more democratic aspects of that country's semidemocracy.

Most dramatically, the armed forces of Nazi Germany overran the European continent. In most of the countries they defeated, the Germans supported local antidemocratic forces. By 1942, once again, very few states had much claim to democratic government.

World War II and Its Aftermath

The victory of the combined forces of the Soviet Union and the western democracies over Germany and its allies in 1945 inaugurated a new, larger wave of democratizations. The German collapse left Soviet forces in control of eastern Europe and U.S. forces dominant in western Europe. Each side refashioned the political systems in the areas under its control in its own image. The United States and its allies restored democratic regimes in the previously democratic parts of western Europe that had been conquered by Germany and installed new democratic systems in Italy, West Germany, Austria, Greece, Japan, and South Korea. As a sort of mirror image, political systems resembling the Soviet Union's were installed in eastern Europe. Unlike at the end of the previous Great War, there were now two intact and very different models of success. Soon the United States and the Soviet Union abandoned their wartime partnership in favor of the most intense and bitter rivalry. Some partisans of the Soviet Union and its allies claimed to be realizing a superior version of democratic ideals, shorn of the colonialism, racism, and social inequality of the "bourgeois" western variant.

Weakened by the great military struggle, the western European democracies began to abandon their vast colonial holdings in Asia and Africa. Often they were challenged by social movements in the former colonies, some of which mounted military campaigns against the occupying forces. The new, postcolonial states often produced democratic constitutions; unlike after World War I, the retreating imperial powers often encouraged the new states to do so. This was particularly true of Great Britain, whose lawyers helped draft the democratic documents of Asian and African states. But those new constitutions also often had sections on fundamental rights and on religion that were not modeled on the practices of the former colonial power. Some ideas in those new constitutions also showed the influence of the two dominant powers of the moment, the United States and the Soviet Union, but also of the Universal Declaration of Human Rights of 1948, adopted by the United Nations, that was set up at the end of the terrible war.[7]

During this democratic moment in world history, popular forces and reforming elites sometimes seized opportunities in Latin America. The significantly named Democratic Action Party came to power in Venezuela in 1948 and attempted the first democratic rule in that country's violent history. Costa Rica stands out among its Central American neighbors for a tradition of peaceful transitions through electoral processes; that tradition can be associated with its constitution of 1949, which settled a civil war fought the previous year. Brazilian generals, also acting in the name of democracy, removed an authoritarian president from office and ordered elections. Some of those Brazilian generals had become very experienced in speaking of the use of military force on behalf of democracy when they participated alongside American and British forces in World War II (the only Latin American military to do so).

The Turkish government, feeling threatened by its powerful neighbor, the Soviet Union, decided to permit competitive parties to contest elections for the first time (apart from some brief experiments) since the constitution of 1924. Various oppositional elements seized the opportunity to organize no fewer than fifteen new parties over the next two years. The most successful of these parties, which seized the spirit of the moment in naming itself the Democratic Party, was voted into power four years later.

While restoring democracies in western Europe, promoting them in defeated countries, and sponsoring democratic constitutions in former colonies, the major western powers themselves democratized. It was in the post–World War II wave, for example, that French women obtained the right to vote; that several U.S. states extended the suffrage to their Native American citizens and a U.S. president ordered the end of racial segregation in the armed forces; and that Great Britain abandoned plural voting.

In this period many Latin American countries also extended the right to vote to women. In some of these Latin American instances, however, the right was not exercised in practice, because the military commanders, not the electorate, decided who occupied office. But once the right was given, however vacuous at the time, it endured to be exercised when more democratic procedures emerged.

The central and eastern European countries that had not extended the suffrage to women in the wake of World War I (as had Russia, Poland, and Czechoslovakia) now did so. Eastern Europe's communist parties organized many elections in which women could vote. Because opposition parties could not field candidates, these women voters were not participating in choosing their government. Nevertheless, as in Latin America, acquisition of the right to vote, even in sham elections, helped define the practices of postcommunist political systems.

Social movements challenging the prevailing order in Asia, Africa, and Latin America sometimes favored the Soviet model. At other times, threatened governments attempted to enlist the United States on their side by claiming that the opposition sought the advance of communism. The result was a series of challenges, often successful, to newly inaugurated democratic and semidemocratic systems by socialist forces supported by the Soviet Union and antisocialist forces supported by the United States. Democratically elected presidents sometimes terminated democracy, as in South Korea or the Philippines, and militaries often seized power, as in much of Latin America, parts of Asia and Africa, and Greece. Such presidents and militaries usually claimed to be preventing the triumph of communism. On the other hand, regimes claiming to represent one or another form of socialism sometimes terminated democratic or semidemocratic constitutions in other parts of Asia and Africa.

The Greatest Wave of All

By the 1960s, multiple forms of antidemocratic rule had come to dominate Asia, Africa, and Latin America, and communist regimes seemed firmly rooted in central and eastern Europe. Many social scientists were becoming convinced that democracy could thrive only under very special conditions, which were found almost uniquely in the more well-to-do countries of the West. This seemed to many almost a self-evident truth: If few countries outside the West in 1965 or 1970 were democratic, surely some special feature of those western societies must predispose them toward democracy. Because the West, for the moment, also included many of the richest and most powerful countries, much of the discussion of the secret of western democracy had a strong flavor of self-congratulation.

The social scientists did not agree, however, on what these special western conditions were that favored democracy. Some thought distinctive aspects of western culture must be the secret, although they could not agree on which aspects. Others held that the prosperity of the West must account for its propensity for democracy, as if democracy were a luxury that people in poorer countries couldn't afford. And still others argued that the West had a distinctive institutional history that had established parliaments at an early stage. Some scholars of Latin America, for example, argued that the absence of democracy there came from roots in authoritarian Iberian cultures while others thought that recent trends in economic development led the powerful to suppress the growing urban working class by installing brutal regimes.

Even as these explanations of western distinctiveness were being elaborated, however, the newest and greatest wave of democratization was gathering steam. By the early 1990s, western Europe's remaining authoritarian regimes had come to an end, almost all Latin American governments had some claim to democracy, the impossible overthrow of communist parties had happened in central and eastern Europe, and African regimes faced democratic challenges on an unprecedented scale—including the spectacular ending of democracy-for-whites-only in South Africa.

Explaining the Ebb and Flow of Democratization

In Chapter 2, I suggested that multicontinental waves of democratization come about through the conjunction of multiple causes: social movement challenges, reforms initiated by elites, and the compound of movements and reforms. Democratizing movements and democratizing reformers must both be seen in their transnational contexts. Movements are buoyed by others' successes and adapt foreign models to local circumstances. Elite reformers sometimes try foreign models to solve local problems, sometimes hope for foreign support, and sometimes bow to foreign coercion.

Recall also that social movements on behalf of excluded groups often aim to reorganize political power; elite reformers, on the other hand, sometimes appeal to democratic notions of legitimation in an attempt to avoid changing the organization of political power. Finally, students of particular moments in the history of democratization are often in great disagreement about the precise roles of elite reformers and social movement challengers. A great deal remains to be learned about these processes.

By 1910, movements advocating change had become a standard, recognizable part of the political landscape in many countries. Access to an expanding literate public through books and newspapers was commonplace. Social movements had acquired considerable experience in appealing to that public and in claiming to represent that public (or part of it). Where representative institutions existed, however weak, movements had learned to try to influence them through their own claims to represent the popular will. But the movements that flourished between the American and French Revolutions and World War I did not always limit themselves to protesting specific policies and demanding others. The movements might demand a reorganization of political power itself.

In explaining the ebb and flow of democratization waves in the twentieth century, I will point first to two of the legacies of the period between the late eighteenth and early twentieth centuries. One is the development of a transnational culture in which the existence of a written constitution was an important claim to international respectability. Twentieth-century crises that replaced one regime by another also brought new constitutions in their wake. A second important nineteenth-century legacy is the development of effective social movements. We will see how these nineteenth-century movements confronted some of the challenges and opportunities of the twentieth century.

However, twentieth-century patterns of democratization were not simply a continuation of those of the nineteenth century. The new century was uniquely favorable to democratic waves of unprecedented geographic scope. The increasing power capacity of states was an essential ingredient in the development of modern social movements, and the interstate system is an essential context for understanding elite reformers. In the twentieth century, states achieved the capacity to concentrate their resources for destructive conflicts on a scale that no sane person in previous centuries could have imagined. Not only did wartime provide a favorable opportunity for movements to pressure elites, but war's aftermath left the victors new opportunities to reshape the world. Finally, to understand the ebb and flow of democratization since 1945, we must pay special attention to the development and sudden end of the Cold War, the long period of bitter U.S.-Soviet antagonism.

The Creation of Constitutional Traditions

The notion of writing constitutions specifying the powers of different branches of government proved to be a particularly powerful notion, for which the United States provided a striking model. This model was adopted first by Poland, in 1791; later that same year, revolutionary France pointed the way for more and more countries. Apart from its specific provisions, which might differ from place to place, a constitution by its very existence is a statement that living human beings can decide how to structure their political institutions; political institutions do not have to depend on interpretations of the divine will or of age-old tradition or of the arbitrary will of a monarch. Social movements developed the habit of demanding a constitution or, where such a document already existed, of demanding amendments or even total revision. The U.S. Constitution, with its provision for amendment and its well-known, almost instantaneous adoption of ten of them—its famous Bill of Rights—demonstrated that constitutions were not only made by human hands but also revisable.

In one important respect, the French revolutionary experience of constitution writing was to prove more influential than the original American model. The French revolutionary National Assembly struggled mightily to write its constitution and did so, by 1791. A year later, that constitution was scrapped and a second constitution, held to be far more democratic, was written. Then it was set aside for what was claimed to be a wartime emergency, which has become known as the Reign of Terror. When the Terror was dismantled, yet another constitution was written. In the second half of the 1790s, the French government ruled by virtue of this third constitution, which that government itself flagrantly violated, until a coup d'etat brought General Napoleon Bonaparte to power. This event, of course, required yet another constitution—and so forth.

The entire French experience encouraged elite reformers and social movement challengers to mark each major alteration in the organization of power with a new written document. Each time human beings wrote such a document, claims that authority derived from divine rather than human sources became less and less credible. Much of Latin America, Asia, and Africa has been following this French model of repeatedly scrapping constitutions. Venezuela, to take an impressive but by no means unique example, produced new constitutions in 1811, 1819, 1821, 1830, 1858, 1864, 1874, 1881, 1891,

1893, 1901, 1904, 1909, 1914, 1922, 1925, 1928, 1929, 1936, 1947, 1953, 1961, and 1999. The Dominican Republic has had even more.

Many in the United States see such constitutional traditions as bizarre and perhaps comical. The American text, although it has been occasionally but very significantly amended, is treated with some of the reverence once reserved for the word of God. In the 1790s, Thomas Paine was already observing that the U.S. Constitution was "a political bible."[8] But it is worth recalling that both the French and American Revolutions were cousins within that same late eighteenth-century wave of democratization; that the American text, so sacred today, is a replacement for a first constitution that was scrapped (the Articles of Confederation); and that some participants in the foundational process of the United States favored periodic, fundamental revision. Thomas Jefferson, for example, held that unless a new constitution was written every twenty years or so, the frozen document would be a vehicle for the tyranny of the dead over the living.

Social movements have played a significant role in constitutional revision. They have not only attempted to pressure hereditary monarchs and assemblies for specific policies but sometimes demanded alterations in the arrangements for making decisions. Defining parliamentary power in relation to monarchs and defining the right to vote for parliamentary representatives became highly significant subjects for social movement action. Where parliamentary institutions were nonexistent (as in Russia before 1905), a movement might press for their existence. Where parliaments were unable to control the appointment of ministers (as in Germany until the democratizing current of the decade of the Great War), a movement might press for such authority. Where suffrage was restricted (as in the United States, where no women and many African Americans and Native Americans could not vote in 1910), a movement like the American movement for women's suffrage might press for its expansion.

The practice of making political change by the writing and rewriting of constitutions helped to focus social movements and elite reformers on fundamental institutional change and thereby contributed to the creation of new institutions for democratization. But new forms of antidemocratic rule could be, and were, invented as well. The writing of constitutions, by making political institutions the outcome of deliberate and explicit acts of human will, made all political institutions revisable and thereby helped prepare the way for democratic and antidemocratic innovation.

The Labor Movement, the Women's Movement, and Wartime Opportunities

In the late nineteenth and early twentieth centuries, in western Europe, North America, and sometimes elsewhere, two kinds of movements were especially active in demanding the enlargement of democratic claims. One was the labor movement, formed in large part around the concerns and claims of workers in the expanding factories. Its unions engaged in struggles over workplace issues and economic concerns and supported political parties that sought to advance worker interests. Socialist parties primarily, but also other parties bidding for the support of industrial workers, came to demand changes in political institutions so that worker interests would be better represented. One important issue on the European continent was increasing parliamentary power over budgets and ministers. Another was eliminating barriers to voting (whether based on some minimal level of tax obligation, ownership of certain forms of property, or particular educational credentials) that left workers at a disadvantage. In some European countries, extra votes for those with certain qualifications or electoral systems in which those with higher incomes got proportionately greater representation in parliament were issues as well.

In the late nineteenth and early twentieth centuries, such parties often made common cause with another great source of social activism, the women's movement. Within all political systems in which parliaments played a significant role, it demanded expansion of the suffrage to include women and frequently supported expanded parliamentary powers to make that suffrage meaningful. As long as parliaments were relatively weak and the right to vote was relatively restricted, the women's movement and the labor movement were often very close to each other. In Germany around 1910, for example, the Socialist Party was the only party that consistently supported women's suffrage.

As industrialization advanced, the capacity of organized workers to disrupt social order increased as well. Rising levels of literacy, slowly but steadily improving transportation and communication networks, and experience acquired in the formation of labor unions and political parties all contributed to an increasing capacity for such organization (and for others with different or even opposed agendas as well).

Sometimes powerholders responded by attempting to contain or suppress such threatening actions. During much of the nineteenth century, for example, labor unions were illegal in France. In 1878 Germany outlawed the Socialist

Party, which lasted a dozen years. In other times and places, powerholders responded to the challenge of popular mobilization by accepting or even championing democratic reforms. In England in 1867, Parliament expanded the suffrage in order to defuse a mass mobilization that it feared it could not control (precisely what those who opposed the more limited expansion of 1832 had pessimistically predicted). By 1910, the capacity of social movements to mount major challenges was very great. Although the power of the lower house of the German parliament was a limited one, for example, the Socialist Party was now the largest party in that body. The growth of such movements in itself, however, does not explain the dramatic jump in democratization in the decade and a half after 1910, for the capacity of powerholders to resist the pressures for democratization remained considerable.

World War I was to make the campaigns of workers' and women's movements for expansion of the right to vote particularly effective in a number of countries, for several reasons. First, the extraordinary mobilization of men to replace the vast numbers being slaughtered resulted in chronic labor shortages. At the same time, the extraordinary expenditure of firepower and the extraordinary destructiveness of that firepower continually threatened shortages of cannons, shells, and ships, thereby creating a tremendous increase in demand for factory workers. Belligerent countries discovered that—although it was widely believed that the gentle, nurturant, and healing characteristics of women rendered them unfit for any connection with martial violence whatsoever—work in munitions plants suited women after all. The cooperation of workers, men and women alike, was needed if the war was to proceed.

As the war ground on, death and destruction seemed assured while victory proved elusive. Powerholders became increasingly sensitive to the continued allegiance of the men in the trenches and the women and men in the factories. Talk about extending the right to vote flourished. Some in Great Britain favored extending the right to vote to all men in combat. But how could their fellows in munitions plants be left out? And if munitions workers were to vote, how could those workers who were women be excluded? The role of the war appears clearly in the Canadian extension of the franchise—first to women in uniform, then to women with close male relatives in the service, and finally, at war's end, to all adult women citizens.[9]

Beyond the fear of disaffection in wartime, however, it is likely that some powerholders felt morally responsible for treating those who suffered in wartime with respect. Some of the previously excluded obtained some political rights after the war, as if in repayment of a debt. In 1919, for example, Native Americans with military service were granted the right to apply for citizenship, a provision that few attempted to pursue.[10]

The postwar expansion of voting rights also owed a great deal to the fact that powerholders in exhausted countries feared social revolution. The revolution in Russia was a particularly frightening example. The central role of Russia's mutinous soldiers and sailors in overthrowing their own government was an ominous sign. The imminent return home of hundreds of thousands of men, millions in the major combatant powers—many of the men mutilated and many more inwardly wounded and all habituated to violence—was a daunting prospect even for those who preferred the prewar social order. Many men in the trenches came to regard the upper classes of their own countries as having not only created the war but also as having supplied the generals who, from the safety of luxurious headquarters, were directing the slaughter; passionate class hatred is, in fact, a central theme of the vast literature of suffering written by the former soldiers of England, France, and Germany. As the veterans returned, many states suddenly expanded voting rights, the powers of parliament, or both.

The achievement of universal and equal voting rights in Germany, for example, was powerfully aided by naval mutiny and socialist revolt in 1918. As the German government recognized its imminent military collapse and its utter incapacity to demand greater sacrifices, it committed itself to a radically limited monarchy, with a powerful parliament that could remove ministers. The continuing threat of revolution led to the further step of terminating the monarchy altogether. Beyond Germany, 1919 was a year of extraordinary labor conflict in many European countries, which reinforced the tendency to give those previously excluded a stake in the political order. And workers were rapidly organizing: Between 1919 and 1921 union membership grew considerably in many countries.

For those conservative politicians who believed that women were intrinsically more conservative than men, enfranchising women suddenly seemed more appealing. If the working classes had to be given the vote, it seemed to some to be safer to give it to women, too. However, in the United States, where the constitutional amendment enfranchising women was ratified in 1920, the motivating force was not so much the fear of a revolutionary workers' movement as the fear of immigrant voters and the continuing concern in the southern states with the political subordination of blacks.

As conservative forces in many countries began embracing the women's movement, the more conservative forces within the women's movement came to the fore. Some believed that by distancing themselves from the movement for black rights, by aligning themselves against newer immigrants, American women could gain the vote. Similarly, women's activism in Germany following World War I was as noted for its alliance with the political right (and even ultraright) as it had been for its links to socialists a generation earlier. In Europe, conservative elites looked on potential women voters as antisocialist defenders of home and tradition. Everywhere, the side of the women's movement that had long stood for moral renewal—as in the campaigns against prostitution and alcohol, which women's organizations took on in nearly every country with a significant women's movement—appealed to conservative forces in the established order. It is striking that an organization called the Women's Christian Temperance Union took the lead in the movement for the vote in a number of countries. In parts of Latin America, some on the left feared women would vote for conservative parties and some on the right hoped they would, with the result that voting rights for women were more likely to be promoted by the right.

By no means did all conservatives support women's suffrage. A continuing reluctance by some to recognize women as full citizens and a continuing notion of women as childlike dependents showed up alongside enfranchisement during this wave. When Iceland extended voting rights in 1915, only women at least forty years old obtained suffrage. In Britain in 1918, only women who met various conditions, including the age of thirty or more, got the vote.[11]

An important lesson of this story is that organizations attempting democratic advance are sometimes engaged in mutually supporting activities but at other times may work at cross-purposes. This is so because democratization has been a large number of separate battles. Supporters of both women's rights and slave emancipation in the mid-nineteenth-century United States sometimes had to decide whether both could be successfully pursued at once or whether it was strategic to support one at the expense of the other. Supporters of women's rights and workers' rights in Europe in the early twentieth century could confront similar choices.

Victors of War: Power and Prestige

War and postwar social crisis increased the capacity of social movements to obtain democratic concessions, especially in the more industrialized countries.

But the democratic wave that lasted into the 1920s probably was helped along by the war in a very different way as well. From the 1790s on, every democratic advance, especially in a wealthy and powerful country, was potentially a model for powerholders everywhere. I suggested earlier that the American and French Revolutions provided, at the most fundamental level, a model of how claiming to rule on behalf of the people was compatible with effective power, could even be the source of effective power. At the end of World War I, the obvious victors had been the major western democracies of the day, and the great losers were what politicians called the "autocracies": Germany, Austro-Hungary, Russia, and the Ottoman Empire. Not only did the victorious powers have an opportunity to attempt to reconstruct the world as they chose, but the claim to democracy now seemed to some desirable in itself or the mark of respectability in the international arena. So new states formed in Europe on the ruins of empires now adopted nonmonarchical constitutions, and continuing monarchical states now generated constitutions providing for limited rule, elected parliaments, and the like. And, as mentioned earlier, some states beyond Europe, notably Turkey and Mexico, incorporated much of the current language into their constitutional documents.

One might suspect that some powerholders sought merely a democratic appearance, in order to appease challenging social movements and appear respectable within the international community. Such a suspicion would be right, and I will return to this theme later.

The international climate exerted great force in the second wave of democratization at the end of World War II (and again in the twentieth century's third and most geographically extensive democratizing moment as well). The fascist powers were defeated in 1945 by the alliance of the Soviet Union and the western democracies. For the western democracies, war's end was an opportune moment not only to restore democracy in the countries of western Europe that had been conquered by the Germans but also to implant or revitalize democracy in Germany, Austria, South Korea, Italy, and Japan. And as the European powers gave up their colonies, sometimes after a bitter fight, some of the new states took on democratic constitutions. The Soviet Union, for its part, set up congenial governments on its own model in the parts of eastern Europe it occupied, supported autonomous communist governments in Yugoslavia and Albania, and provided aid to revolutionary movements in various other places, among which the most spectacular success was China. It was common to think of the planet as divided into different social worlds:

there were the prosperous western democracies, there was the "eastern bloc" under communist rule, and there was the Third World, the generally poorer countries, many recent colonies, the setting for the bitter rivalry of the United States and the Soviet Union.

The general climate sometimes provided an opportunity for democratization even in difficult circumstances. It would be hard to find a country whose historical track record looked less promising, for example, than Venezuela. Its war of independence from Spain, in the early nineteenth century, was the setting for great violence. A profoundly divided white elite was torn between a desire for autonomy from Spanish rule and a fear of revolt by the large black population. The militarized and violent tenor never left Venezuelan politics; long stretches of internal warfare were occasionally punctuated by successful tyrants. In the 1940s, the global struggle between "democracy" and "fascism" provided a chance for a party called Democratic Action to press its case. At war's end, the Venezuelan military permitted that party to try to launch a new and democratic Venezuela. Unhappy with the results, the military threw them from power three years later but permitted them to return again in 1958.

Labor militancy, in conjunction with the military triumph of the democracies, played a significant role in democratization at the end of World War I. Widespread labor militancy may have played a significant role after World War II as well. A study of worldwide labor conflict shows the postwar period to have involved very high levels of unrest throughout North and South America, western Europe, much of Asia, and parts of Africa.[12] Wartime fears of labor strife had already led the British to support union organization in their colonies. It seemed better to make some concessions to organized labor in return for worker effort than to try to hold the line against unions and risk disruption. Labor agitation both at home and abroad probably contributed to postwar European abandonment of empire and perhaps helps account for the democratic elements in the constitutions of some of the postcolonial regimes.

In the wave of democratization following World War I, the ability of the victors to reshape many countries played a considerable role, even a predominant one. Following World War II, the victors again had considerable sway, and local forces were also able to reshape their own countries, making use of the transnational legitimacy of democracy and of socialism. But consider the situation of lesser players on the world stage a few years later and the sorts of appeals represented by the two superpowers. Eastern Europe was under the domination of the Soviet Union, and the countries of the region were hardly likely to suddenly transform themselves. Many other states in Asia, Africa, and Latin America depended on the United States or the Soviet Union or both for military or economic support and were thereby likely to attempt to please their patrons. Not surprisingly, the post–World War II democratization wave was succeeded by a new countercurrent.

The Ambiguous Role of the United States: Mid-1950s to Mid-1970s

The support of the United States during the Cold War was hardly a clear inducement to develop democratic forms. The policy of the United States was more clearly directed against its great enemy, the Soviet Union, than it was in favor of democratization. Indeed, the United States was an important source of support for ending democratic forms in a number of Latin American instances, out of dislike for policies that it held to be dangerous. Military establishments sometimes found that Washington was extremely sympathetic to their claims to be preventing a socialist revolution, particularly after a genuine revolution had taken place in Cuba.

As an example, consider the coup that ended the presidency of Brazil's João Goulart in 1964. Many Brazilian generals and political figures had serious grievances about Goulart, including his closeness to labor unions, his advocacy of the suffrage for rural illiterates, and his reluctance to suppress the activism of leftists in the lower ranks of the military. The U.S. government reduced aid to Brazil sharply in 1963. Brazilian military planners, whose unusually close ties to the U.S. military derived from common participation in World War II, were well aware of U.S. sympathy. That sympathy was later demonstrated in a congratulatory message from the U.S. president to the coup leaders.[13]

Several years later, U.S. antipathy to Chile's elected socialist president, Salvador Allende, was manifest in a much more active effort to support anti-Allende forces. The Chilean situation was a very difficult and increasingly tense one, involving land seizures by poorer country people, factory occupations by workers, and countermobilizations by those injured by economic turmoil. Plots and counterplots were everywhere, with increasing fears or hopes, depending on one's position, of action by Chile's armed forces, despite their deserved reputation for being far less prone to political action than their fellows in other Latin American countries. The United States, anxious about the effect of socialist revolution on U.S. investments (especially in copper mining), had attempted to get the military to prevent Allende from assuming office in the first place. When Allende was nonetheless installed as president, the United States helped deepen the crisis by supporting Allende's enemies, cutting off aid and encouraging others to do so, and promoting Allende's removal in 1973.[14]

These two military actions, incidentally, were quite significant components of the multicontinental antidemocratic wave that began in the 1950s. The Brazilian coup—the first time in the twentieth century that the country's military went beyond tossing out a president to stay in power and take the reins of government itself (for two decades)—was an inspiring model to many other Latin American militaries. The Chilean coup had been especially shocking to many because that country had such a long democratic history and a military with a reputation for nonpolitical professionalism that was believed to distinguish it from militaries in neighboring countries. But the Chilean regime turned out to be the longest holdout in South America against the democratizing currents of the 1970s and 1980s. And unlike other military regimes of that historical moment—which are remembered, sometimes even on the political right, for their corruption and mismanagement as well as their brutality—the Chilean regime is remembered, even by some on the left, for the partial success of its economic policies as well as its violence.

At the same time the U.S. government was supporting military coups, it was also claiming the mantle of world leadership in a global struggle on behalf of democracy. During this time, Americans continued to think of their country as profoundly democratic, and American history classes in U.S. schools tended to tell the story of a progressive democratization. American social scientists tended to think of nondemocratic political systems as somehow defective; foreign students in the United States were exposed to this undercurrent of disdain. The U.S. government drew on such values to strongly denounce human rights abuses and even curtailed aid to some of the very regimes the United States had helped to establish. The United States protested the treatment of prisoners of the Brazilian military, for example.

With such a mixture of motives in play, U.S. policies understandably varied from one presidential administration to the next and from one government agency to the next—as well as differed with regard to one country and its neighbors. Thus the United States played a very ambiguous role at this historical moment: It sometimes supported antidemocratic regimes, and it sometimes contributed to their delegitimation. In light of this ambiguity, U.S. claims to be the leader of the world's democracies seemed false to numerous political figures and intellectuals in poorer parts of the world. When the United States supplanted France as the dominant power in Indochina during the 1960s, to take one very important example, many people in Vietnam would have found it difficult to believe that U.S. military actions in their country were on behalf of democracy.

Disaffection in the "People's Democracies"

During this period, the Soviet Union claimed to be encouraging a superior brand of democracy, modeled on its own institutions. Its allies, in fact, often described themselves as "people's democratic republics." The pattern of elite dominance within communist parties and of party domination over other institutions was widely referred to as "democratic centralism." These democratic claims appeared as false to many citizens of the United States and western Europe (and some of those in poorer countries who admired the western allies), as did U.S. claims to defend democracy appear to many in countries where the United States encouraged generals to remove elected presidents.

The great difficulty of organizing meant that social movements rarely engaged in open public protest in the Soviet Union and its allies. But people seized even risky opportunities. After the death of Joseph Stalin in 1953, there was a certain relaxation, almost immediately followed by explosive protest in East Germany, which was suppressed by force. When the first Secretary of the Communist Party of the Soviet Union, Nikita Khrushchev, repudiated the Stalinist past in 1956, a new sense of possibility led to explosive protests in Hungary and Poland, which also were suppressed by force. Although largely hidden after the violence of 1956, disaffection in central and eastern Europe was widespread.

The general sense that the government lied all the time made claims of simple truth telling powerful weapons for opposition intellectuals like Václav Havel in Czechoslovakia and Adam Michnik and Jacek Kuroń in Poland. Small networks of dissenting intellectuals began to form, to meet in one another's apartments, to develop unofficial publications. Factory workers found especially galling the public claim that theirs was a "worker's state" when they knew perfectly well that they had no power. When a Hungarian dissident published a book dealing with the world of factory workers, he was arrested and sociologists he had shared the text with were harassed. The irony of the English translation's title—*A Worker in a Worker's State*—was obvious to all.[15]

Although public displays of opposition were very limited, groups of friends, neighbors, relatives, and co-workers privately shared their jointly held dismay.

In central and eastern Europe, the communist regimes were often seen as Soviet impositions, adding a nationalist's critique to the other complaints. All that was needed for an oppositional explosion was a new opportunity to mobilize. Poles created such an opportunity for themselves in 1980, and the Soviet government provided one for everywhere else in 1989.

New Challenges

Some scholars see the long period of U.S.-Soviet rivalry—the Cold War—as the central force impelling the antidemocratic wave that lasted from the 1950s into the 1970s. During this time, many in poorer countries who had hoped for democratic government had their hopes dashed. But new social movement challenges were also forming. As supporters of the West and of the Soviet Union and its allies denounced each others' claims to be promoters of some version of democracy, many citizens of western countries adopted very critical viewpoints toward the limitations of their own institutions.

In the United States, the civil rights movement that had begun in the 1950s and flourished in the 1960s challenged the exclusion of African Americans from equal access to education as well as public facilities ranging from restaurants to restrooms and limitations on the right to vote. The numbers of participants in this and allied movements swelled enormously with rising opposition to the Vietnam War in the 1960s, especially on college campuses. In western Europe, dissenters, with an important student core, challenged the reality of "participation" in their country's affairs. One of the things that probably made the western countries vulnerable to challenge to expand the meaning of democracy at home was their governments' claims to be promoting democracy abroad.

At the same time, many in central and eastern Europe were also experiencing a painful gap between official rhetoric and dismaying reality. Although the difficulties in organizing a sustained challenge were very much greater than in the West, challenges were mounted nonetheless.

These various challenges to the authorities, in the West and the East alike, coalesced on a multicontinental scale in 1968. Students and others staged major protests in many places, including New York, Paris, Warsaw, Prague, and Mexico City. By now radio and TV broadcasting brought sounds and images of protest in one place to many other places, even when governments attempted to block those sounds and images. The major disturbance outside the United States and Europe took place in Mexico, whose claims to democratic procedures, which go back to the time of World War I, had long been widely experienced as fraudulent. Young people, and others, in the prosperous western democracies joined protests in enormous numbers at the same time young people, and others, in Poland, Czechoslovakia, and Mexico challenged the failure of their governments to live up to the principles they claimed to stand for. The pattern of regime change in the world from the mid-1950s into the 1970s, then, shows a series of triumphs for military coups and authoritarian socialisms, as well as a striking series of movements for democratization. These movements tended to be as effective in sustaining protest in countries where many citizens already thought of themselves as living under democracy like the United States or France as they did in countries where few people believed the official democratic claims like Poland or Czechoslovakia.

In the general climate of protest, participants raised a wide array of issues: minority participation in social and economic life, the arms race, the situation of women, deterioration of the environment, continuing poverty in wealthy countries, middle-class lifestyles, the university curriculum. Some of these issues continued to inform social movements well after the peak moments of protest. (Some sociologists came to write of "new social movements.") Those unhappy with student occupations of universities, traffic snarled by demonstrations, and harsh criticism of government policies—or shocked by the unconventional dress and impolite language of the protestors or the startling music they enjoyed—sometimes saw the protestors as enemies of well-established democratic institutions. Against the Cold War background, some, especially in the United States, saw protestors as supporters of the Soviet Union—although in western Europe, even communist parties were sometimes seen by protestors as part of the political establishment. In Poland and Czechoslovakia the central issue was the domination of society by communist parties backed by the Soviet army. Those who marched for civil rights or to get governments to behave more responsibly thought of themselves as deepening democracy when they called for "power to the people," to use a slogan much heard in the United States. In western countries, some people saw protestors as enemies of the democratic practices that were already in place and were baffled or angry that enormous numbers of demonstrators did not seem to respect existing institutions. But those filling the streets or occupying the campuses denounced those in power as hypocrites and frauds who were perpetuating social injustice and blocking a more genuinely democratic order. In the university where I taught in the late 1960s, when a student strike brought classes to a halt, some among both the strikers and their opponents called those in the opposite camp fascists.

Transnational Financial Networks

The 1960s and 1970s also saw the strengthening of powerful international financial networks, which provided enormous sums of money for development projects in Latin America, Asia, and to some extent central and eastern Europe. When these countries experienced severe difficulties in repaying these loans, many in those indebted countries that had significant democratic features came to believe that the democracy that had developed in the postwar wave was to blame for their problems. Democratic governments, so it was widely held in Brazil and Chile and many other places, were incapable of being sufficiently tough: They put too many people on the public payroll, were too generous in providing subsidies for the poor, were too active in supporting labor's wishes for higher wages, and were too generous toward inefficient national industries that ought to be shut down. All these forms of foolish generosity, it was held, came about because politicians needed to win elections and sacrificed proper economic management for that purpose.

Bankers' demands for repayment led some in poorer countries, particularly on the political right, to favor ending democracy. Some in banking circles and in Washington agreed, seeing the termination of democracy as just economic good sense. So both the wish to protect investors and fears of communist revolution contributed to U.S. support for the termination of democracy in various places.

At the same time, others in poorer countries, especially on the political left, had their own diagnosis. In this analysis, foreign loans were supporting projects with little benefit to poorer people, some benefit to the well-off, and much benefit to corrupt politicians—who managed to enrich themselves, often concealing their new wealth in foreign accounts. These same politicians then cut social services and increased taxes to meet the creditors' demands for repayment. This diagnosis saw the democratic claims of current governments as inadequate or downright fraudulent. In Latin America, the left's skepticism about democracy, the admiration for the Cuban revolution, and the embrace of a revolutionary course by some only added to the antidemocratic propensities of rightist opponents who wanted to head off potential revolutions. The few revolutionary movements that did attain power did not seem to be delivering democracy either. The resulting series of military coups added to the widespread pessimism of the time about the future of democracy in the world.

The 1970s and 1980s

Several aspects of the 1970s and 1980s transformed the world scene radically: democratization in southern Europe, Third World economic disaster, and social movements' seizure of opportunities in eastern Europe following Soviet reform. In the end, the language of democracy was widely embraced in the Third World.

Democratization in southern Europe. The nondemocratic states that bordered democratic western Europe—Spain, Greece, and Portugal—were refused admission into the economic institutions of this increasingly prosperous region until they developed democratic practices. Moreover, exclusion from the rest of Europe was widely experienced as shameful (I recall taxi drivers and hotel clerks in Francisco Franco's Spain apologizing to me because their country was not like the rest of Europe), and social movements were able to use such sentiment to help keep alive the notion of democratic restoration. In the 1970s, dramatic events led to institutional reform, and in the favorable atmosphere of a prospering and democratic Europe, in each case a democratic model was followed. Thus began the most recent worldwide democratic wave.

Third World economic disaster. By the 1980s, much of the world was in severe economic difficulty. In Latin America, for example, tens of billions of dollars per year were removed from the local economies and returned to foreign investors. In Africa, widespread poverty led to desperate overgrazing and deforestation, ultimately leading to vast famines and general economic collapse. The authoritarian governments in place drew much of the blame, which permitted democratic movements to revive and reforming elites to urge militaries to step down. A few years earlier, charges of economic irrationality had joined with fears of communism to favor military overthrows of democratic and semidemocratic regimes in Latin America. Now those militaries were blamed for mounting economic disaster.

The degree to which social movements and democratizing elements among the powerholders were responsible for generating reforms varied enormously from country to country. Sometimes both reformers and challengers acted in tandem, as internal reforms opened up opportunities for democratic movements and democratic movements led regimes to open up. In Brazil, for example, by the early 1980s some in the military sought to leave power and social movements held many demonstrations with hundreds of thousands, even millions, of persons, the largest demonstrations in the history of that country.

Soviet reform and eastern European opportunity. At the same historical moment, a major reform current was challenging the patterns of rule in the Soviet Union. In central and eastern Europe, as well as in the Soviet Union itself, opposition forces were able to use the international climate to keep their opposition alive and visible.

The Soviet Union had entered into an international agreement with the West, the Helsinki Accords, that provided for the monitoring of human rights abuses. (The Helsinki Final Act was signed in 1975.) The Soviet Union assented to this agreement in return for improved economic relations with the western countries. The legitimating power of democratic ideals was by now so profoundly entrenched in western countries that the western governments were finding it difficult, in terms of their own publics, to improve their economic relations with the Soviet Union without getting a human rights agreement.

It is very difficult to know if anyone on either side actually expected the Helsinki Accords to be honored. In retrospect, however, the agreement provided that bit of opportunity required by dissident social movements all over eastern Europe. The Helsinki Accords made it profoundly embarrassing for the Soviet Union or any other government to suppress citizens totally. In Poland in particular, an enormous movement called Solidarity demanded the right to establish autonomous trade unions, independent of government control. In the summer and fall of 1980, what began as a strike of shipyard workers galvanized millions of Poles into protest, whose central demand for a workers' organization independent of state control challenged a regime that claimed it was a workers' state. Although the regime did manage to contain that challenge (by martial law), it was unable to destroy Solidarity under the watchful eyes of a human rights–conscious world.

In other countries, especially in Czechoslovakia, Hungary, and the Soviet Union itself, smaller groups of dissidents became active. In 1989, when the Soviet Union made clear that it was no longer prepared to defend by force the central and eastern European regimes against their own people, hundreds of thousands took to the streets in East Germany, Czechoslovakia, and Romania. One regime after another collapsed. The Soviet Union itself splintered into many distinct republics. In the general world climate, with democratic states riding high, the new leaderships of all these countries quickly announced their intention to develop democratic forms. Elections were held, parties were organized, parliaments became active, and new constitutions began to be written.

The end of alternative models: The Third World embraces democracy. In poorer parts of the world, governments that had looked to the Soviet Union for help adjusted to the impossibility of obtaining aid from anywhere other than the richer democratic countries. Revolutionary forces that had hoped to overthrow governments and had sought assistance from one or another member of the increasingly fragmented "socialist bloc" came to the same conclusion. Suddenly democracy movements and democratic promises were everywhere.

Let us survey the world political scene in the mid-1990s. We see that, for the first time in memory, every country in Central America had an elected head of state. African regimes in the 1990s were holding multiparty competitive elections, some for the first time (although some of these regimes, unhappy with the election results, refused to honor them). A particularly striking case, because of its wealth and power, was South Africa, where the white minority had enjoyed democratic procedures from which the great majority of their fellow citizens were totally excluded. A long and bitter struggle between various groups and the whites-only regime led to a process of negotiation. In 1994, for the first time in South African history, the black majority participated in elections.

Recall the background to these dramatic changes: Just as a variety of antidemocratic forces had gathered themselves to overthrow democracy after the post–World War I democratization wave, so too was the post–World War II era of democratization followed by a time of democratic collapse. The antidemocratic wave of the 1920s and 1930s took some of its striking features from the European fascist movements of the era. Even when the antidemocratic forces were not predominantly fascistic, they had often worked closely with fascist allies or borrowed from the Italian or German constitution. The Brazilian "New State" established by its constitution of 1937, which borrowed much from Benito Mussolini's Italy, is a good example of the power of fascist models. The postdemocratic states of the 1960s and 1970s were profoundly shaped, on the contrary, by socialism. The Soviet Union, like the western democracies, had been a victor in World War II, and revolutionary socialist movements were enjoying spectacular battlefield successes in China and Vietnam. Many in poorer, weaker countries saw socialism as the wave of the future. With economic failures, some in poorer countries looked to socialist models for solutions and to the Soviet Union for support. The propensity of the United States to support the wealthy strata of poorer countries and the view of western European powers as recent (or even continuing) imperialist conquerors contributed to a rejection of western models. Thus when governments fell, some new regimes opted for authoritarian socialism. Other democratic systems, especially in Latin America, were overthrown by those fearful of socialism, often with U.S. support.

With the declining appeal of the Soviet Union as a model and the collapse of the Soviet Union as a source of aid, the revolutionary impulse slackened; governments that had claimed "socialism" embraced other, often western, models; and antidemocratic regimes could no longer use the threat of communism to justify repression. Thus both Albania and Mongolia held elections to inaugurate postcommunist regimes, and Brazil and Chile held elections to launch postmilitary regimes within a few years of each other.

By the late 1980s, democracy had taken on the characteristics of what Samuel Huntington calls a "prevailing nostrum."[16] Powerholders were seeing democratization as part of the cure for all manner of ills, sometimes in places little known for supporting democracy in the recent past. The managers of the transnational financial networks, who had played a significant role in undermining democracies in the 1960s and 1970s in indebted Third World countries, were now coming around to a new political theory. A quarter century earlier, democracy had been seen as a source of silly development projects, wasteful spending, political corruption, and massive borrowing to cover the costs. Elected politicians, so this theory went, would create jobs for potential voters, support unproductive enterprises in return for campaign contributions or bribes, and try to enrich themselves at the same time. They would favor getting loans over raising taxes to finance their projects. So democracy looked bad to international bankers. But the new authoritarian regimes in Latin America or Africa turned out to be just as prone to failed development policies, corrupt officials, wasteful spending, and unpayable debts. Or even more so. Maybe democracy, with at least some level of accountability, was actually better. And maybe democracy was a better preventative measure against revolution, too. According to one study of the World Bank's decision making, by the 1990s there was some sentiment inside the bank for making the democratic accountability of governments a condition for receiving financial aid.[17]

If favorable views of democracy had penetrated into many previously inhospitable high places, small wonder that weaker players on the world stage joined in. Consider an African example: In June 1994, readers of the *New York Times* learned of the first multiparty elections held in several African countries. Britain and France had informed their former colonies that support "would be tied to political pluralism."[18]

Consider yet another sign of the times: In the 1990s the established elites of many Middle Eastern countries were facing a severe challenge from movements claiming to restore Islam to its proper place in public (and private) life. Western political scientists had rarely attributed democratic characteristics to the elites of those countries, but the political scientists saw the movements they called "Islamic fundamentalist" or "Islamist" as profoundly antidemocratic as well. Yet both the establishment and the challengers were now sometimes claiming the mantle of democracy for themselves. Jordan's King Hussein, for example, supported Jordanian democratization in 1992: "We perceive Jordanian democracy as a model and an example . . . from which there will be no turning back."[19] The head of Tunisia's banned Islamist movement spoke in equally positive tones: "We accept [the fact that we must] work within the legal framework in the hope of making it more democratic and pluralist."[20] Doubters at the time wondered at the depth of such commitments. But, genuine or not, those commitments showed that more and more states and more and more opposition movements in more and more parts of the world found the claim of embracing democracy to be the way to go.

Conclusions

In this chapter we have seen an oscillation in the twentieth century between democratic and antidemocratic currents on a global scale. We have also seen that ordinary people and powerful elites have promoted democratization in a wide variety of ways. Finally, we have seen that the very meaning of democracy has been continually debated, fought over, and changed. By the middle of the 1990s, a far larger proportion of the governments of this planet were claiming to be democracies than ever before. How would things look as time passed? Was a new antidemocratic countercurrent already gathering steam? And what sort of democracy was in the process of being created?

What is the state of democracy early in the twenty-first century? And what are the prospects for the future? To answer these questions, we must try to discern the possibilities within the current movement. To do so intelligently, we need to step back from the broad lines of the story sketched in the past two chapters and reflect further on their main themes: the power of democratic legitimation for governments and social movements alike, the capacities of powerholders to maintain their position within new institutional forms, and the capacities of social movements to seize opportunities present in the rhetoric and the institutions of democratization.

CHAPTER 5
SEMIDEMOCRACY, PSEUDODEMOCRACY, DEMOCRACY

Toward the beginning of the modern era of democratization, in the late 1780s, the French monarchy was floundering in a profound crisis. Its resources were depleted, its credit was gone, but its expenses were great. Rather than just accept its demands for taxes, powerful social groups were insisting that the king convene the Estates General, an old representative body that had not met since 1614, to consider his tax demands. Many hoped to be able to use the Estates General as a vehicle for bringing about changes, and the king was forced to go along.

But who was to sit in the Estates, and how was the Estates to reach decisions? Conservative forces demanded that the Estates be constituted in such a fashion that conservatives could be sure to dominate. Their proposal, modeled on past procedures, was to have three separate bodies. The first would represent the clergy, the second the nobility, and the third the remainder of the population, perhaps 98 percent of the people of France. Each chamber would have one vote. Thus, 98 percent of the people of France would be represented by a body that could be outvoted 2 to 1 by delegates of the privileged orders.

Those who spoke for drastic reform had a different proposal: The Third Estate would have as many delegates as the other two combined, and decisions would be made by all the delegates sitting as a single body and voting as individuals. Thus the deputies of the Third Estate, plus liberal minorities among the deputies of the clergy and nobility, would often be able to get more than half the total votes, and reform programs would carry the day. This was one of the early modest battles over election rules and parliamentary procedures in the long, unfinished struggle for democracy.

The unfolding of this drama is instructive to us. The French government—hoping for peace without losing control, for some reform but not too much—decreed that the number of delegates of the Third Estate would be doubled, as the supporters of extensive change had demanded, but left unsettled the question of the voting rules at the Estates General. If voting would be "by order" rather than "by head," in the terminology of the debate, the modest democratization involved in allowing 98 percent of the French people to be represented by 50 percent of the delegates would not be translated into a liberalizing program. This is an early instance of a *democratic facade*—that is, of the existence of an institution associated with democracy (a larger share of the delegates for the great majority of the French people) in an overall context that could easily empty it of its power.

The next step in the story is also instructive. The delegates of the Third Estate showed up and insisted that they would participate only in a body that met as a whole and voted as individuals. After some hesitation, they took the bold step of proceeding to act as if that were possible, calling themselves the National Assembly and inviting the other deputies to join them. The king was plainly considering putting a stop to this step by military action, but he backed down after an uprising by the people of Paris. They were determined to support their National Assembly, now constituted along the lines desired by the Third Estate delegates.

Sometimes elites, under pressure, grant more democratic structures but do so in ways aimed at neutralizing the democratic potential, just as the king went along with expanded representation but not democratic voting. Sometimes democratic forces are able to use such facades as opportunities for further democratic openings, as the deputies of the Third Estate and their allies did in claiming that they were the nucleus of a National Assembly. And sometimes elite reformers get nowhere without support by ordinary people in the streets and fields, as happened when the Old Regime was revealed as vulnerable to the concerted action of the Parisians who stormed the Bastille, the city's famous prison fortress, in July 1789.

Facade Democracy

Students of Central American politics are familiar with the concept of the democratic facade: the regime with an elected legislature and an elected president, a constitution specifying their powers and guaranteeing all sorts of rights for citizens, a judicial process to which citizens can appeal, and political parties that engage in campaigns—all the elements of democracy, indeed, but one. That one is an effective reality based on the formal rules.[1]

A number of devices may be used to undercut the rules:

- The elected president's authority may be limited. In much of Central American history, for example, the leading generals and the U.S. ambassador have often wielded far more genuine authority than the elected president. The U.S. ambassador has sometimes been even more powerful than the generals.
- The capacity of opposition parties to conduct campaigns may be severely curtailed by a variety of means. Registration laws might be interpreted by a corrupt judiciary to prevent a party campaigning at all, or, less subtly, party campaigners might be threatened, beaten, or killed.
- As for the actual vote, voters have often been intimidated, and fraudulent vote counts have been even more common.
- Finally, but not less importantly, a more powerful state has sometimes "intervened" militarily when sufficiently unhappy with political life in the client state.

The United States has a history of such interventions, as when it sent expeditions to Mexico in 1914 and 1916 or when it occupied the Dominican Republic from 1916 to 1924, Haiti from 1914 to 1934, or Nicaragua from 1912 to 1925, and sent marines to Cuba from 1917 to 1923. In more recent years, the United States overthrew the government of Guatemala in 1954, occupied the Dominican Republic in 1965, invaded Grenada in 1983, seized the head of the Panamanian government in 1989, and occupied Haiti in 1994. Whether the United States was deposing a government (elected or otherwise) or, as in Haiti, reinstalling an elected one, with every action it demonstrated the limits to the autonomy of any weak regime so close to the greatest economic, military, and cultural power in the twentieth century. The turn-of-the-century Mexican tyrant Porfirio

Díaz is supposed to have observed, "Poor Mexico—so far from God and so near to the United States."

Few observers would regard a political system with these features as very democratic, even in periods with elections, a generous suffrage, parliamentary bodies, parties, and constitutions. Why bother with such a farcical, meaningless "democratic" political structure, one might well ask. Because powerholders often need to justify their power—sometimes to their own people, sometimes to potential foreign benefactors, perhaps to themselves. To the extent that the claim to democracy is an essential element of a legitimate political order, and we have seen that this has been increasingly the case on a global basis from the 1790s on, political systems have been cloaking themselves in democratic guise. The most significant point here is that the modern history of democracy and the history of fraudulent claims to democracy are inseparable. One powerful impulse to restructure institutions is to achieve a democratic appearance, which is, however, quite distinct from actually altering the distribution of power. These appearances, however, are far from meaningless, for they sometimes create opportunities for further change.

It may be helpful at this point to introduce a somewhat different vocabulary. It is not enough simply to describe particular political arrangements as democratic or not democratic. By the prevalent standards of the day, whether that day is in 1890, 1920, 1950, 1995, or 2015, we may find political systems with some significant democratic components but some significant antidemocratic components as well. Let us, provisionally, call such systems *semidemocracy*. We may also find other political systems that have democratic elements but that in no way and to no degree actually have governments controlled by their citizenry. Let us call such systems, like those that have been common in the history of Central America, *pseudodemocracy*.

The point of this language is not to definitively classify existing political arrangements as democratic, semidemocratic, pseudodemocratic, or nondemocratic but more modestly to call attention to important aspects of social realities. When we look for semidemocracy, we are looking for the ways in which democratic and nondemocratic processes may coexist or even intertwine. When we speak of pseudodemocracy, we are looking for the ways in which the mythic substructure of political life (such as the belief that "the people rule") differs from how power is actually acquired and how power is actually used.

Democratic-Authoritarian Hybrids: Elections

Let us borrow the term *hybrid* to indicate the mixture of democratic and nondemocratic elements that can be found in political systems. A survey of the political systems of the twentieth and twenty-first centuries would reveal a great variety of such hybrids. We can get some idea of this variety by looking at the relationship of electoral processes to political power. The mythical substructure of democracy tells us that the people rule, and it has become generally accepted that through elections the will of the people is made known. The notion that individual citizens freely choose among candidates for positions of power may be a mythical distortion of more complex realities, however, in three broad ways:

- There may be constraints on the capacities of individuals to choose.
- There may be constraints on the range of choices that are possible.
- There may be constraints on the degree to which elections determine who holds power.

In addition to these issues of how powerholders are chosen, there are some very difficult questions of the degree to which those who are chosen actually carry out the will of electorates, a subject that will be touched on in Chapter 7.

Let's look more closely at each of these three limitations on the expression of the popular will through elections. There are many examples of each. Sometimes the deviations have been very obvious, but some have been more subtle.

Limitations on Individual Freedom to Choose

These limitations come in two varieties: limitations on which individual citizens are allowed to do the choosing and limitations on the freedom with which those who do the choosing are able to make their choices.

Every political system in the world today that has voting places some limitations on who has the right to vote. In not a single country do children vote for national officials, although countries differ in the minimum age for voting. Most countries deny voting rights to those who are not "citizens," even if those noncitizens are long-term residents, participate in the national language and culture, work there, and raise their children (who sometimes are citizens) there. Beyond these very widespread limitations, there may be others. In various countries that have called themselves democracies since the nineteenth century, large numbers of people have been excluded from voting rights because they were not men, because they had insufficient wealth or property, or because they belonged to a particular ethnic group. For example, throughout most of the twentieth century, women did not have full voting rights in Switzerland, the aboriginal peoples of Australia could not vote in that country, and the overwhelming majority of South African people could not vote because of their race.

Restrictions on electorates may be more subtle as well. Those who belong to particular groups may have the legal right to vote yet be discouraged through violence from exercising that right. This mechanism has been important in limiting the rights of African Americans at various times and places in the history of the United States. In some villages in India, members of the lowest rung of the caste system, the "untouchables" (those who do what is considered to be the dirtiest work), have sometimes been confronted by extreme violence if they attempt to exercise voting rights that are guaranteed in the constitution of India.

From the point of view of the intimidated, who are perfectly aware of the forces arrayed against them, nothing about any of these tactics is very subtle. But if such practices are largely confined to the rural areas, away from the curiosity of reporters and the glare of television spotlights, many people will be unaware of the extent to which the electorate in practice is constituted differently than it is in law. Even a country's citizens may be unaware of the difficulties some of their fellow citizens face if they should try to exercise their legal rights. For foreign journalists, sociologists, and historians, the likelihood of misunderstanding real limitations to democracy are even greater.

A different sort of restriction is found in the twenty-first-century United States. In the late nineteenth century, many states began to develop relatively complex procedures to register voters, which dramatically reduced the proportion of legally eligible people who actually voted. These restrictions were long a major cause of low voter turnout in the United States. Estimates vary, but the number of unregistered U.S. adults in the mid-1990s was certainly in the tens of millions. (Since then, however, the number has fallen dramatically as the result of legislation simplifying registration, but turnout continued to be low compared to other wealthy democratic countries.)[2] In the period leading up to the presidential campaign of 2012, some states were introducing varied procedures that would again make registration more difficult, including requiring government-issued photo ID. One major party claimed that the purpose of this legislation was to reduce fraudulent voting, but the other claimed that it sought to keep poorer people—less likely to have cars and therefore driver's licenses—from voting. As often, social conflicts may redefine how democracy works.

In more than a dozen countries (including Belgium, Australia, Sweden, Italy, New Zealand, and Germany) voter turnout has commonly been over 80 percent. In the United States, fewer than three out of five eligible voters turned out in the bitterly contested elections for president in 2012; and far fewer vote in nonpresidential elections. A great deal of research has shown clearly that those who do not vote in the United States tend to be from relatively poor backgrounds. Thus those who actually vote are not a cross-section of "the people" but tend to be better off economically.

The subtlety of this particular barrier to voting may be seen in the claim that the United States practices universal suffrage, a claim that is rarely questioned. The term *universal suffrage* comes out of the mythical conception of democracy. As I pointed out in Chapter 3, before the Civil War, when few blacks and no women could vote, the term *universal suffrage* was already used to characterize the U.S. political system. But in no country today is suffrage literally universal, because there are always some restrictions on who is included in the universe.

The freedom of an individual to choose may be constrained in many other possible ways as well. The absence of a secret ballot, for example, exposes individuals to punishments and rewards from communities or the powerful, making voting more of a collective and less of an individual act. Nineteenth-century voting was frequently public. In the 1840s, for example, voters announced their vote out loud in Virginia, Kentucky, Illinois, Arkansas, Missouri, and Texas.[3] In some of the elections held in the former Soviet Union, a voter had the right to enter a booth and cast a ballot in secret, but doing so was an individual choice and an unusual one at that. Choosing to vote in secret strongly suggested some sort of dissent, a suggestion that few were prepared to make. Even where secret ballots are legally mandated, they sometimes have been not so secret in practice. My grandfather's older brother was once paid for his vote by a party worker in New York City and was beaten up after he cast his "secret" ballot for another candidate.

A particularly interesting version of such practices has been found in countries where the pattern of social relations is "clientelistic." When there are many poor people with considerable economic insecurity—perhaps jobs are scarce, perhaps claims to land are uncertain—powerful "bosses" are often able to exchange modest rewards, such as a job or a spot of land, for votes. Those who are unwilling to comply may be subject to the violence of privately employed gangs, often recruited from the same poor people. The bosses not only tell their followers how to vote but also may provide transportation to the polling places and have their followers bar others from voting. Using the image of animals led by their owner, Brazilians used to speak of the "halter vote." One Brazilian story tells about the man who asks the local boss "whom I voted for"; the boss admonishes him to remember that the vote is secret.[4] Such practices were common in nineteenth- and early twentieth-century Spain and southern Italy, as well as in much of Latin America. In communities with a clientelistic organization, voting may well be unanimous, reflecting the will of a powerful individual and not a consensus of autonomous voters. Democratic rules, indeed, may be a central mechanism in the maintenance of the boss's local tyranny because in return for delivering the right vote regional and national powerholders would support the boss if challenged.

Limitations on Competition

A very different kind of constraint on electoral processes comes out of the ways in which competition for the allegiance of the electorate is organized. Some restrictions on political competition have to do with the formal rights, embodied in laws, of people to form themselves into parties for the purpose of competing for votes. A more subtle form of restriction involves the way such competition is carried out in reality.

Legal restrictions. Some states control competition by legally restricting the formation of political parties. For example, parties with particular religious or ethnic programs may be barred from public life. Parties that advocate particular political positions might also be banned. Communist parties have frequently been prevented from contesting elections; fascist parties have been restricted in Germany since the end of World War II. At one point in the modern history of Argentina, the party that supported the exiled Juan Perón was prohibited by that country's military from appearing on the ballot in most of the elections held from the mid-1950s to the mid-1960s. This was a rather striking limitation, because the Peronist party was the one with the largest popular support at the time.

A less sweeping variant is the barring of particular individuals from holding public office. These are usually people who have been active in public life and whose policies have antagonized the powerful. Brazil and Turkey are examples of countries where such deprivations of political rights have been far from unusual.

A very significant practice in this vein is the "licensing" of parties.[5] A regime not only may decide which parties to permit but may even create one—or more than one or perhaps all of the parties allowed. In the 1970s, when the Brazilian military after a decade in power began to reopen the political system, it created not only a party designed to support its policies but also the only opposition party. Brazilians said that the difference between the two parties was that one said "yes" and the other said "yes, sir."

An array of more subtle practices is possible, especially in regulations governing electoral campaigns. Laws may make it easier or more difficult for new parties to enter the political arena, may make it easier or more difficult for candidates to have access to the mass media during election campaigns, may make it easier for some parties than others to have complaints about irregularities taken seriously, may define and redesign electoral circumscriptions to produce particular outcomes, and so forth. In the United States, Americans take it for granted that the dominant party in a state legislature will redraw the map of electoral districts to give that party an advantage in the next election. In the elections for the U.S. House of Representatives in 2012, for example, if we add up the total votes for all 435 House seats nationally, the Democrats got more votes than the Republicans yet 234 Republicans were elected to 201 Democrats. This was partly the result of the way Republican-majority state legislatures drew district boundaries.

Resource disparities. Not all citizens are equally able to take advantage of the formal rules for electoral competition. Let us first consider the question of resources. Imagine a country with significant disparities of wealth among individuals or significant differences in the wealth held by organized bodies. Would someone with millions of dollars have exactly the same opportunity to influence the opinions of others as someone in poverty? Of course not. Nor could a small business be expected to provide the same funds to a political party as a giant corporation could. Political campaigns are costly. Candidates need to be able to provide for themselves, first of all, but also need to travel; to pay printing costs; to hire political consultants, lawyers, and accountants; and nowadays, to obtain access to the mass media and pay for expensive advertising. The wealthy are more able to bear such costs. Even if all are equally free by law to enter the electoral arena themselves, to join or form parties, and to give funds to the parties of their choice, in a society characterized by inequality of wealth, some are able to give far more of their time, energy, or money than others. And what society does not have significant inequalities?

There is no country where electoral competition is carried out on a level playing field. One symptom of this situation is the degree to which very wealthy people are more likely to be candidates for public office than very poor people. In 2011, for example, about 48 percent of legislators in the U.S. Congress were millionaires.[6] But probably more significant is the degree to which the vast expenses of modern campaigning are sustained by contributions from the wealthy. In the hard-fought U.S. presidential campaign of 2012, the two rival candidates together raised more than $2 billion.[7] Adding in the costs of the congressional campaign makes the total enormously larger. To avoid the issues presented by such astronomical sums in politics, some countries limit campaign spending by law.

One very important question, then, is the way the rules of the political game permit or encourage parties and candidates to raise resources. When James Madison was formulating his ideas about the U.S. Constitution in the 1780s, he was concerned initially with how it might be possible to ensure that those elected to office were the sort of well-to-do, educated men he trusted. Fears of what one Virginia delegate to the Constitutional Convention called "the turbulence and follies of democracy"[8] weighed heavily on many others as well. Madison and his associates were especially concerned about the capacity of debtors to democratically violate the rights of creditors and of the propertyless to disregard the rights of property.[9]

Madison hit on the notion that, if a congressional district encompassed a fairly large territory, only a prosperous person would have the leisure and the resources to make himself well enough known throughout his district to win an election. Even with a very wide right to vote, Madison reasoned, and even with a free choice of candidates, the triumph of a certain kind of person would be assured. In the ensuing debates over the Constitution, critics charged it with being the instrument of "aristocratic tyranny," with being a plan to "raise the fortunes and respectability of the *well-born few,* and oppress the plebeians."[10] Two centuries later, in the early twenty-first century, campaign expenses are astronomical, and those individuals and organizations with wealth have a great advantage, even within an electoral process legally open to all comers. The same is true in many other countries but it is particularly characteristic of the United States because restrictions on how campaigns are financed are so limited. Those opposed to restrictions have been able to argue that they would violate free speech principles and have been getting sympathetic responses from the Supreme Court.

One important resource in the twenty-first century is access to the communications media that carry messages to the electorate. Many scholars of electoral processes urge us to consider the nature of the media of communication. They particularly note that the immediacy of television, combined with the impact of images and words flooding into one's living room or den, provides an unrivaled opportunity to get across simple messages. If the government controls access to television, the parties, positions, and candidates that the government favors may thus have an enormous advantage. Governments have sometimes organized elections in which opposition parties are given limited or even no opportunity to present their case before the cameras, leaving the government's own message virtually unchallenged. Even when communication media are not government owned but are in private hands, we can ask whether those who control those media have a substantial advantage over rivals. No doubt one of the reasons for the triumph of Silvio Berlusconi at the polls in Italy in 1994 was his position as the head of a vast communications empire, which controlled about half of Italian TV programming, several publishing firms, and almost three dozen magazines.[11] To the extent that an electorate makes decisions based on the facts known to the public, the capacity to shape those facts, to conceal some and interpret others, may have a significant impact on the outcome of elections.

In the early twenty-first century new electronic communications media were coming into their own. Some saw this as the beginning of a great democratization of access to information. Words and images could spread with lightning speed through email, YouTube, Facebook, and Twitter. The challenge to the hopes of authoritarian regimes to tightly control public information led some of them, like China, to devote great efforts to try to limit access in general and for regimes faced with active protest movements, as Egypt was in 2011's Arab Spring, to try to shut down the new media. In more democratic countries, politicians were trying to figure out how to make the new media work for them and social movements found a new issue in mounting efforts to prevent governments from curbing the new tools.

Some observers held that the new media meant that citizens were becoming better informed. Others held that they were increasingly paying attention only to communications from those who felt the same way as themselves and were getting exposed to a narrower range of information. Still others thought that the gap between the well-off and the poor who cannot afford the new media and who live in places with less Internet access was producing what they called a "digital divide."

Limitations on the Capacity of Electoral Processes to Determine Powerholders

In numerous ways "the will of the people," as expressed through the ballot, may not be well translated into who holds power and what policies are carried out. If positions that confer real power are occupied neither by elected officials nor by those subject to the authority of such officials, electoral processes are not capable of determining effective power. In the nineteenth century, as we have seen, hereditary monarchs in much of Europe shared the public stage with elected parliamentary bodies. Yet for much of the nineteenth century, many of those monarchs still had the upper hand in appointing ministers and other officials, in determining budgets and taxation, in controlling military and police forces, and in issuing decrees.

In much of Latin American history, not only were military officers unelected (military officership has hardly ever been elective anywhere), but they were often subordinate to elected officials only to the extent the military officers cared to be. The main barrier to military seizures of power or concealed dictation of policy from the sidelines was not the secure dominance of a civilian president but the internal divisions within the military itself. In Turkey, the military has for decades seen itself as the guardian of certain principles on behalf of which it is prepared to depose elected governments. These principles include the defense of secularism against Islamic-oriented parties as the army reaffirmed in 2007. As an indication that their ability to shape politics has significantly declined, more than forty officers were arrested in 2010 and charged with planning a coup.

If an elected parliament's laws are subject to the scrutiny of a council of military officers (as was the case in Portugal in the 1970s), or a religious body (as in Iran in the 1980s and beyond), or if military officers are free to threaten coups to get their way, then there are significant political actors whose power does not rest on popular will. Unelected kings, religious authorities, and military councils are, however, merely the most obvious of such mechanisms. In the case of some weaker countries that depend on a powerful foreign government, elected officials may often have to yield to that foreign power. Many observers of Central America at many historical movements, as pointed out earlier, have viewed the single most powerful decision maker in many instances as the U.S. ambassador, whether the president of the country in question was an elected politician or a general at the head of a coup.[12] Sometimes force goes beyond threats. In 1989, for example, after an opposition movement failed to end the rule of Panama's General Noriega, 24,000 U.S. troops were sent to do so, successfully.

The degree to which major decisions are in the hands of political figures who are accountable to citizens is a critical issue. It is worth considering whether recent economic, social, and political trends on a world scale are likely to place major decisions in the hands of unelected powerholders. We will consider this question more carefully in Chapter 7.

Democratic Sham

If laws can exclude people from the vote or threats can deter those allowed to vote by law, if parties can be banned or some parties have advantages in waging campaigns, it may be quite difficult to assess the degree to which the actual selection of powerholders approximates popular choice. Small wonder that scholars often disagree on whether or not to call particular political systems democratic.

In the late eighteenth century, claiming that governments should derive their powers from the consent of the governed was a dramatic and daring act. In the early twenty-first century, making such a claim is commonplace, but determining what reality there is to such claims is often rather difficult. Those in government, those with wealth, and those with some capacity to intimidate others have many ways to push expressions of the voice of the people in one direction rather than another. Some would question whether there is ever any reality to democracy at all, whether all claims to democracy are merely fraudulent—whether democracy is a sham.

In the 1920s, some people in countries with formal democratic rules but with extremely clientelistic social structures—countries such as Italy, Spain, and Brazil—elaborated a critique of democracy—as it existed in reality in their country—as a sham. With some accuracy, they pointed to the degree to which local elites actually controlled all major social institutions and used the mechanisms of elections to do so. It was out of such considerations that some looked to fascist and other movements of the political right as a superior alternative. Democracy was seen not only as corrupt and backward but also as entirely hypocritical in its claims to represent "the people." Mainly, the political bosses were represented. Although it still exists, this particular critique of democracy as a sham is much less common in the early twenty-first century than it was in the 1920s, partly because such clientelistic structures are weaker in many countries (or at least less obvious in the far more urban setting that most people now live in, rather than the impoverished countryside of the past) and partly because the fascisms with which this critique was often associated were deeply discredited by the horrors of World War II.

On the other side of the political spectrum, some on the left have at times criticized the reality of democracy in the wealthier countries by pointing to the consequences of uneven distribution of wealth, the role of costly mass media in molding opinion, and the hidden access of the wealthy to elected politicians. Some on the left, like some on the right, have sometimes regarded claims to democracy as essentially fraudulent and these critiques have gained strength in the early twenty-first century. We will return to this in the next two chapters.

We can build on the earlier chapters to look at this question in a different perspective.

A Two-Edged Sword

In earlier chapters, I suggested that claims of democratic legitimation on the part of powerholders provide opportunities for challengers. If powerholders assert that they rule by the will of the people, challengers can assert that they speak for at least some of the people. The challengers may try to show that they represent a significant contingent by demonstrating their numbers through petitions or at the ballot box, by staging visible demonstrations, or by contending that obviously their position on some issue is supported by large numbers. Powerholders claiming the mantle of democratic legitimation may have trouble totally suppressing such activities. It could well happen, then—and in fact often has happened—that semidemocratic and even pseudodemocratic governments have been successfully challenged by more democratic elements, often much to the surprise of the rulers of the day.

Let's consider a few examples. Mexico, in the late nineteenth and early twentieth centuries, was a tyranny presided over by Porfirio Díaz. Díaz organized periodic elections that, by virtue of fear and fraud, were sure to provide the desired vote counts. In 1908 he announced in a newspaper interview that, as a supporter of democracy, he really hoped that the next electoral campaign would be a vigorous one. He thereby encouraged the emergence of an opposition that ultimately became the focus for a vast and varied group of challenges. Those challenges became the Mexican Revolution, which overthrew Díaz.[13]

In the mid-1970s, Brazil's military rulers, in power for a decade, attempted to attach some measure of democratic legitimation to themselves. They set up a party, which was expected to control the Brazilian Congress, made up of politicians supportive of the military regime. They also set up an opposition, which was in the unenviable position of being a minority in Congress while having to run for office under rules designed to impede their success. Over the next few years, three processes managed to spoil this scheme. First, the progovernment party turned out to be much less docile than the military had wished; it never wanted to reduce Congress to a rubber stamp for the military's ideas. Second, no matter how the electoral rules were written, and rewritten again and again, the opposition party did much better than expected. (Many in the opposition itself had initially debated whether or not to participate. Some felt that they would provide the generals with a slim layer of democratic legitimation, without any chance of actually gaining power.) The third process was the degree to which the staging of election campaigns—however limited, controlled, and unfair the rules made them—implied some opportunity for political debate in the press, in the universities, and inside professional organizations. These opportunities eventually led to an unprecedented level of popular mobilization against the government, with demonstrations by hundreds of thousands of people in major Brazilian cities. Instead of providing the controlled, limited opening they appear to have been after at first, the generals wound up returning power to civilians.

Rather frequently, antidemocratic governments organize elections or plebiscites they hope to win, discover that they have lost, and find it impossible to set aside the elections. In 1980 the Uruguayan military, having terrorized the population, organized a referendum to legitimate a constitution that permanently gave the military power. But the military lost, to the amazement of both itself and the opposition. Chile's General Augusto Pinochet sponsored a vote on Chile's future in 1988, asking for eight more years of power, and was widely believed likely to win. Having observed the regime survive in spite of economic troubles, few Chileans of any political persuasion expected to see democratic institutions restored in Pinochet's lifetime. But Pinochet lost—and stepped down. In 1990 the socialist government of Nicaragua organized elections that it expected to win, in part to counter criticism from European socialists about its nondemocratic character. It lost and, further surprising both supporters and enemies, relinquished power. After a decade of bitter struggle with the opposition movement Solidarity, Poland's communist government agreed on a compromise in which elections would be held under rules designed to prevent a complete defeat for the regime. Solidarity did much better than expected by either side, winning ninety-nine out of one hundred seats in the Senate. We could find many other examples.

So common are such occurrences that the political scientist Samuel Huntington regards what he calls "stunning elections" as a regular part of the twilight of nondemocratic regimes.[14] We might well ask why such regimes often mistake the way the electorate will actually vote. More important for the themes of this book, however, we should note three other aspects of these situations:

- Many nondemocratic regimes desire at some point to drape themselves with the democratic mantle and sponsor elections or plebiscites, relax press censorship, permit (or even, as in the Brazilian case, actually organize) an opposition to resume its activities. This is powerful testimony to the force of democratic claims at certain moments in history.
- Even with some degree of censorship, restrictions on campaigning, violence and threats of violence, and electoral fraud, opposition forces on occasion manage to triumph, sometimes stunningly.
- The surprised regime, often after some hesitation, frequently accedes to the decision of the vote counts. It is less surprising that some regimes simply ignore the elections, as the Burmese and Algerian governments did in 1990. But in other cases, the government accepts the result.

What we see happening here are rulers attempting to use democratic legitimation as a shield against actual alteration in who exercises power and how, as well as oppositional movements managing to find in that very attempt the strategic opportunity to force democratization well beyond the regime's intentions. These examples, focusing on the "stunning election," point toward a much more general observation: semidemocratic and even pseudodemocratic situations often contain opportunities for democratic mobilizations that challenge the regime.

Conservatives in France in the summer of 1789 feared that if the National Assembly issued a Declaration of Rights of Man and Citizen (it did) then the lower classes would be encouraged to go beyond the intentions of those who voted on that document (they did). Conservatives in England in the early 1830s feared that expanding suffrage from a very small portion of the population to a proportion a bit less small would eventually result in "democracy," a word used quite negatively in those debates; the limited expansion of 1832 did indeed prove to be the first of several steps toward a vastly greater expansion. And conservatives in the United States in the 1780s feared the results of a very wide right to vote; the United States soon turned out to be, so Gordon Wood has argued, a rather more democratic place than those who wrote the Constitution were expecting.[15]

In each of these cases, the misgivings of conservatives were borne out. Small changes and large changes alike often have opened the way to further changes. Sometimes, with very small democratic openings, social movements have been able to bring about far greater ones (sometimes in concert, to be sure, with reforming elites). Why have movements been able to seize limited opportunities and make them less limited? Why are social movements so often able to operate effectively even under pseudodemocratic and semidemocratic circumstances? I want to stress five reasons:

- The claim that the people rule makes it difficult to totally suppress all manifestations of discontent. Although regimes purporting to be democratic or even merely to be democratizing may attempt to limit opposition, others are unlikely to take such claims seriously if no opposition at all is tolerated. The Brazilian military attempted to organize a tame opposition in the 1970s; the Nigerian military attempted something similar in the 1990s. The Brazilian case ultimately saw the military step down. In Nigeria, military rule ended in 1999, but ensuing elections were widely regarded as seriously deformed by fraud and violence. In both cases, the regime plainly felt it needed an opposition of some sort, thereby providing the possibility of a more effective opposition than it had counted on.

- The specific practices that indicate some level of democracy make it easier for groups of various persuasions, including groups trying to bring about greater democratization, to organize and press their claims. Election campaigns, if allowed, are opportunities to get dissenting messages out to the public and to elect people who will be foci of opposition within the government. For example, when the Brazilian military government in the 1970s permitted competitive elections under restrictive rules, which were always subject to change, many in the opposition thought it an error to participate at all. But others campaigned for the Brazilian Democratic Movement, which ultimately grew into a significant force.

- If opposition parties can operate, however unfreely, they may be able to mount a significant challenge when some favorable opportunity—international difficulties, economic crisis, scandal—presents itself. The German Socialist Party, which was able to operate legally from the 1890s on, grew enormously before World War I and was able to play a major role in the great crisis at the end of the war that led to a new and significantly democratized constitution (although the new democratic regime was overthrown in the early 1930s).

- If elections are held but voting rights are limited, an existing party is often tempted to seek the support of those currently denied representation. Thus, as discussed in Chapter 4, some very conservative political figures supported women's right to vote at the close of World War I in the United States and elsewhere because they expected that women would vote conservatively.

- More generally, democratic claims impart legitimacy to social movements as well as to governments. The notion that the movement (or the government) represents "the people" has been a powerful one for the past two centuries.

Thus the two-edged sword: A governing elite may attempt to invoke the notion that it rules on the basis of popular will. But even the most limited acknowledgment of democratic values and practices may open the way to powerful demands for more. On the other hand, the success of a movement in promoting democratic rhetoric or in creating democratic institutions may be contained by elites who manage to retain their power under the new circumstances. Democratization opens the door to more democratization; but elites may protect or even enhance their own positions under democratic auspices.

Democracy ... or Democratization?

In the dialogue—sometimes violent, sometimes peaceable—between the well-off and those less so, between the authorities and the powerless, new institutions may be created under the democratic label. In the late eighteenth century, few of those who called themselves democrats in that first multicontinental democratic wave would have been enthusiastic about secret ballots, which were commonly held by democrats to be a tool for aristocratic rule. A true champion of the people, democrats believed, would hold his head high and vote in public. Nor would anyone have thought much of political parties competing for office. Indeed, in France in the 1790s, to refer to someone as a member of a party was a step short of denouncing him as a traitor. The patriot speaks for all the people, so it was held, not for a part of them. George Washington, in his farewell address, warned his countrymen of the dangers of what he called "faction," expressing a similar disregard of political parties. Votes for women? Forget it: Women, so many democrats held, were inherently dependent creatures, needing the support of a man and unable to reason through the affairs of state. The same reasoning has justified at various times and places the exclusion from voting rights of servants and the poor and still justifies the exclusion of children.

As the era of modern democracy was launched in the social revolutions at the end of the eighteenth century, rival conceptions of democracy confronted each other. People used to meeting with neighbors in local assemblies or with fellow guild members sometimes did not think highly of parliamentary bodies, because elected representatives could become a new aristocracy. In many towns in revolutionary France, militant citizens met, deliberated, and acted, sometimes regarding themselves as more authoritative than the national parliament because they themselves were the people rather than mere representatives.

In the early twenty-first century, however, we can hardly even think of the word democracy without thinking of elected representatives, secret ballots, multiparty competition, and voting rights for nearly all adults. Notions of which institutions embody democracy, then, have changed a great deal. In the early twenty-first century, some social movements are again challenging the equation of democracy with representative bodies.

The established authorities commonly think of democracy as already existing, as having been achieved in past struggles. Social movement challengers, availing themselves of opportunities as they find them—election campaigns, freedom of assembly, an uncensored press—protest their exclusion in the name of the democracy that remains to be created. At moments of heightened conflict, each side may denounce the other for perpetrating a cruel fraud by destroying democracy while claiming to defend it.

It is hard to imagine an end to this sort of conflict. Changes in economic life, political organization, and culture ensure that some, and sometimes many, will call for more democratization in the future.

Consider economic changes. Technological transformation will continue to make certain skills irrelevant and new ones mandatory; some people will have expected opportunities closed to them, and others will find unanticipated possibilities. The depletion of traditional sources of raw materials will impel both the discovery of new sources and technological creativity in devising substitutes; the geographic location of valued materials in the world will thus continue to change. Changing tastes will lead to new products and therefore new chains of economic interconnection, as raw materials from various places are combined in new ways in new places. Some of those in difficulty will seek their fortune elsewhere and join in the enormous migrations of modern times. The relative well-being of various groups is always shifting, so political systems that embody the compromises from last year's conflicts will always be challenged by someone. Those losing ground may resist and find the rules of the political game inadequate to protect their needs. Those whose stars are rising may find new resources with which to press their case.

Just as shifting economic circumstances lead to reappraisal of political rules, so do cultural processes. The sense of belonging to a group and the sense that this group suffers particular indignities that need to be addressed are cultural phenomena and thus subject to redefinition. Even a political system that changes in order to give those who feel excluded a sense of belonging may be subject to challenge down the line—by those newly injured by economic change, newly aggrieved by political decisions, newly aroused to a sense of indignity by a redefinition of their own sense of belongingness. Democratization eases the task of mobilizing social movements, and change assures fresh supplies of grievances to be pressed. Democratization reliably generates demands for more democratization. Democratization does not bring societies to a terminal point of political development; it merely opens the way for further conflicts and new, but always provisional, resolutions.

The definition of democracy will continue to be debated. Political scientists and sociologists are often fond of classifying countries into those that are democratic and those that are not. Sometimes they develop an even finer classification, which distinguishes different types of democracy or different types of nondemocratic regimes. Yet even the most renowned scholars disagree when they try to categorize the real governments of the world. These debates will never be settled—that is, will never be settled as long as democratic movements exist. For one thing, it is often very difficult to know precisely how particular institutions operate (consider the realities of voting, for example). More profoundly, disagreements about what democracy is are part of the fabric of democracy. As long as democracy is alive as a justification for rulership, governing elites will sometimes claim that democracy has been achieved and social movements will sometimes claim that it has not.

Why Democracy Cannot Be Reduced to Elections

Electoral processes are central to democratic legitimation, but in no state is political life limited to elections. Modern governments include large bureaucracies that issue regulations and administer policies; that employ professional experts in such matters as the design of roads and bridges, the control of epidemics, the testing of weapons, and the development of new strains of wheat; and that respond to requests and threats from citizens as well as requests and threats from other governments.

Political scientists have described in great detail the ways in which powerful agencies develop their own kinds of politics and resist effective supervision by ministers and legislators. The question of effective control of such agencies by political figures who are accountable to electorates is one of the classic questions of modern political science. Many political scientists recognize bureaucracies as a major challenge to legitimating claims that government action is a manifestation of "the will of the people." The voice of the people may be heard on election day, perhaps, or one may think one has heard it or may agree to claim one has heard it. But it is not obvious that the voice of the people is heard in decisions about how much to charge to deliver different sorts of mail or how to certify the safety of new drugs or whether to allocate more money for soldiers' boots or which new jet fighters to buy or the hundreds of thousands of other decisions made by governments. If one way of characterizing democracy is by whether a government is responsible to the people, many political scientists would agree with Carl Friedrich that "the task of our industrial age" is to achieve "a responsible bureaucracy."[16]

The role of professional experts in government is also a challenge to democratic notions, even if these professionals do not make lifetime careers in bureaucratic agencies. "Professionals," as defined by the sociologist Andrew Abbot, are people who have a claim to be listened to that is based on some abstract body of knowledge acquired through a period of specialized education and training.[17] Economists, to take one important group making a mark on government service, spend years in the study of the academic discipline of economics. One important element in the world of such professionals is that they have acquired a devotion to the theories that form the core of their discipline. As a result, professionals may be open to violating the will of electorates or disagreeing with bureaucratic superiors. Professionals can easily take the body of ideas that they bring with them into government service into other forms of employment if those ideas become political liabilities.

Leszek Balcerowicz, a professional economist who served in newly democratic Poland as finance minister and vice premier, observed that economists in government, unlike traditional politicians, may find their academic reputations actually enhanced following political failure if they were upholding the prevailing academic wisdom. Balcerowicz's point is that professional specialists in positions of power may be highly motivated to defy the will of voting publics, because their careers do not depend on their political fortunes alone.[18] Since leaving office, Balcerowicz served as an adviser to the government of another country, been a professor, published a book, and written a regular column for a Polish magazine. We may sometimes value such specialists precisely because they have some independence of mind, but they complicate the issue of democratic control over officials.

Political scientists have also demonstrated that government agencies and legislatures do not act in isolation. Individuals and organizations are continually trying to persuade government bodies to act or not act on a nearly infinite variety of matters. Individuals and organizations offer suggestions or information, promise electoral support or campaign contributions, and provide gifts and bribes. Neither the workings of government nor the diverse influence processes take place under the same glare of publicity as do election campaigns. Lobbying—whether open or hidden, whether following legal practices, questionable ones, or downright illegal modes of influence—is an important element in every political system with democratic claims. Opportunities for elected or appointed powerholders to use their positions to feather their own nests are numerous, and hardly limited to democratic government. But they are a special problem for democratic legitimation since such practices challenge the democratic notion that the purpose of government is to serve "the people" rather than to be an instrument by which a special class of people, "the politicians," enrich themselves.

In modern democracies, the practice of secret ballots means that the vote of one person has the same weight as another's in the same electoral district in deciding who is elected to office. But what of influence on the actions of those elected? Research comparing the policy preferences of U.S. citizens to the legislation actually enacted by Congress clearly demonstrates that those with higher incomes may not always get what they want but that they are far more likely to than those of more modest means. Americans are plainly not all equally influential in the formation of policies by those they elect.[19]

Among the many forms of influence, the activities of social movements deserve particular attention. If all political systems have mechanisms by which some people can influence policy, systems claiming to be democratic are unusually open to mobilization campaigns outside of and even contrary to official channels. We may try to define democracy by some set of formal procedures for choosing officials and for defining what powers those powerholders have. But we will never find that democratic practice is limited to those electoral mechanisms and parliamentary practices. Social movements may threaten unfavorable consequences on election day, but they may also threaten disruption long before election day, in the form of strikes, picketing, demonstrations, blockages, badgering, and other embarrassing actions.

Just as the politics of powerholders is never limited to trying to win elections, so the actions of oppositional forces are never limited to the electoral arena. And just as those with the appropriate resources will sometimes attempt to use them outside the official rules (an offer of a campaign contribution by a rich corporation in return for a desired decision, for example), social movements will sometimes violate the laws regulating their behavior. They may demonstrate without a permit, strike in defiance of a court injunction, disrupt the plans of officialdom, and sometimes initiate violence. The image

of people deciding policy at the ballot box is violated by the reality of bureaucratic power, by the behind-the-scenes views of technical experts—and
by the actions of disruptive oppositions.

The bureaucrats and experts behind the scenes and the protestors in the
streets and fields often consider each other illegitimate. No matter how elections are organized, some will always believe that their influence is inadequate
and their interests are unrepresented, and some of those people will have
the capacity to form movements and initiate actions. Bureaucratic officials,
whose doings are mysterious to the protestors, are seen by those protestors
as undemocratic: Who elected them? When did "the people" adequately
debate their policies? But to the beleaguered officials, it is those parading in
the streets, occupying the campuses or factories, or blocking the roads who
are undemocratic, because they do not accept the actions of the government
whose top officials have been chosen by properly organized elections. Where
is democracy? In the 1960s, those involved in challenging the authorities in
the United States used to say, "Democracy is in the streets." Sometimes it is.

The "Invention" of Democracy

As social movements and governing elites redefined the meanings of democracy, people in certain countries and at certain historical moments developed
new ways of thinking about democracy and new institutions to embody those
ideas.[20] Some of these pioneering ideas and institutions were later borrowed
elsewhere. Sometimes social movements in one place borrowed the goals,
tactics, or organizational methods first tried somewhere else. And sometimes
those in power followed the example of powerholders elsewhere.

Which innovations were so widely borrowed by social movements or by
governing elites that they became part of how we think about democracy
today? A definitive answer to this question is not possible, in part because
scholars inevitably differ on what they think democracy is but also because our
knowledge of the histories, on a world scale, of many of the relevant institutions is incomplete. But here is a tentative list of democratic breakthroughs:

- *Self-identification of a social movement with "democracy"*: This innovation seems to have arisen in Belgium and Holland in the 1780s, as people
  described political conflicts as a clash of "aristocrats" and "democrats."

This usage was soon recognized all over the European world and in the European colonies in the western hemisphere.

- *Constitutions explicitly describing and limiting the authority of power-holders*: The Constitution of the United States, ratified in 1789, was the model, inspiring numerous successors. Important precursors include some of the documents produced in the course of the English revolution of the 1640s and the eighteenth-century Swedish constitution. The first European country to follow the U.S. example was Poland in 1791. The French constitution of 1791 and the subsequent constitutions of that revolutionary decade were widely imitated by neighboring countries or imposed by French military forces. In the early nineteenth century, Spanish colonies in the western hemisphere wrote constitutions after achieving independence, influenced by Spain's new constitution of 1812, itself triggered by the French military occupation of a great deal of Spanish territory.

- *Political parties that compete for votes*: By the late eighteenth century, political parties had been a part of political life in England for a long time, as various groups and personalities contended for the right to sit in Parliament. Yet this practice was widely spoken of at the time as the corruption of an ideal. In 1738 Lord Bolingbroke observed that a "patriot king" would unify his people: "Instead of putting himself at the head of one party in order to govern his people, he will put himself at the head of his people in order to govern, or more properly to subdue, all parties."[21] James Madison commented in 1787 "that the public good is disregarded by the conflicts of rival parties."[22] It is hard to be sure where and when the idea of a party began to change, but the early nineteenth-century United States is a very likely possibility. By the 1820s, adherents of New York State's Democratic Republicans were openly proclaiming their loyalty to the party: "When party distinctions are no longer known and recognized, our freedom will be in jeopardy, as 'the calm of despotism' will then be visible. . . . We are party men, attached to party systems."[23] By the middle of the nineteenth century, those who called themselves democrats in Europe had generally accepted the notion of party as a proper form of organization rather than the corruption of some ideal.

- *Responsibility of all powerholders to an electorate*: This idea was plainly pioneered in the new United States, whose Constitution of 1789 rejected both a hereditary monarch and a hereditary aristocracy. No one was president or could sit in Congress by right; powerholders were to be either elected or appointed by those who were elected. The history of democracy in nineteenth-century western Europe, in contrast, was marked by the coexistence of elected parliaments and hereditary monarchs, who battled over their respective powers. The unhappy history of the French constitution of 1791, for example, ended with a new, republican constitution and the king's being tried and executed by the parliament. In some countries, this conflict was compounded by the inherited right to sit in an upper house of parliament. The first countries to follow the United States in radically eliminating hereditary claims to authority were the newly independent states of Latin America, which threw off Iberian rule in the early part of the nineteenth century. Most of their new constitutions followed the U.S. example in this regard, Brazil being the most important exception.

- *Conflation of democracy with representative institutions*: This was another American innovation, closely related to the preceding one. Thomas Paine recognized the significance of this step almost instantly, characterizing the new U.S. political model as "representation ingrafted upon democracy."[24] In the 1780s, many writers had thought of representative institutions as something quite distinct from democracy. James Madison distinguished "republics" like the American states from "pure democracy" precisely because they had a "scheme of representation."[25] The common European notion of representation envisaged some mechanism, not necessarily electoral, by which delegates presented the views of the ruled to the ruler. Democracy, in contrast, was often perceived as the direct involvement of citizens in decision making. Few thought Britain's Parliament had much to do with democracy after the upheavals of the mid-seventeenth century gave way to a restored monarchy. And in the 1790s, French democrats were profoundly suspicious of elected legislators. But in the new United States, by the time the Constitution was completed, many Americans felt that they had created a new kind of government, and some were using the word democracy to describe it.[26]

- *Elimination of property or wealth qualifications for voting*: This is a difficult matter to assess, because many countries have both national and local elections to consider; in some, like the United States, state or provincial elections must be considered as well. It is also difficult to distinguish what the voting rules were in law and what the actual practice was, particularly in remote rural regions far from the scrutiny of the central government. Nevertheless, the French constitution of 1793 may have been the first to eliminate property or wealth qualifications, superseding the constitution of 1791, which had established a minimal tax payment as a requirement for voting in national elections. The constitution of 1793, however, never went into effect. By the early nineteenth century, many of the states of the new United States had eliminated property and wealth requirements for white men. An election held in Mexico City in 1812 seems to have had a very wide suffrage in practice, because officials did not enforce the legal restrictions.[27] Some other early nineteenth-century elections in Latin America had very broad suffrage. In 1848, Switzerland may have been the first country to formally and fully eliminate such requirements, but the actual application of the law is not clear. France's Revolution of 1848 eliminated property qualifications for men, but a more restrictive set of rules was soon reintroduced, before France's Second Republic was shut down by its elected president. In Latin America Argentina, Colombia, Mexico, and Venezuela adopted universal male suffrage during the 1850s, although in some places restrictions were introduced later on.[28]

- *Women's right to vote*: New Zealand was the first country to secure women's voting rights in national elections (in 1893); Australia followed suit in 1902, although women could not vote in all elections at the state level until 1908. Perhaps the shortage of women in these two frontier societies and the desire to attract women immigrants from Europe played a role. This hypothesis is buttressed by a state-by-state look at the campaign for women's voting rights in the United States: The western territories of Wyoming (1869) and Utah (1870) took the lead prior to becoming states, followed by the western states of Colorado (1893) and Idaho (1896). Perhaps the smaller numbers of women in these frontier areas made women's votes a bit less threatening. In addition, conservative upholders of propriety saw women as an important moral force for taming the wild frontier culture, which was often characterized by fighting, drinking, gambling, and cursing. An important component of the women's movement, the Women's Christian Temperance Union, embraced this identification. The New

Zealand and Australian branches of this organization were important in demanding voting rights in those countries.

- *Secret ballot:* Secret voting was widely known for many years and sometimes used in very specific contexts. But no country seems to have required it uniformly until two Australian states adopted the secret ballot in 1856, after which it was adopted throughout Australia. A key element was a written list of candidates' names distributed by election officials. When similar provisions became law in various countries in the western hemisphere (for example, in many parts of the United States in the 1880s), the mechanism was known as "the Australian ballot."
- *Personal freedom for all:* At the onset of modern democracy in the late eighteenth century, large numbers of people were enslaved all over the western hemisphere. A Haitian slave revolt brought slavery to an end along with Haitian independence from France after terrible warfare. Spanish American countries ended their own slaveholding after achieving their own independence. Among the European empires, it was among the least of them, Denmark, that pioneered in 1792 in ending the slave trade in its colonies. Revolutionary France was early to abolish slavery, then reinstated it a few years later.

So where and when was democracy "invented"? The list of innovators and early followers of those innovators includes a very interesting collection of places: Belgium, Holland, the United States, Australia, New Zealand, Poland, perhaps Switzerland, parts of Latin America, Denmark, Haiti. The great powers of the world are not very strongly represented. England had some important innovations in the revolutionary seventeenth century, and France had some stillborn pioneering developments in the revolutionary 1790s. The United States is on the list, certainly, but in the late eighteenth and early nineteenth centuries, when it was hardly the center of world power it was to become. On the other hand, the very poorest and weakest parts of the world are not much represented on this list either. This little list also suggests a different kind of answer to when and where democracy was invented: many times, in many places.

Let me offer a hypothesis about the sources of political creativity. Political creativity in the greatest powers tends to be diminished by the sense that everything is fine—or at least that everything is fine for the wealthy and powerful of those countries. When seriously challenged, political elites tend to be able to protect their own interests by mobilizing support for the re-creation of the glories of the past. Among the poorer regions of the earth, on the other hand, realistic hopes for rapid transformation are blighted by the sense of failure. It is among those countries that are lesser players on the world stage but have moderate wealth—where the hope of progress runs strong while the barriers to change may be weaker—that the great breakthroughs that have redefined democracy have tended to take place. And where will they take place in the future? With that question, we can turn to the final chapters.

Conclusions

In this chapter we have seen that democratic practices and undemocratic practices can exist side by side. Established elites and social movement challengers will often attack each other's democratic claims. In the course of these conflicts, democracy has been redefined, and the places where new institutions have been pioneered are often not the wealthiest and most powerful of countries.

If social conflicts have been leading to redefinition of democracy for over two centuries, can we say anything about the sorts of conflict in the early twenty-first century that will be important for democracy's future?

CHAPTER 6
BEYOND THE GREAT DEMOCRATIC WAVE

Hope and Disappointment: A Haitian Example

In 1994 a U.S. military force returned a Haitian president to power. Jean-Bertrand Aristide, governing Haiti as a democratically elected president after a long string of dictatorships, had been removed from power by the Haitian military. After a period of diplomatic maneuvering, he followed some 15,000 U.S. troops back into office to complete his interrupted term as head of the government of one of this planet's poorer countries. At the time, U.S. officials described this sequence of events as the restoration of democracy. A closer examination shows how ambiguous that democracy was.

We have seen in previous chapters that powerful elites often manage to maintain their positions within democratic frameworks and that social movements are able to use democracy as an opportunity. Both processes were part of the Haitian story. Let's look at two news items from Haiti under U.S. military occupation. In the first, from the fall of 1994, we learn that despite the U.S. presence in major cities, out in the countryside little had changed. A reporter from an area three hours by car from the capital noted, "Jean-Bertrand Aristide may once again be President of Haiti, but in this poor but verdant valley, Jean Lacoste Edouard is still the boss and he enforces his will with fists, clubs, machetes, and guns."[1] On the other hand, poor people were feeling emboldened, as never before, to occupy land. As a government official explained, "[Because] we are living in a democracy now," ordinary people know that violence will not be used against squatters.[2]

A decade after his return, Aristide's second, very turbulent term as popularly elected president saw declining U.S. support and mounting opposition violence. When the United States eventually flew him out of the country in 2004, his supporters described this not as rescue but as kidnap. In 2011, he again returned to his still desperately poor and politically troubled country.[3] It would be hard for champions of democracy to find much inspiration in these developments, except perhaps for that first election.

Stepping back from this Haitian story, we may ask to what degree the hopes that surrounded Haitian change were borne out in other places as the great burst of democratizations played out or whether the disappointments that set in soon after were repeated elsewhere. To what extent have traditional antidemocratic practices been revived or new ones invented? To what extent did the powerful manage to empty democratic claims of any meaning? To what extent have social movements or reforming elites (or some combination of the two) managed to give democracy a new meaning? We may ask an even larger question. We have seen that there is a world history of democracy. We have seen that the meaning of democracy has changed as social movements and powerholders in different countries have reacted to one another. Stepping back from the case of Haiti, or any other particular instance, what forces will shape the future history of democratization?

Even the Great Wave Had Limits

We have seen that in one country after another, on one continent after another, democracy was spreading in the late twentieth century. In the 1970s the spotlight was on the transformation of western Europe's few remaining authoritarian regimes, in the 1980s Latin American militaries left the presidential palaces and went back to the barracks (to use an expression from that moment), in 1989 and beyond communist regimes fell, and change was happening in parts of Asia and Africa as well. In some of the world's antidemocratic regimes there were major movements marching under the banners of democracy, and to some observers it seemed just a matter of time before they triumphed as well. With eastern Europe's communist regimes tumbling, one scholar asked whether it was "The End of History?" as he entitled an enthusiastic article. It would be the end because the world was heading to a single political model, and a desirable one at that. By the early 1990s, his book-length version was even more confident and dropped the question mark.[4] He spoke for the optimism of that moment.

By the early twenty-first century, students of democracy had become less sure. New examples of major democratic transition had become much less frequent. In some places, the end of a nondemocratic regime turned out to mean a transition to a different one, not to something that was especially democratic. And in some places, democratic change had gone into reverse. If there had not been a major, antidemocratic wave flowing over many countries as in the past (although some were wondering if that might yet happen), many saw the democratic wave as having crested, as having gone into a stall. Some spoke of a "democratic recession." Scholar Larry Diamond sees some thirty-five cases of reversal between the mid-1970s when the great democratic wave began and 2010. In 2014 an increasingly authoritarian Russia organized a Eurasian Union as a counter to the economic weight of the European Union, joining an economically dynamic China to form a solid, geographically vast bloc of antidemocratic states. Nonetheless both older and newer democracies were proving fairly durable. Despite the recession, Diamond reckons there were 116 democratic states as the twenty-first century entered its second decade.[5]

But equally troubling as such reversals, some instances of democratization were accompanied by other, disturbing trends, so that democracy was not delivering all that people hoped for. And it was troubling in a different way in that it was not only in places where democracy was a recent thing, but in older democracies as well, that there were signs of considerable disappointment with how it was working in practice. The question of how well democracy was working was being raised not just in places where democracy was shaky, or new, or in the poorest parts of the world, but in the relatively well established wealthy democracies, too. What all this was suggesting to some observers, was that democracy was facing some new challenges that were likely to play out in hard-to-foresee ways in the years ahead.

In this chapter I'm going to explore the limits of that greatest (so far) of all democratic waves, paying attention, as in earlier chapters, to the interplay of social movements and powerholders, and to connections across national borders as well as within them. In the next, final chapter, I will look at the significant issues that are challenging the democracy of today and that will do so tomorrow, consider opportunities as well as obstacles, and suggest several very different imaginable scenarios for the future.

Containing Democratization

If we compare the countries of the world in the early twenty-first century to their situation at the beginning of the 1970s, as we have seen in Chapter 4, a very large number of countries have become significantly more democratic. They include South American countries like Argentina, Central American countries like Panama, western European countries like Portugal, eastern European countries like Poland, Asian countries like Thailand, and African countries like Mozambique. They include countries that had been under military rule like Brazil and communist rule like Mongolia. They include countries that had recently been colonies like Senegal, countries that had been independent states for centuries like Spain, and countries that did not have an independent existence before the great democratic wave like Bosnia. With so many countries embracing democracy in so many parts of the world and coming from very different national histories—and with very different cultural traditions and income levels, too—it was easy to think of this as a worldwide trend that would soon cover the entire planet. But in the period since the last South American military regime to do so returned power to civilians in Chile in 1990, a variety of limits to the world's greatest democratic wave were in evidence.

Defeating Democratic Movements

In some countries democratic movements were crushed by governments and in others governments managed to at least contain them. The enormous country of China is an important instance. A significant protest movement emerged in Beijing in 1989, largely composed of students, and when the regime sent in military forces angry crowds in the Chinese capital tried to impede the troops' movement. Effective government violence broke the protests with significant loss of life. In subsequent years, the Chinese government invested great energy in developing ways to break up potential protest movements, including keeping the new electronic communications technologies in check. Chinese activists speak of the great firewall of China, referring at the same time to the amazing Great Wall built long ago to repel northern invaders and to today's technology for blocking unwanted Internet connections.⁶ Twitter, for example, has played a significant role in some important twenty-first century movements but it is barred from China. The government has authorized a Chinese version that does pretty much the same thing, with the big difference being that the server is in Beijing so the government can manage, when it wishes, to monitor its use and identify those sending forbidden messages.

China's rapid growth has been making China a major player in the world economy; its military strength preoccupies its neighbors; and its cities are places where new wealth is flamboyantly on display. Some have therefore argued that China is becoming a new model of wealth and power without democracy, a potential inspiration to powerholders elsewhere who hope to follow suit. Recall that countries' political systems have often been imitated when they seemed models of success, whether they were democracies or something else. When it was disclosed in 2013 that the U.S. government was keeping track of the use of social media by its citizens, some wondered whether even countries generally regarded as democracies were taking a leaf from China.

Next door to China, Burma is an extremely poor country whose military rulers kept it isolated from what they saw as dangerous influences for a half century. A British colony occupied by Japan during World War II, its new postwar independence saw an increasingly repressive military in conflict with armed ethnic minorities, separatist forces, revolutionary movements, and mutinous soldiers. By the 1970s the military rulers confronted not only this variety of armed rebellions in the countryside but also growing urban mobilizations by students, factory workers, and Buddhist monks deploying a range of nonviolent and violent tactics. In the late 1980s economic crisis galvanized a huge movement under the leadership of Aung San Suu Kyi, daughter of a murdered hero-general from those early postcolonial days. Despite its scale, and the admiration it found among the publics of the wealthy democracies (demonstrated by the Nobel Prize for Peace awarded to its leader), the movement was crushed by the violent regime that tightly controlled travel to and from Burma, shut down the universities that were bases for student protestors, and arrested and tortured protesting monks. Another movement of monks was crushed in 2007 and became known, for the color of their robes, as the Saffron Revolution, this time documented on video by underground journalists.

If I were writing this book a few years earlier, this Burmese story would simply have been another dramatic example of the apparent crushing of a democratic movement. But to observers' great surprise, a fraudulent election for parliament and president in 2010 was followed by dramatic moves from inside the ruling regime in 2011. Press censorship was radically dialed back, dignitaries from the wealthy democratic countries were invited to visit, opposition figures were freed from prison and house arrest, cease-fire negotiations were begun with armed rebels, and Aung San Suu Kyi's party was allowed to contest forty-five parliamentary seats—it won forty-three of them. At that point, more open elections were promised for 2015.

So Burma becomes an example of both the apparent crushing of a democracy movement and the sometimes surprising political openings promoted by powerholders that encourage a previously failing movement.[7] Observers debated the causes: Did the regime hope to acquire resources by improving relations with the democratic western powers, a hope perhaps made sharper by nervousness about dependence on China? Did it fear a new round of massive protest, a fear made sharper as it noted the Arab Spring of early 2011? Had regime insiders simply become exhausted by the evidently dead-end character of the policies of isolation and impoverishment? Was the change prefigured by the shock of a vast storm in 2008 that killed 130,000 people and led the regime to relax temporarily the restrictions on foreign connections and local organizations so that foreign aid and local groups could work together to relieve the vast, sudden misery? Whatever the cause, this example teaches us that oppositional movements that have been harassed and contained are not necessarily destroyed and sometimes may surprise us when they reemerge. (We can also use these Burmese events to remind us of another lesson from democracy's turbulent history: democratic advances can raise new questions. Observers were noting that at the same time the democracy movement was reviving, there was increasing persecution of a Burmese minority, the Muslim Rohingyas.)

Creating New Authoritarian Regimes

The rapid fall of authoritarian regimes did not necessarily mean the equally rapid construction of democracies. Eastern Europe furnishes a whole cluster of instances, because the political transition that began in 1989 had led by the early 1990s to the breakup of Czechoslovakia into two new states, Yugoslavia into five, and the Soviet Union into fifteen, with further fissioning imaginable. In addition there were five European states previously ruled by communist parties that remained intact. Some of these countries rapidly formed democratic institutions and others did not. As we have seen repeatedly in the history of democracy, in a moment of democratic advance in many parts of the world, authoritarian powerholders sometimes found ways of sustaining their rule despite adopting some apparently democratic features. In some parts of the postcommunist zone elections were held, but political rivals intimidated; the press threatened and journalists harassed, beaten, arrested, or killed; severe limits placed on opposition campaigning; funds extorted from business interests; and election results falsified. These new regimes might in many ways have worked differently than what had preceded them, but no one could have called them democratic. By the mid-1990s, postcommunist countries included not only new democracies but new pseudodemocracies, too.

Postcommunist eastern Europe also illustrates how the transnational wave of democracy energized effective pro-democracy movements as well as new varieties of authoritarianism, as described by scholars Valerie Bunce and Sharon Wolchik.[8] In Romania and Bulgaria, participants in the previous communist regime were far better organized than opposition movements and the democratic transition brought them to power. Opposition movements then developed a potent combination of election campaigning and protest, gaining advice from European and U.S. sources, but also from veterans of the highly dramatic and successful campaign to unseat the Marcos regime in the Philippines in 1986. Veterans of the Romanian and Bulgarian campaigns lent their support to democratic movements among their neighbors, contributing their experience to the successful campaign to challenge the new ruler of the new country of Slovakia. Vladimír Mečiar and his allies put together a system in which elections would be held, but opponents were intimidated, voting was skewed, electoral tabulations were suspicious, and the press was threatened. But in 1998, he was defeated at the polls anyway and a far more democratic Slovakia emerged. Veterans of the Slovakian campaign, as well as foreign sources of ideas and training, then lent a hand to the even more elaborate struggle to unseat Slobodan Milošević in Serbia, who also staged rigged elections, and whose means of power included jailing, beating, and even murdering opponents.

By now a basic model for unseating tyrants had emerged: opponents studied carefully how to conduct an election campaign, including inviting international monitors and foreign journalists, and, very importantly, how to energize citizens who were so disaffected and disillusioned that they hadn't been bothering to vote. A striking feature of all these campaigns was the mobilization of youth movements with "Rock the Vote" campaigns to get younger people to join in. Milošević was defeated at the ballot box. But unlike his counterpart in Slovakia, he refused to accept defeat. The opposition then organized huge nonviolent protest mobilizations that, in the end, the army and police refused to mow down by force. This pattern was then imported elsewhere in the postcommunist zone: into Ukraine, Georgia, and Kyrgyzstan as well as (with much less success) Armenia, Azerbaijan, and Belarus. So here was a specific, transportable model for challenging a new tyrant whose rule combined questionable elections with intimidation and violence.

So successful was this model in some places, that movement activists seeking to unseat tyrants far from postcommunist Europe sometimes took note. One Egyptian organization, for example, the April 6 Movement, got in touch with the major youth organization from the Serbian campaign for advice on how to organize massive nonviolent protest to topple the regime of Hosni Mubarak, and they participated in the huge demonstrations in Cairo's Tahrir Square in 2011. On the other hand, such campaigns failed to bring down tyrants in other postcommunist places, like Belarus. It is a very interesting question to explore why they worked in some places and not others.

The habits of protest and the skills of social movement organization could take root. Enormous protests following questionable election counts in 2004 were dubbed Ukraine's Orange Revolution and ushered in a democratic con- stitution, but also considerable conflict over Ukraine's mineral wealth, its pe- troleum pipelines, its economic connections eastward to Russia and westward to the European Union, and the place of its diverse cultures in its national identity. In 2013, when its elected president moved to restrict parliamentary independence, arrest political opponents, and orient foreign policy toward his eastern rather than western neighbors, another huge protest movement formed and occupied a great square in the capital, Kiev, for months, ultimately driving the president from office, reversing the recent antidemocratic constitutional changes, and triggering enormous pressures from Russia. It was symptomatic of this moment in the world history of democracy that both sides announced themselves as the democratic one: champions of the deposed president declared that a democratically elected head of state had been driven from office by Ukrainian fascists in collusion with western powers; those sympathetic with the rebellious crowds hoped that democracy was being revived and that Russia could be kept away; and the leaders of the established parties hoped that they would be able to hang on to power somehow, despite a huge social movement that was unsympathetic to the corruption of the established parties and a Russian government that was unsympathetic to a more democratic Ukraine.

Elections and Not Much Else

Let's look back at the whole history of democracy since people began using the term *democrats* in the 1780s in order to see something remarkable about the recent period since the great democratic wave that began in the 1970s. Many more countries than ever before in all major world regions were making use of competitive elections as the mechanism by which people attained high national office even in comparison to the high points of previous democratic waves. However, a sober look at other features that were widely understood to be part and parcel of what was meant by democracy in the early twenty-first century showed important gaps. The big generalization is that contested elections, an important piece of democracy, had spread far more widely in the world than had civil liberties, so not all the new elections were credible contests. A free press, with protections against intimidation and freedom to organize opposition parties or protest movements had expanded along with credible elections. But elections with mysterious vote counts, intimidated oppositions, or violence against journalists were far from unusual, sparking frequent claims of electoral fraud.

Africa furnishes many striking examples. When the various European colonial powers abandoned the goal of retaining their colonies in the generation after World War II, hopes for democracy ran high. But those democratic hopes were often dashed by successful leaders erecting single-party governments, disgruntled military forces staging coups, or corrupt states controlling scarce resources and using them for political coercion. What is more, competing political factions readily attained weapons from rival Cold War powers and turned from ballots to bullets, if, indeed, they ever bothered with ballots at all.

By the late 1980s, by one count, only six of forty-seven African countries were holding contested multiparty elections and of these only two held elections that could reasonably be described as "free and fair," a phrase commonly used to distinguish some electoral practices from others. But the great wave of democratization touched Africa, as it did other regions. By the late 1990s, some forty-three countries were holding contested multiparty elections and eight of them were reasonably free. Over the next decade the quality of elections improved in several other countries as well. But if Ghana or Mozambique, for example, was deepening its democratic life, in other places, like Kenya, power-holders manipulated electoral results, and in still other places like Zimbabwe, opposition movements or parties were crushed, journalism was controlled or intimidated, and violence was a principal mechanism for retaining office.

One could summarize this as large but limited change that came from the conjunction of many of the sources we have been exploring in this book. With the ending of the Cold War, western powers, and especially the United States, became more committed to promoting democracy. Sources of foreign aid for everything from health care to road construction were insisting that African states, like other states, conform to democratic practices. African movements took heart from democratic changes and from democratic movements in other places. Severe economic troubles in the late 1980s led governments to seek foreign loans, and as we have seen, this was a moment when global financial institutions were favoring democratic practices and in a position to push them on desperately poor countries (let us remember that many African countries rank among the world's poorest). But in addition, the economic austerity favored by the International Monetary Fund and the World Bank was widely seen in Africa as additional suffering on top of the economic problems that led to asking for the loans in the first place. This also meant that political leaders who negotiated such terms, commonly held to be humiliating as well as painful, became targets for local social movements, some advocating more democracy. So the combination of all these causes made the late 1980s and the next few years a favorable time for democratization, as in other parts of the world.

But we learn a number of other things from the African story. While many countries exhibited the most readily recognizable sign of democratization—the holding of contested elections—in some countries those elections, carefully manipulated, became vehicles of continued domination by the same people. Scholars of Africa were writing of "low quality democracy" or even "electoral authoritarianism."[9] And beyond elections, press freedoms—or the freedom to form oppositions—did advance in some places, but were often significantly limited or even nonexistent in others. In other words, as we have seen throughout the entire history of democracy, powerful people were able to use ostensibly democratic mechanisms as an instrument to continue their own rule. On the other hand, as we have also seen, in some places and at some times democratization went well beyond that and in other cases social movements were able to make use of even limited democratization to demand more, sometimes with success.

Particularly notable in Africa was the enormous increase in activity by movements on behalf of women's rights. Women in Ghana, for example, actively participated in movements for democracy and went on to mobilize for expanding the rights of women.[10] According to one count, in 2005, Africa had ninety-four organizations working for women's rights, almost three-quarters of which were founded since 1990.[11]

So one can be impressed by how much change had taken place by the early twenty-first century by noting that most rulers in Africa could now lay claim to having won an election. One can be impressed at the capacity of rulers to stage elections in their own interest. And one can be impressed at the capacity of mobilized citizens to make democracy more real.[12] Organizations have been developing to monitor elections, lobby for control of corruption, and defuse ethnic conflict. And these organizations support each other across national borders through the African Democracy Forum or the transnational activism of South Africa's Institute for Democracy.[13]

Some simple tabulations show the extent and also the limits of change. From the 1960s into the 1980s, African leaders had been far more likely to leave office through violence than through peaceful negotiation, natural death, or electoral defeat. That figure began to change dramatically in the 1990s and has continued to change in the early twenty-first century when the great majority of leaders were leaving office peacefully.[14] Most African states had by then adopted some democratic features but sometimes only in limited ways, something we have seen repeatedly in the history of democracy. Yet however fraudulently this was happening in some places, the entire history of modern democracy also suggests that we be on the lookout for the kind of social movements that have sometimes been able to use such democratic trappings to successfully demand more reality and less sham. As one study of African politics put it, "[e]ven flawed elections worked as a force for democracy."[15]

Democratic Reversals

In a geographically diverse group of countries, elected presidents or victorious parties found ways to enlarge their powers including curtailing the independent authority of courts or parliaments, restricting the possibilities for electoral opposition, contracting press freedoms, and blocking the formation of independent social movements. The rationales varied: some claimed to be acting on behalf of an ethnic or territorial group, others claimed rival political parties were illegitimate, still others that an oppositional grouping was an agent of a foreign enemy, and some even claimed to be embodying a truer version of democracy.

As an example, consider developments in Hungary following its democratic elections of 2010. The big winner was a party whose 53 percent majority in the popular vote earned it 68 percent of parliamentary seats thanks to an electoral law disproportionately favoring larger parties (a measure enacted in some democracies in order to guard against the sorts of instability produced when it is difficult to have a majority government). This meant that under Hungary's constitution, the now dominant party had the two-thirds majority needed to alter any constitutional text. Over the next months it severely reduced the authority of key institutions that had provided checks on presidential power, including the Constitutional Court, the National Election Commission, and the previously independent Ombudsmen, whose job was to protect citizens' rights. In addition, party loyalists were appointed to bodies such as the Media Authority (given new powers to demand what was called "fairness" from journalists). When organs of the European Union found that the new rules violated European human rights standards, Hungary's leaders replied that these measures had been enacted properly under democratic laws and that the now dominant party had the clear support of a majority of the Hungarian people. In addition to serving as a reminder that democratic processes can contract as well as expand and democracy sometimes can be contracted through legal procedures, the Hungarian example helps us see something else. The general prestige of democracy by the early twenty-first century was so great that regimes engaged in contracting democracy claimed to be doing so democratically or even to be improving democracy, not ending it.[16]

Especially common was the appeal to a more or less democratically conducted election that had been followed by the successful expansion of presidential powers through asserting media control; restricting opposition parties; contracting judicial independence; limiting the role of legislatures; and ignoring, encouraging, or even organizing violence against opponents. When oppositional movements managed despite these restrictions to stage massive protest demonstrations, supporters of the regime would say that these demonstrations were orchestrated by foreign powers and were defying a democratic regime. The Ukrainian and Venezuelan governments were challenged in 2014 by enormous sustained demonstrations whose participants claimed to be fighting for democracy while the supporters of those governments claimed that the crowds were in rebellion against democratically elected leaders and instigated to do so by foreign enemies. The Ukrainian and Venezuelan governments were in many ways extremely different but some of the claims of their defenders were strikingly similar. All sides in these very bitter, serious quarrels were claiming the democratic mantle.

Democratic Disappointment

So some observers in the early twenty-first century suggested that extensive as it was, the great wave of democratization had about run its course. Some countries, including giant China, had resisted it, some had kept it very limited, and a few places that had participated had seen it soon eroded. Scholars began to note that recent democratizations had often left major social problems unresolved and in some cases probably had exacerbated them, raising concerns that frustrated, angry, and disappointed citizens might come to support antidemocratic alternatives that promised to fix things. Many African countries adopted electoral practices, as we have seen, but maintained their reputations for corruption. Brazil's military returned to the barracks, but its impoverished urban neighborhoods came under the control of narcotraffickers. Guatemala's long, bloody civil war came to an end and parties competed in reasonable elections at the ballot box, but its murder rate skyrocketed.

Let's dwell a bit on Mexico's experience. Its elections became genuinely competitive as its long-dominant party—the Institutional Revolutionary Party—finally, and peacefully, surrendered power after many decades. That dominant party had won the presidency in every election since 1929 and every state governorship, too. But in 1989 the great wave of global democratization touched Mexico and for the first time another party won a state governorship, and as things continued to open up, in 2000 another party won the presidency. Social movements flourished. A free press engaged in lively debates. Many democratic theorists favored a less centralized style of rule to curb presidential abuses and a democratizing Mexico followed suit. Mexican states got more power and the central government became less dominant; following similar advice, Mexico's president became less strong and its Congress stronger, too. So democracy was on the march.

At the same time, however, the vast transnational trade in illicit psychoactive chemicals was having an extraordinarily malicious impact that was made worse by these changes. The body count of the drug wars was extraordinary for a country not at war: between 2006 and 2011 about 50,000 Mexicans were killed.[17] Drug lords were finding it easier to outgun and to bribe local police forces and state governments than national police and the national government. Some social scientists expressed concern that with corruption booming and violence unchecked, people might turn away from democracy in search of some "strong hand," to use a phrase often heard in these discussions, so that they could send their kids to school without fear those kids would be kidnapped for ransom, killed in some shootout among gangsters, or victimized by corrupt police.

The Mexican experience also suggested that perhaps no national government could manage problems that were as much transnational as national. Mexican citizens in a democratic Mexico may have acquired some say in who governed their country but they had not gotten any input into U.S. drug policies or into U.S .firearms laws, yet U.S. demand for drugs funded the gangsters, the U.S. "war on drugs" guaranteed that prices were steep and profits astronomical because it was a very risky business, and U.S.-origin firearms were devastating Mexico.[18]

To step back from the Mexican specifics, in some places political systems were becoming more democratic (to varying degrees) at the same time as the national state seemed less and less effective in providing some basic things, like security from violence, that citizens had come to expect from a state whether democratic or otherwise. In some places democratization itself was experienced as among the plausible causes of the problems.

Small wonder that along with the great boost in democratization, citizens were showing signs of disaffection, not with democracy in the abstract, but with how things were actually working. Doubts were expressed to pollsters about fundamental institutions—presidents, parliaments, judiciaries. And central institutions of democracy as it has evolved since the democratic revolution at the end of the eighteenth century were showing signs of decreasing public engagement. In country after country, membership in political parties was in decline. Voting rates were down in many countries, too. So there was concern that another antidemocratic wave might be in the offing as the newer democracies failed to satisfy citizen expectations for a decent life and more generally seemed incapable of solving very serious problems. If citizens saw elections as fraudulent, officials as corrupt, and governments (even if recently democratic) as unable to protect them from violence, this would be very important but perhaps not surprising. But what was even more striking, this disappointment was showing up not only in poor countries that had recently developed democratic institutions, like Mali—one of the poorest of countries whose recent development of multiparty elections was, in 2012, troubled by an armed secessionist movement, local and imported Islamists, a restless military, and French combat troops—or in places recently emerged from horrendous civil war—like Guatemala—or in countries with long histories of antidemocratic regimes—like Hungary. In the wealthy countries that had long democratic histories to boast of, that included places that were central to the eighteenth-century democratic explosion, that had fought wars that were at least partly on behalf of democracy, places like, for example, the United States, signs of disenchantment and disengagement were emerging as well. We will try to make sense of this in the final chapter.

One message of this chapter is that we can see the most recent democratic wave as a great triumph for democracy, despite the limitations that I have just traced. The scale of change was enormous. Political scientists commonly take note of a variety of characteristics of democratic government and combine them into an index to attempt to measure quantitatively the extent of democracy. By two of the most commonly used measures, between the early 1970s and the middle of the first decade of the twenty-first century, sixty-three countries had become significantly more democratic and a mere five significantly less so.[19] In this chapter we have also noted some of the limitations of this great wave of new or renewed democracy. So it may not be all that surprising that some people were not altogether happy with the quality of the democracy thus far achieved. But why were the more established democracies troubled as well? We shall see in the next chapter that new challenges have been emerging that will shape democracy's history in the twenty-first century.

New Movements for Democracy

Remember how often even knowledgeable observers have proven to be wrong about the future prospects of democracy. Democracy seemed on a roll after World War I, but by the mid-1920s seemed in retreat and its survival looked very far from assured in the face of the advances of fascist powers and their allies. Then it seemed once again to many to be the wave of the future after World War II, though seriously challenged by the Soviet Union and its allies.

The end of European colonial rule opened up many new possibilities for democracy, too. But by the 1970s, after a wave of military coups and presidential arrogations of power, it again looked to many as though democracy had crested—but the greatest wave of democratization soon followed. So let us not conclude too hastily that the signs that this great wave has about run its course, serious as they are, are telling us what the future will bring. In fact, the second decade of the twenty-first century has seen renewed strength in democratic movements. Iran was challenged by the Green Revolution that followed its disputed election of 2009. The Burmese democracy movement had been failing to make much headway (as we just noted), when in 2010 the winners of a typically rigged election announced significant liberalization. And few democracy movements captured world attention more than did the Arab Spring later that same year.

The Middle East had an established reputation among social scientists as among the most resolutely undemocratic among large world regions. Scholars debated why. Some argued that there was an inhospitable culture. Others stressed the legacies of colonial rule. Still others pointed to a toxic mix of oil wealth funding despotic regimes and massive poverty making other concerns far more salient to most people. And others yet again argued that the main goal of western powers in the region, including the United States, was to prevent any boats being rocked, especially in the wake of heightened concern with Muslim terrorists after the attack on the World Trade Center in 2001. They wondered if the increased focus on democracy as a post–Cold War policy goal on the part of the wealthy, established democracies was being eroded. So whatever the explanation, democratic prospects were not looking great.

Few people outside of Tunisia had heard of Sidi Bouzid, a provincial town where a street vendor set himself on fire on December 17, 2010, after being humiliated by local police. Unexpectedly, large numbers of Tunisians came into the streets, taking this death as emblematic of their own experience of an arbitrary, brutal, corrupt, and unaccountable state. Just a few weeks later, after the police refused to shoot the rising numbers of determined citizens, the tyrant fled, news that galvanized protest across the Middle East and North Africa. Huge numbers in Cairo occupied Tahrir Square and soon that county's leaders were toppled as well. Tunisians and Egyptians set about forming new parties, writing a new constitution, and planning elections. Similar movements went down to defeat in other places (like Bahrain) or morphed into civil wars (in Libya and Syria).

Two years downstream from the huge demonstrations, the places where the Arab Spring started were showing how differently even successful overthrows of despotic regimes could play out. These were a turbulent two years in both Tunisia and Egypt and in each a party claiming an Islamic identity came to the fore in new elections. But in Tunisia, faced with continuing turmoil, the various parties were still negotiating the shape of a new political system. In Egypt, the military stepped in and was moving to crush all the many forms of opposition that had emerged. Social scientists were spending much energy trying to figure out whether these developments could or would lead to democratic outcomes in the future, but what was clear was that there had been a huge, new democratic movement in places not noted for them. Where will democracy movements gather strength next? And with what consequences?

So it is important to conclude this chapter with the reminder that even those who have devoted much careful thought do not have a terribly good track record of predicting when democratic movements will erupt, when powerholders will decide to seriously change, and what the longer-term outcomes of these dramatic moments will prove to be. No one alive at the beginning of 1914, only months before the horrors of World War I began, had any idea of the ebbs and flows of democracy that would characterize the next hundred years. In 2014, no one can see the next hundred years any more clearly. But we can say something of the challenges democracy will face even though we are not going to be able to foresee very well the failures and successes.

CHAPTER 7
INTO THE TWENTY-FIRST CENTURY
NEW CHALLENGES, NEW OPPORTUNITIES

An Election Campaign in Democratic Spain, 2011

As the campaign for local and regional elections that were to take place on May 22, 2011, neared its end, anyone paying attention to events in Spain could see the simultaneous occurrence of two recurrent features of modern democracies: first, the competition among political parties according to established rules, and second, the unexpected emergence of a movement calling for a rethinking of what democracy is and ought to be. Starting a week before election day, tens of thousands of (mostly) young people in dozens of Spanish cities camped in public spaces, organized themselves into committees, formulated dramatic slogans, expressed their disgust with established practices, set up websites, and debated among themselves what the "real democracy" they called for would look like. TV commentators on Spanish politics over the next few weeks were not only holding forth on such standard themes as the enormous electoral defeat of the Socialists but were also trying to understand who were the people occupying the squares, what they stood for, and why they carried out their actions at that particular moment. Newspaper readers were not only reading columns helpfully explaining the ways Spanish electoral rules shaped outcomes but were also encountering articles telling them how the occupation of plazas by the *Indignados*—the

"Outraged"—was like or unlike the typical patterns of Spanish protest since the democratic transition, like or unlike protests against economic austerity elsewhere in Europe, like or unlike the wave of Arab revolts that had taken place just a few months earlier.

When protestors toppled Egypt's long-term ruler early in 2011, observers wondered if this was going to kick off a new wave of democratization in the world; some authoritarian regimes grew nervous. But what do we make of that huge wave of protest in already democratic Spain soon afterwards that called for "real democracy"? We have seen repeatedly throughout the history of modern democracy that protestors have sometimes vigorously criticized existing democratic institutions and in so doing have sometimes altered them and even sometimes reshaped what we mean by democracy. Some people in Spain and beyond were wondering whether this was the beginning of another such moment. Others, noting that Spain was one of the first countries that had kicked off the great democratic wave in the 1970s, found the protest unsettling.

A few months later in 2011, a movement in some ways very similar occupied public spaces in many U.S. cities, calling itself the "Occupy" movement. Occupy aroused just as much controversy, enthusiasm, bafflement, and hostility as did its Spanish predecessor. A year and a half later it was the turn of Turkey, a country that many scholars judged to have significantly democratized in recent years. Then Brazil. Enormous protests under military rule in the mid-1980s had hastened the ending of military rule there, one of the major episodes in that decade's return to civilian authority and democracy all over Latin America. Democracy brought varied movements, as always, with varied reactions, also as always. In speaking for some of those most marginalized throughout Brazilian history, the Movement of Landless Workers seemed to some a deepening of democracy and to others a threat to it.[1] Then to the surprise of Brazilians in the summer of 2013, huge numbers of protestors were raising signs and chanting slogans passionately criticizing how Brazilian democracy was working. So early in the twenty-first century there have continued to be dramatic movements calling for democracy in places that do not have very much, but also critical movements within more democratic countries as well. In this chapter we will explore some of the challenges democracy confronts in the twenty-first century and will try to understand why there are significant democratic protest movements in countries that already have had long democratic histories.

Recapitulation

Social movements are likely to appear periodically with great force, especially under governments making democratic claims. An important consequence is that the meaning of democracy is itself subject to change. During the more than two centuries that we have been considering, some older sources of conflict have survived despite economic and political transformations. But at the same time, new ways for people to organize and mobilize and new bases on which people identify with other people have generated some newer conflicts.

Technological change continues to regroup people in new ways. Workplaces get larger or smaller as those who control the new technologies search for profitable ways to put them to use. People migrate from rural to urban places and cross national frontiers and even oceans seeking new opportunities as old ones die. And the structure of the workplace itself keeps changing, as does its geographic location as investors seek new places for their enterprises. Bureaucratization of work routines places many people in the same situation as each other. Economic downturns see people on the move. This has been the case for centuries and continues today. When financial crisis engulfed Argentina between 1999 and 2002 and unemployment rose to near 20 percent, there was a significant migration to Spain. But a few years later, in the wake of the international financial crisis that broke in 2008, Spain experienced even higher unemployment rates, reaching 27 percent in 2013—so people were moving from there to Argentina.

Changing economic roles are complemented by changing political structures. As power has passed from local elites to central bureaucracies, local identities have given way to regional and national ones. The authorities we deal with today are the tax collector, the recruiting sergeant, the police officer, the government inspector, and the welfare worker, all in the pay of central authority. To these agents of the state bureaucracy, we are all alike regardless of which "village" we come from.

Multicultural contacts are now a part of everyday experience—because of the colossal migrations of people induced by economic change or political conflict, the capacity to maintain contacts across oceans through ever more elaborate communications networks, and the increasingly distant orientations of economic and political elites dealing with distant businesses and distant governments. An awareness of other cultures is part of daily life. It also energizes movements for cultural change as people embrace or reject options that seem exciting or threatening. So part of modern life includes "nationalist," "tribal," "traditional," and religiously "fundamentalist" attempts to reembrace an imagined (and sometimes fictive) past.

In this world of transnational and transcultural contact, some hope to borrow admired elements from afar, others hope to create something profoundly new, and still others hope to defend something threatened or even to re-create something valued from the past. Examples of these processes include democratic movements in the late eighteenth century and fascist movements in the 1930s, which were inspired by distant examples of success. Conservative movements in the nineteenth century hoped to limit the damage done by the great democratic breakthrough. And women's movements have often fought for a future different from the past or present.

Some movements manage very effectively to fuse appeal to past and future, to the local and the transnational. Chinese students in Beijing in 1989 managed to appeal to the swelling global democratic wave; my colleague Larry Glasco photographed a demonstrator in Tiananmen Square with a sign reading "Democracy World Trend," in English. But the students also carried reminders of a Chinese protest tradition going back to the May 4 Movement of 1919. Were Beijing students who sold T-shirts with the slogan "Democracy and Science"[2] identifying with current world trends, with the modern history of Chinese protest, or with both?

Collective identities will continue to change as workers in rising or declining industries, inhabitants of waxing or waning political entities, and champions of cultural futures or pasts find common cause. There are and will continue to be groups whose interests are not politically represented to their satisfaction. For such groups—whether they are economically marginal guest workers, inadequately consulted businesspeople, or participants in stigmatized subcultures—the attachment to mythic democracy makes the sense of exclusion particularly poignant.

For centuries new communications technologies have been altering the capacity of people to coordinate their actions even when separated in space. We have seen the role of growing literacy and the development of journalism for the history of social movements in the eighteenth and nineteenth centuries, the significance of radio, cinema, and TV in the twentieth. By the early twenty-first century, the proliferation of inexpensive, personally owned electronic devices, from cell phones to computers, and of software permitting near-instant transmission of messages, from email to Twitter, was altering the tactics of movements and governments alike. Cell phone photographs of protestors in one Chinese village were immediately known in others despite the efforts of the state to limit Internet access; images from Tahrir Square were known in Spain, the United States, and other places at once. For their part, governments were doing their best to limit such communication or to monitor it. The U.S. government, in 2013, for example, acknowledged that it had gotten a court order to get all of the telecommunication company Verizon's phone logs, thereby revealing a vast data collection effort to keep tabs on its citizens.[3] Protestors in many places were using their cell phones to guide each other around police barriers; police were using protestors' cell phones as location devices to track them down.

Democratic liberties and contemporary communications technologies permit the disappointed to band together; accountability to electorates encourages political leaders to seek the support of the excluded. The result is continued mobilizations, periodically overflowing available electoral channels. Those who take to the streets and the less adventurous who identify with them decry the fraudulent character (thus far) of democratic claims. Those who resist find democracy (as they understand it) to be threatened. Thus both opponents and supporters of the current institutional approximation of the mythic democratic order defend their positions (and denounce each other) in the name of democracy. For example, in the wave of social protests of the 1960s in western Europe and North America, both those who embraced the politics of the streets and those who greeted it with fear and anger denounced each other as enemies of democracy. The same mutual denunciations happened in the Spanish protests of May 2011. The protestors who camped on the plazas toward the end of an election campaign for parliamentary representatives displayed banners reading "They Don't Represent Us" and called for "Real Democracy—It's Time," but indignant political figures were telling TV audiences that it was the protestors who were in defiance of real democracy as practiced through those elections and in that parliament. We have seen that over the past several centuries, out of such confrontations evolve new forms of participation in political life and new understandings of democracy.

I have attempted in earlier chapters to show some of the creative junctures at which democracy generally came to mean parliaments, near-universal adult suffrage, competitive parties, and so on. At those junctures, issues of control over political figures, rights of participation, and channels for institutionalizing conflict within limits came to the fore. No one can foretell the institutional innovations that may characterize future elaborations of democracy, but it is possible to identify some of the tensions early in the twenty-first century to which such innovations may respond. Underlying much of the ferment were emerging global issues that were posing challenges not only to countries recently democratized but to places where people were proud of long-developing democratic traditions, too.

Transnationalization

Let me briefly sketch a cluster of interconnected processes that seem likely to transform the character of democracy. These processes transcend the boundaries of national economies, national politics, and national cultures.

Today, without leaving their living rooms, people can be culturally plugged into formerly distant places. In the new democracies that had emerged by the 1990s, and in the older democracies as well, people were in touch with words and images from far off. In post-military Argentina, the press was reporting the family scandals of U.S. movie stars. In the wake of communism's collapse in central and eastern Europe, when foreign culture flowed in, some aspects of the previous cultural scene fell into deep trouble. In some countries, Russian-originated programming vanished virtually overnight, and the rising costs of paper led publishers to radically cut back on books targeted at smaller audiences. On one Saturday in Warsaw, in 1993, on the two former government-run television networks, twelve of the sixty-four programs originated in the United States (including every program for kids). On the competing privately owned networks, the proportion of foreign programs was still larger. In any event, Poles with cable television or satellite dishes could watch practically anything shown abroad.[4] By the early twenty-first century, Poles could watch news programs from Germany, soap operas from Latin America, travel shows from Asia, and music programs from the Middle East. And shows from Russia, too.

Simultaneously, the development of new means of communication has made it possible for enormous flows of investment to move almost instantaneously on virtually a global scale. Businesspeople in New York can almost instantaneously respond by telephone and email to economic problems in Mexico. Sophisticated computer programs tell them at once just how all their investments might be threatened by the bad news from Mexico City.

If appropriate, the computers can instantly withdraw resources from Mexico and move them elsewhere, perhaps to Brazil and east Asia. This is not a futuristic, hypothetical scenario, but was already happening by the 1990s and is even more characteristic of the new century. The profound significance of the incredible mobility of capital is that national states now have more limited capacities to shape their own economies. An extra, European twist is that many countries have adopted the euro as their common currency, which means that one important tool used in managing past financial crisis (manipulating the value of the national currency to get a desired mix of imports and exports) is no longer under their control. This was felt very acutely by many citizens in hard-hit countries following the financial crash of 2008, when it became painfully evident in Greece, for example, that the capacity of their own government to fix things was severely limited.

Powerholders' loss of control over an increasingly transnational economy leads some of them to try to develop new, transnational mechanisms of coordination for economic and other issues. The variety of transnational governing structures that we see emerging is a powerful symptom. The European Union that had grown to include twenty-eight countries by 2013 (with further enlargement possible) is the most elaborate to date. It means for the residents of those countries that there is another, very significant, government above their national states. The United States, Mexico, and Canada have entered into a North American Free Trade Agreement. The countries of southern South America have set up a similar common market (Mercosur). The African Union plays a significant role in regional peacekeeping.

Transnational economic institutions play an extraordinary role in channeling the vast flow of global resources. Institutions like the International Monetary Fund and the World Bank control billions of dollars on their own. Even more importantly, they have formidable influence within the transnational financial community. When the IMF approves a loan to some country, multinational consortia of banking institutions and even governments feel investment in that country is a relatively safe bet. Vastly more investment then follows. Of course, if the IMF decides that a country is a poor risk, then that country is threatened with disaster. In the early twenty-first century, almost every country in the world labors to satisfy the requirements of this transnational community of finance. The World Trade Organization can impose significant sanctions on countries whose economic policies violate its notions of what constitute unfair economic practices that give some illegitimate advantage in international trade, and member states, including the most powerful among them—the United States—take this threat seriously.

The division of the world's countries into richer and poorer remains sharp, although there are significant disagreements among scholars about whether the gap is widening or shrinking because there are differences about how it is to be best measured.[5] In the early twenty-first century it was clear that the rate of population growth in the poorer countries was far exceeding the rate in the richer countries, although in many places that rate of growth has been declining. The overwhelming majority of the additional billions of people living on this planet as the twenty-first century advances will be born in poorer countries.[6] The twentieth century was an era of vast population displacement due to economic catastrophe and war, and our new century continues to see extraordinary transnational migrations of people. The richer countries' immigration policies differ enormously, but many who live in North America and western Europe were born elsewhere. Some are permanent residents of the country they have moved to, some have legal but temporary status, some are illegal residents. In fact, despite extensive policing mechanisms and elaborate legislation, millions of people live illegally in the United States.

Some political leaders have endeavored to develop new mechanisms for transnational political action, to control a world that is sliding from their grasp. But other leaders have attempted to keep out the foreign capital, block the new immigrants, or expel the older minorities and limit the inroads of alien cultural practices, in order to preserve something of the national essence in the face of a denationalizing world. On the one hand, a newly denationalized professional elite is emerging, moving among universities, government posts, and international agencies; U.S.-born advisers, for example, poured into post-communist eastern Europe to instruct local politicians on getting a market economy to work properly. But other political figures, not coincidentally, were proclaiming that only a return to purer religious traditions or the removal of the foreigners will permit national renewal. In some countries, advocates of human rights were denounced for spreading alien ideas associated with the European Union or the United States. In some African states or in Russia, for example, advocacy of gay rights was not only denounced as contrary to national cultural traditions but claimed to be associated with foreign plots against national sovereignty.

These forms of transnationalization are not primarily either economic, political, or cultural processes—they are all of them at once. The increasing complexity of transnational economic networks, the declining capacities of national states (in spite of the enormous firepower at their disposal), and the multitude of cultural mixtures, borrowings, innovations, and reactions all interact. But they pose anew the question of the relationship between democracy's legitimating myths and the realities of political institutions.

Awareness of transnationalization in many forms was augmented by a growing sense in many quarters that in the twenty-first century, humanity was confronting some extremely serious problems that were not easy to solve by the national states separately, not even by the wealthiest and most powerful among them. Failure to manage these problems effectively would make the century ahead a grim one for many people. Governments that fail to act effectively will face serious challenges and if those governments are democratic ones such failures could give new strength to antidemocratic movements. In Europe after World War I when democracies and semidemocracies failed to rise to the economic and social crises of the day, powerful antidemocratic movements formed. This is an imaginable twenty-first century scenario if failure continues. But since success in managing these problems will involve concerted action on a transnational scale, success, too, will challenge existing notions of democracy, bounded as these are within the frontiers of the national states. Let us look at some of these challenges and their implications for democracy.

A Small List of Big Questions[7]

1. *Global climate change* requires concerted transnational action if anything ever did. There is no sign that such action is coming in the near future and much reason to doubt that it will be. By the early twenty-first century severe consequences were beginning to be glimpsed: storms of increasing severity too numerous to ascribe to the usual year-to-year fluctuations (like Hurricane Sandy that ravaged U.S. East Coast cities in 2012); challenges to complex ecosystems; resource scarcity as a potential source of warfare by the desperate (probably prefigured by deadly violence in Sudan as some peoples found their traditional livelihoods threatened and moved into places where others were living); the appearance of serious tropical diseases (like dengue) in new locations. This is a profoundly transnational problem. Junk dumped in rivers pollutes the waters downstream across national borders; junk pumped

into the atmosphere circulates worldwide. It has proven extremely difficult to get international cooperation on this partly for fear that some other country will gain advantage in economic competition. In some countries public opinion support for effective action is weak because the dangers seem remote and abstract, and they defy what one expects from everyday experience (the oceans will rise: are you kidding me?).

2. *Threat of economic disruption with rapid flow of investments from place to place.* In 2008, an enormous financial crisis began with the collapse of financial institutions in the United States and rapidly engulfed many countries. In the United States and western Europe unemployment rose rapidly, hitting figures over 25 percent in several countries in Europe. Housing values fell and people found themselves with mortgages worth more than their homes and often laid off from income-providing jobs. Businesses starved for customers as people guarded their reduced incomes. Governments were unable to collect taxes to provide their usual services, since citizens were out of work and businesses out of customers. For all the attention paid to this issue in the press, by dueling political parties, by economists attacking each other's explanations, and by powerholders claiming to be improving things, the world's wealthy democracies were not putting in place effective barriers to the otherwise certain next crisis. Not that the present crisis was resolving itself: For years after the crisis broke, U.S. rates of home eviction and unemployment ran way above normal with no end in sight. In many European countries things were much worse as those countries found themselves trapped within a European Union unwilling or unable to promote effective measures and utterly unable to manage things on their own. Citizens in the wealthy democracies wondered why government policies were supporting the very financial institutions that had triggered the disaster while cutting funding for the services that support people in emergencies and also cutting investments for the future like road and bridge repair, education, public health, and research.

3. *Transnationalized criminality,* trafficking in narcotics and weapons and even human beings, corrupting the civic life of entire countries, increasing the insecurity of everyday life at the same time as governments have been democratizing. We've taken a look at how this has been playing out in Latin America in the previous chapter.

4. The *likelihood of deadly global epidemics* that spread as easily as cheap plane fare permits. AIDS was a warning sign. A serious new disease, it migrated from animals to humans in Africa, then spread around the world beginning in the 1960s with especially devastating effects in poorer countries whose medical systems have no capacity to provide the expensive treatments that were eventually developed. Many worry that the next illness that, like AIDS, migrates from animals to humans may be far easier to contract and far more speedily lethal. In the early twenty-first century, the world was terrified of the possibility of the bird flu that originated in Asia developing the capacity to migrate from human to human. We readily recall the good fortune that the H1N1 flu virus of 2009 was not far more deadly than it proved to be. The only thing that seems certain is that more dangerous disease threats lie ahead.

5. *Nuclear proliferation,* likely to mean, sooner or later, weapons of mass destruction in the hands of criminals, terrorists, vengeful states, or the deranged with money to buy them. In the early twenty-first century, several countries that saw themselves as threatened by significant enemies were trying to acquire at least the capacity to build them and maybe were planning to actually build them, like North Korea, a prospect that will only add to the general threat.

6. *The propensity for globalized capitalism to develop and deploy new tech-nologies with potentially far-reaching destructive consequences in the relentless pursuit of profits,* examples of which we see in the destruction of agrarian traditions through industrialized monocultures, the haz-ardous use of chemicals to increase meat production for market, or the reckless hunt for petroleum on the floor of the ocean. In large areas of the United States, older patterns of farming have been displaced by the vast production of a few crops and the fertilizers and insecticides to sustain this, with unknown long-range consequences. The vast use of antibiotics in large-scale stock-raising has speeded up the develop-ment of drug-resistant microorganisms with enormous perils to human health, exacerbating the risks of global epidemics just described. The relentless search for new sources of energy has led to risky technologies to extract fuels from deep underground or below the sea. The risks (and benefits, too), have border-crossing consequences.

7. *Inequality.* The wealthy democracies have differed notably for decades in the extent of their income inequalities, with Scandinavian countries

having less, the United States more, and other countries in between. Early in the twenty-first century observers noted that the levels of inequality were increasing, very much so in some of them. In the United States, for example, in 1981, the top 1 percent of taxpayers earned 23 percent of all income; in 2005 that number had risen to 37.2 percent.[8] Essentially this means that the wealthiest Americans were getting much wealthier and other households, on the average, were at a plateau or even losing out. Economists have been debating the causes of this reversal of the previous long-term trend toward greater equality.

This pattern, which has led some to speak of a new "gilded age," borrowing from an earlier period in U.S. history of very uneven growth of enormous personal wealth, raises important issues for democracy. If the extremely wealthy are able to use their very much greater political clout to promote policies in their interest alone, for everyone else the quality of the U.S. political system may seem significantly wanting. Public opinion polls were beginning to show that there was a growing belief that government, even in the more democratic countries, primarily serves only a narrow stratum of its citizens. For the United States, for example, a comparison of people's views on a wide variety of issues between 1981 and 2002 revealed that only the views of the upper one-tenth of the U.S. income distribution seemed to be influencing legislation passed by the U.S. Congress.[9] Let us remember that over two millennia ago, classical Greek thinkers were of the view that democracy could only work well if there weren't obviously huge differences in wealth. If there were such huge differences, the despair and envy on the part of the many poor would lead them to revolt and the consequent fear of this prospect on the part of the wealthy and powerful few would lead them to oppression—either way, democracy would not be viable. Are we confident that the wealthier democracies are not heading toward such difficulties? The United States may be the most extreme among the wealthy democracies in this regard, but the trend both toward growing inequalities and citizens' belief that their political system strongly favors the better off is characteristic of other countries as well.

But there is a second form of inequality that is notable, namely, those structures that separate opportunities available to people in different parts of the world. The growing importance of connections across national borders means that people in many countries are aware of considerable differences in the wealth and power of different national states and may find that even a democratic government of their own country does not secure significant influence in shaping the circumstances of their lives. What will the consequences of this be for people's commitments to democracy?

8. Finally, let me note the transnational *flows of people*, which have been posing some very contentious issues within the wealthy democracies and in other places as well. With poorer and richer countries side by side, with more peaceful places accessible from places where lives are threatened by incredible violence, and with richer countries confronting low birthrates and aging and ailing populations, nothing is going to stop people escaping from poverty and violence into western Europe, the United States, or Japan, posing many troubling ethnic, cultural, and other issues that all by themselves challenge the meanings of democracy and raise anew questions of inclusion and exclusion. All over western Europe people are debating whether preserving European democracies means excluding those believed to be different and sometimes deficient in democratic values, or including them by virtue of adhesion to universalistic conceptions of citizenship. And people were debating what some saw as threats to national traditions and identities while others welcomed new ideas and practices. The interplay of exclusion and inclusion is once again a central theme of debate in the wealthy democracies.

If democratic states fail to adequately manage these challenges it would not be surprising to see a revival of arguments that democratically accountable politicians are not capable of acting for the public good. Some of these challenges have the potential to excite plainly antidemocratic movements. In the 1920s and 1930s, when Europe's democratic states failed miserably to relieve the suffering from that era's economic crises, movements to replace democracy with something else gained strength. The ongoing ineffectiveness of governmental policy in many places in confronting the challenge of the deep unemployment triggered by the crash of 2008 may have such a potential. In Greece, especially hard hit, a movement was blaming the political elite, the European Union, the immigrants, and the banks for producing misery among the Greek people and was targeting foreigners for violence.[10]

Or think about the awful possibility that someone, for whatever reason, manages to explode a nuclear weapon against any city anywhere in the world. When terrorists turned four aircraft into flying bombs in the United States on September 11, 2001, the consequence was a stepping up of police practices that previously would have been seen as contractions of democracy, not just in the United States but in many other places as well. Governments expanded their powers to monitor the communications of their citizens, for example, and fearful citizens largely accepted this. In pursuing what was called the War on Terror the United States developed secret courts, tortured prisoners, and enhanced police powers. Now imagine the likely aftermath of even a single nuclear attack, anywhere.

These sorts of challenges to democracy, stemming from failure—failure to make people feel safe from a wide variety of dangers—are familiar from the past, although no less serious for their familiarity. And these challenges in combination are especially potent. If economic conditions seem bad, foreign immigrants are particularly likely to be seen as a problem rather than an asset, for example. And as in the past, we may see ahead both movements rejecting democracy and movements to deepen democracy, movements to junk it and movements to fix it. But the deeper point here is that even success at managing these transnational challenges will raise questions about democracy.

The very development of effective mechanisms for dealing with these transnational issues will increase the presence of transnational institutions in people's lives even more than they already are. The growing significance and visibility of transnational and global processes, whether economic, cultural, or political, raises some important questions about the kinds of democracy that have been achieved in large parts of the world by the early twenty-first century.

New Democratic Challenges

The new forms of transnationalization already pose several important challenges for claims of democratic government and will do so even more sharply as the presence of the world beyond national borders increasingly impinges on the lives of those within them. While as we have seen, much has changed about democracy since the late eighteenth century, one thing has not—the core notion that the very idea of democracy has to do with the capacity of a defined people on a defined territory to govern itself freely in accord with certain values and practices. But in the twenty-first century transnational processes were raising questions about whether people in separate national states could control the conditions of their lives regardless of whether they had democratic constitutions. Transnational processes were reopening questions about who these people were as well.

Where Are Decisions Made?

The first great challenge arises from limits on the power of national governments to make significant decisions. Decisions increasingly are being made by such regional structures as the European Union, whose bureaucratic officials ("Eurocrats") issue thousands of regulations affecting the economic life of all Europe; the United Nations, which, among many other activities, now oversees the deployment of military force in various places; and a variety of transnational financial institutions, which make decisions of momentous consequence.

None of these institutions is particularly democratic. The European Parliament, the legislative component of the European governing structure, is a very weak body compared to the European Union's regulation-issuing agencies. This situation is reminiscent of the weak nineteenth-century parliaments we encountered in Chapter 3. One of the reasons some Europeans are dubious about their own country's membership in the European Union is unhappiness about participating in a nondemocratic structure.

Weak as they are, the democratic elements of the European Union are a good deal more evident than any democratic elements of many other transnational structures. There is at least an elected parliament, however weak. The decision-making apparatuses of the powerful financial networks have no democratic elements at all. The World Bank, for example, is managed by a board of "executive directors"; some of the directors are named by wealthy member countries, and others are chosen by the bank's "board of governors," which is composed of major finance officials of all the member countries. The actual votes of most of the executive directors are not publicly disclosed, so accountability to citizens is nonexistent. The U.S. government is one of a few that release information about the positions taken by the directors they name.[11]

Although more people since the mid-1990s have been living under national governments with some claim to democracy than at any other point during more than two centuries of modern democratic history, the actual power of those states may be slipping away, passing to these emerging transnational structures. The impact of the World Bank's decisions, for example, is often much greater than the impact of many government decisions. Rare is the government that actively defies the World Bank's conditions for access to its financial resources. Two students of the World Bank have concluded that, for many countries, national sovereignty "has become a fiction."[12] Under these circumstances, although a far greater proportion of the people of the world participate in more or less democratic selection of national political leaderships, it is not at all obvious that they have thereby acquired a greater capacity to shape the central policy decisions that affect their lives.

Recall that the great wave of democratization was kicked off in the 1970s in Portugal, Greece, and Spain. Since the great economic crisis that began in 2008, try telling people in those places that since they now live in democratic countries, they are in charge of the critical conditions that shape their lives. You would be laughed at because they know that the European Central Bank, other institutions of the European Union, the World Bank, the International Monetary Fund, and the government of Germany—the most powerful member of the European Union—make decisions that are more important for daily life in Greece and Spain than those made by their own democratic governments. Some may ask what democracy is worth or even go beyond asking to form antidemocratic movements, as was happening in Greece. But others may ask whether this state of affairs is really democracy and some may go beyond asking to form movements aiming at improving democratic institutions, as was happening in Spain, and Greece, too.

In this most recent wave of democratizations, national governments are sometimes developing political practices that are adaptations to the great power lodged in these transnational networks. Let us consider the recent democratizations in Latin America. In the early twenty-first century, every country in Central and South America has an elected civilian government, and coups, even the threat of coups, have become far less common than in that region's past. (In Honduras in 2009, however, rather than await the results of an imminently scheduled election, the army deposed the president.)

Yet what is the character of these newly democratized (or redemocratized) countries? As a rough generalization, one may say that elected parliaments in these countries are engaging in considerable debate on issues that are also discussed daily in the knowledgeable, free press; that parties are freely campaigning for office; and that elections are often more honest than in the past.

However, on critical issues of economic policy, already by the 1990s in some places observers noted the country's president often ruling by decree rather than by submitting an economic plan to his country's parliament. Often the presidential plan was formulated by an economic team composed of technical experts with little involvement in party politics but with great sympathy for the economic ideas that underpin the decision making of the powerful transnational financial institutions. Indeed, key members of the president's economic team may have been selected with an eye at least as much on pleasing the International Monetary Fund as appealing to an electorate. The record holder in this particular style of governing seems to have been Argentina's President Carlos Saúl Menem, that country's president in the 1990s, who issued more than three hundred emergency decrees.[13] Some of his critics suggested that Menem used his decree powers even when he would have won in Congress without them, to clearly demonstrate who was the boss.

The tendency toward expanding presidential powers was continuing into the new century. In some cases this would pit a president whose claims to represent poorer, indigenous, or marginalized people had paid off in impressive electoral victories against an opposition claiming that democratic liberties were being endangered by that president. These conflicts could grow very tense, as in Venezuela in 2014 when opposition movements and government supporters confronted each other in the streets in many parts of the country over several increasingly violent months.

Over time observers could notice that countries in Latin America were not all going the same way. Brazil provided effective programs to expand access to education and public services to its poorer citizens. Venezuela defied Washington. Several countries moved to more fully incorporate their darker-skinned citizens, symbolized by the election as president of Peru of Evo Morales. And other countries in the region were trying out new ideas about democracy. As social movements in several Latin American countries pressed with increasing success for rights for the indigenous peoples who have been marginalized for centuries, they also brought new ideas about how to practice democracy, drawing on indigenous ideas and practices. They commonly stressed new mechanisms for participation.[14] Brazil developed "participatory budgeting" in which assemblies of local citizens—everyone is welcome—after much discussion, made real decisions about municipal spending, something well beyond asking ordinary people to speak up as input into decisions made by governing authorities. So some Latin American countries cannot be described as just borrowing democratic practices from elsewhere. They were inventing new practices. Some countries were practicing democracy more or less like western Europe even as things were working poorly in others. In some places democracy was contracting again as elected presidents managed to amass more power and weakened parliamentary or judicial institutions; in others some new ideas about how to practice democracy were being put into action.

Regardless of the precise style of decision making, the challenge of re-creating democracy in the emerging world of transnational decision making is a serious one. But there are opportunities as well.

Opportunities to Reinvent Democracy

In earlier chapters I suggested that, while growing state power in late eighteenth-century Europe was reorienting the focus of popular protest from local concerns to national governments, transformations in communications technology were increasing capacities for large-scale and prolonged social mobilization. Today's newer technologies permit contact among persons in ever-shifting networks on a multicontinental scale. I can send a copy of this book electronically to interested people in eastern Europe or Australia a great deal faster than it will be distributed in bookstores. The possibilities of rapid transnational flows of information and sympathetic identification with distant people are no doubt much greater in our era of email, Twitter, Facebook, and the other, proliferating new technologies than ever before.

One sign of the significance of flexible means of communication is the discomfort of nondemocratic regimes with the prospect of people being able not only to inform themselves but to organize themselves. The former communist regimes of central and eastern Europe were sometimes noted for the limited development of their telephone networks. In the early twenty-first century, the remaining states ruled by communist parties, like China, were similarly and deeply ambivalent about the proliferation of personal computers. So were some other nondemocratic regimes. Without such technology, their powerholders plainly see a bleak economic future. But with such technology, individuals can hook into foreign news sources, communicate with others outside the country on all sorts of matters, and develop computer-linked opposition networks within their countries. As a sign of things to come, when Iranian protestors known as the "green movement" challenged their government in 2009, and again when in many Arab countries the huge wave of protests known as the

Arab Spring was launched at the end of 2010, protestors' use of the new electronic technologies was widely noted, including by the governments of Iran and Egypt, who tried to shut them down. As movements are learning how to use the new tools, governments are working on eavesdropping and blocking technologies. Of course, such new communications mechanisms will be used by, and will shape, new antidemocratic movements as well.

Another very favorable circumstance in the current conditions is previous experience with democratization. The democratic models of legitimacy still run strong, however eroded in practice they are by the shift in power away from the national states. A great deal of public opinion research in countries of recent democratization from the 1970s on shows that in most places people in formerly communist Europe, Latin America, Asia, and Africa say that democracy is the way to go. This does not mean that they are satisfied with the democracy they actually experience in their countries, but it does say that they do not favor a return to previous forms of authoritarian rule or the creation of some new form of authoritarianism.

Thus the new transnational institutions may be facing a legitimacy problem. Public opinion polls have been showing for some time that Europe's citizens are critical of Eurocrats' unresponsiveness to the wishes of Europe's citizens. Such feelings intensified dramatically with the financial crisis that began in 2008 and led to severe and widespread hardship for many Europeans. Such feelings have slowed enactment of the hopes for a deeper European unification that were common two decades earlier, or perhaps ended them altogether. Might one anticipate a recapitulation of Europe's nineteenth-century struggles over democratization on a larger scale, in which the power of the European Parliament in Strasbourg in relation to the European bureaucracy becomes a central point of contention? Strategic openings for democratization within the networks of transnational financial decision making may be far less obvious, but social movements in the past have been very creative in exploiting improbable opportunities.

When I was writing the first edition of this book in the early 1990s it seemed important to point out that despite such potential, social movement action still seemed largely confined to attempts to influence national centers of decision making—even within western Europe, which has visible and significant transnational governing structures. Europeans were generally attempting to alter the policies of the European Union by pressuring their own national governments to take some position within the European Union much more often than they were organizing across borders to directly challenge the key institutions of the European Union itself. There were some important exceptions. For example, the human rights movement tended to be organized transnationally. Amnesty International was organizing people in letter-writing and petitioning campaigns directed at halting torture in countries other than their own. The environmental movement had an important transnational component as well, and the same could be said of the women's movement.

But these trends have continued to grow. Many movements are now addressing transnational issues. Consider for a moment the very notion of "human rights." During that late eighteenth-century revolutionary explosion that kicked off the modern era of struggles for democracy, the French National Assembly in 1789 proclaimed a famous "Declaration of the Rights of Man and Citizen," whose very title suggested that it was hard to distinguish what were the Rights of Man (and Woman) everywhere from what were the rights to be accorded the citizens of one country. The French Revolution was happening at a moment in which people were increasingly thinking beyond what sorts of rights one had as an inhabitant in a particular village or as a member of a particular guild or as a member of a particular legal order (like the Nobility). They were asking what rights one must have simply as a citizen of France or as a member of a large category, like "Women." Some women, in fact, produced a "Declaration of the Rights of Woman and of Women Citizens." In our own era of transnational connection, for many people the question of what are one's rights as a fellow citizen of a particular country (like the United States) is now clearly different than what rights one ought to have regardless of where one happens to be born or reside. The modern human rights movement is making an appeal across borders to our common humanity.

Some movements are therefore addressing the transnational structure of inequalities. To take one very prominent example, more than 15,000 activists from many countries met in Brazil in 2001 to call for change in world structures of wealth and power with the optimistic slogan "Another World Is Possible" and named themselves the World Social Forum. They not only continue to meet periodically in different countries but have inspired dozens of regional, national, and local gatherings of activists (including a U.S. Social Forum), acting as a mechanism to exchange ideas and strategies for challenging transnational inequalities and to serve as a catalyst for new movements. Their discussions raise important questions about what democracy could and should mean in our global age.[15]

Who Belongs?

If the transnational structure of decision making poses one sort of challenge for claims of democratic legitimation, issues of collective identity pose another. We have seen a long series of struggles over who is to be fully included in political life within a democratic political order, powerfully symbolized by conflict over the right to vote. It is probably fair to say that in the early twenty-first century, claims of democracy imply that the electorate includes virtually all adult citizens. No one yet proposes denying that a state is democratic because it excludes small numbers of convicted criminals or all children, although the age of attaining the right to vote varies. (The United States is unusual in the large numbers denied the vote because they are convicted felons, a condition that in some states endures virtually for life. Since the great expansion of the prison population that began in the 1980s, this has been a very large number of people—5.85 million in 2010.[16])

This broad consensus is by no means the end of struggles over the right to participate, for the question of who is a citizen of what is being reopened in a very big way. The equation of "nationality" with "citizenship" is the crux of the matter. Let's connect this important subject with one of the classic themes of democratic ideology developed in Chapter 3: the conception of popular sovereignty. Such a conception became transformed into the practical question of who, precisely, were the sovereign "people" and how was their "sovereignty" demonstrated. By identifying a portion of those in some territory as citizens with political rights and by identifying as one of the central rights the right to vote, the issue seemed solvable—once it was agreed who were the citizens.

The claim that, ideally, the citizenry were a group whose common heritage made of them a nation was one sort of abstract answer. To each nation a state, and within each state one nation: in a world thus organized, distinct peoples could democratically rule distinct states. When Woodrow Wilson was promoting democracy, he was simultaneously promoting national sovereignty. In the wake of World War I, he proposed breaking up the Austro-Hungarian Empire along supposedly national lines. The Ottoman Empire also would be dismantled, with its Arab dominions severed and the frontier between Greece and Turkey redefined. The successful secession of Finland, Latvia, Lithuania, and Estonia from the Russian Empire could easily be accommodated within this framework. Poland was formed out of territories previously held by Russia, Austria, and Germany. Thus the state became but half of a newer concept, the nation-state.

Nation-states are, however, almost entirely mythical. The British Isles comprise at least four very distinct national identities (English, Irish, Scottish, Welsh), Spain a like number. The United States (a phrase whose odd singular use of a plural noun is symptomatic) is full of hyphenated, multiple self-identified groups. And what of Canada? Switzerland? Belgium? the former Soviet Union? The notion that states and nations should correspond has produced endless suffering for those subject to expulsion, coerced reidentification, diminished rights, or death. It has also added a democratic rationale to interstate warfare, because state boundaries rarely coincide with national identities. There are Serbs in Croatia, Hungarians in Romania, and so on. Moreover, new identities are formed out of social struggles. The pressures of labor migration in a world of vast differences between richer and poorer places induces millions of people born in Mexico to live and work in the United States, millions born in Arabic-speaking North Africa to live and work in France, millions of Turks to live and work in Germany. About one-fifth of those who live in Switzerland are noncitizen "guest workers" and their families. In addition, the extraordinary destructiveness of modern warfare continually uproots vast numbers of refugees and the more prosperous countries have developed complex policies for those seeking asylum.

The rich capacity of human beings to define and redefine themselves makes all labels too simple and all attempts to align territory and nationality subject to new challenges from aggrieved minorities. Some of the North Africans in France speak Berber, not Arabic; some German "Turks" call themselves Kurds. Imagine a breakup of Britain aimed at giving states to English, Scots, and Welsh, something actively promoted by some. Where do the Cornish fit in? And what of the divisions between lowland and highland Scots?

Questions of who "belongs" create a good deal of tension when "the people" are supposed to rule. These tensions are not easily resolvable. For example, although Arabs with Israeli citizenship, a significant minority, have a right to vote in Israel's parliamentary elections, no Israeli government makes crucial decisions on national security issues if it will depend for a majority on the votes of Arab deputies in Parliament. In richer countries, the presence of millions of noncitizens means that the "sovereign people" excludes significant numbers of the resident population.

In countries with strong traditions of identifying the state with a nation, democratization may lead the majority group to press for the eviction of minority groups held to be inappropriate bearers of the rights of citizen-nationals;

reactive, defensive movements for autonomy on the part of the threatened minorities may follow. Or movements advocating more rights or even independence for some region may galvanize a reactive assertion of its own identity by dominant groups. In the early twenty-first century, for example, a significant movement for sovereignty in Scotland, for centuries a part of Great Britain, was met in England by increased display of English flags, previously far less likely to be on view than the flag of Britain. In 2014, a long-debated referendum on the possibility of Scottish sovereignty was scheduled. These British events were followed closely in other countries where regional sovereignty sentiments ran strong, as in Catalonia in Spain, where regional party leaders announced their own referendum, declared illegal by the Spanish government.

The ferocious warfare that broke out in the former Yugoslavia in the 1990s, to take another example, is in significant measure a product of democratization. In an independent and democratizing Croatia, some Croats wanted to eliminate various guarantees (jobs, for example) for minority Serbs. Their desire was matched by the desire of some Croatian Serbs to have their own state or to join with Serbia.

In this light, it is sobering to note how many governments have constitutions identifying the state with some specific people. The 1990 constitution of democratized Croatia affirms the "right of the Croatian nation to self-determination and state sovereignty," the Slovenian constitution speaks of "the state of the sovereign Slovenian nation," the Macedonian text speaks of the "national state of the Macedonian people."[17]

Beyond constitutions, one might look at national anthems, flags, coats of arms, or holidays for statements of national identity that include some (but exclude other) residents. Israel's national anthem, for example, deals with the history of the Jewish people and, therefore, could hardly constitute a focus of identity for that country's large Arab minority.

The transnational structure of economic, political, and cultural forces that is rapidly emerging may well exacerbate tensions around issues of identity. People may feel their jobs threatened by either impoverished immigrants or distant workers in other countries. They may fear that their country is losing its capacity to determine its own policies in the face of the World Bank or the United Nations. They may resent that local television programming is being invaded by U.S. game shows and Brazilian soap operas. In western Europe, fear of immigrants has been a major part of politics in recent decades; for France's National Front, it has been the most important issue. For the near future, movements to purify the national culture, gain a grip on economic policy, and belligerently assert sovereignty in the world will have powerful appeal in many places.

In the wake of the economic crisis of 2008 and beyond, in parts of Europe reaction against both immigrants and the European Union ran strong. In Greece the crisis was especially severe, with daily life devastated by unemployment and business failure. The governing parties accepted the onerous terms demanded by lenders although these policies produced more unemployment and more business failures. In this climate, the new Golden Dawn movement found support for its claims that the major parties, the bankers, the European Union, and the immigrants were destroying the country; garnered 7 percent of the popular vote in parliamentary elections in 2012; and organized violence against immigrants, sometimes with the complicity of the police. Observers were struck by the resemblance of party symbols with those of the fascist movements of the past.[18] Such movements may easily connect themselves to political visions that are ferociously antidemocratic, particularly in places where democracy can be portrayed as one of the alien imports to be purged from national life.

What's Next?

For all the power of the democratic idea, even the most recent, greatest wave of democratization has not taken hold on the entire planet. Indeed, in each wave, in many countries democratization has been very limited. Explaining why countries have participated to different degrees in this latest wave is a very big question that I have not addressed. But clearly, even in the early twenty-first century, when claims of democracy are more widespread than ever before, democracy is still denounced in some places. These places may constitute nuclei of new antidemocratic movements. The government of prosperous and authoritarian Singapore, for example, has proclaimed itself a social model superior to the corrupt West and has sought international support for its vision of an orderly, wealthy, anti-individualistic state managed by enlightened experts.[19]

As for the many states with democratic claims, they have new challenges to face, as well as a long history of democratization to build on. The oscillating fortunes of democracy over the past two centuries give us insight into the present moment. On the one hand, we have seen an increasing adhesion to the claim of popular rulership and a great deal of inventiveness on the part of reforming powerholders and challenging movements in developing social institutions to embody that claim. We have also seen powerholders succeed in limiting the play of democratic politics while maintaining legitimizing fictions.

We certainly cannot presume that the more wealthy and powerful democratic states invariably support democracy and oppose authoritarian rule beyond their own borders. We saw that U.S. armed forces during World War II and U.S. postwar aid had a major impact on restoring or implanting democratic practices in postwar western Europe and Japan. But we also saw that during the Cold War that soon followed, U.S. support for democracy was a lot less reliable than U.S. support for anticommunism, including anticommunist tyrants. This meant that with the Cold War over, U.S.-backed efforts were far more likely to push for democracy (though not everywhere) during the 1990s, a very favorable circumstance contributing to the enduring character of recent democratic transitions.

With fears of terrorism in the name of Islam after the attacks of September 11, 2001, and the growing challenge of maintaining energy resources demanded by the economies of the wealthy democracies, by the early twenty-first century those wealthy democracies' support for democracy elsewhere were competing with other objectives. In regard to Muslim countries, they were sometimes favoring good relations with tyrants and not rocking the boat rather than supporting potential democratic challengers or pressing established governments for democratic reforms. This was especially so for countries seen as strategic allies—and in light of the great global reach of U.S. strategic concerns, this meant a lot of countries. For example, the United States provided significant resources to the deeply authoritarian regimes in post-Soviet Central Asia, in the countries that were coming to be known as "the stans"—Kazakhstan, Turkmenistan, Uzbekistan, Tajikistan, and the less authoritarian Kyrgyzstan. In return, the United States got some help for its military activities in neighboring Afghanistan.[20] In addition, it would be hard to claim that the extended U.S. military actions in Afghanistan and Iraq that began early in the new century had led to high-quality democratic outcomes. But it is striking testimony to the power of the idea of democracy that the military invasions and occupations of those countries were in part justified by claiming that one purpose was building democracy.

On the one hand, governments on every continent have been claiming a democratic mantle for their rule. On the other, we have also seen that while they may have adopted elections much else is sometimes missing. But let us recall that throughout the history of democracy, when governments have claimed that their authority rests on democratic principles, social movements have frequently seized their opportunity to challenge those in power to make democracy more real. And, in fact, we have seen that in the early twenty-first century, new movements calling for a truer democracy have sprung up in some of the more democratic countries as have movements calling for a more democratic world. But we have also seen in the early twenty-first century that there are states whose leaderships denounce calls for democracy, human rights, Internet freedoms, journalists' independence, freedom of worship, and rights for women or gays as hypocritical attacks on their countries' traditions and sovereignty by western powers attempting to maintain or reassert claims of regional or world domination. Those making such claims include active players in world and regional affairs like Russia and China.

We have also seen significant issues confronting democratic states, and not just newer democracies, and not just in countries with shaky democratic histories, but in those with the proudest of democratic traditions as well. And we have seen that a very big question is whether people will continue to accept that democracy can be thought of as a reasonable way of governing our own national state without also thinking about what a more democratic world might look like, something that may make future discussions of democracy different from those of the past.

Some past issues live on, too. Consider the full political representation of women. Of all legislators sitting in parliamentary bodies worldwide in 1945, only 2 percent were women. By the start of the twenty-first century, that figure had grown sixfold to 12 percent. Since then it has accelerated and in 2013 was up to 21 percent.[21] So women's place in political systems continues to change, but seemed likely to continue as an issue for some time to come.

We have also seen that innovations kept happening in new places, too. It wasn't just the countries that pioneered in the democratic explosion of the late eighteenth and early nineteenth centuries where women's representation was advancing. Early in the twenty-first century, the country with the highest proportion of women as legislators was Rwanda with somewhat over half, well above the numbers in any of the world's wealthy democratic states.

We have seen that in the early twenty-first century movements challenging democracy as it is currently practiced have mounted dramatic protests. The tens of thousands who camped out in public spaces in Spain in 2011 struck a responsive chord with the Spanish public when they challenged the current forms of parliamentary representation. These plaza occupations struck a responsive chord as well in other countries with democratic governments, like Italy, where the political system, too, was the focus of major protest, or Israel, where the core issue was housing, or Chile, where it was about access to education. In each country, large movements of mostly young people occupied public spaces. The U.S. version, the Occupy movement, called attention to the persistent and growing inequalities of wealth and their consequences for U.S. politics. We have also seen the development of movements addressing human rights across national frontiers and movements addressing the global distribution of wealth and power. Our era is characterized by a collision of forces challenging democratic rule and movements for renewing democracy. Not surprisingly it is full of new ideas, ranging from new ways to participate in local decision making (having citizens themselves make major decisions about budgets, for example, as developed in Brazil), to ways of involving citizens in decisions on a wider scale (taking advantage of the possibilities of electronic communication, for example).[22]

There is no crystal ball that works well in the social sciences. It is unclear whether the future will bring new forms of collective action to democratize the transnational structures of decision making, continuing a tradition of reinventing democracy that is now more than two centuries old; whether it will bring more national states with democratic structures but limited power to make many important decisions, emptying democracy of significance; or even whether it will bring new forms of openly antidemocratic practice. Ongoing failure of the world's democracies, including the best established among them, to effectively deal with a broad range of difficult issues may discredit them (it's happened before). Ongoing growth of unaccountable transnational institutions may weaken democratic states, too. And on the other hand new movements are continuing to spring up and new ideas are being offered. Some propose deepening the democracy of the national states. Some propose challenging transnational power hierarchies. Some ask us to rethink what we mean by democracy. (That's happened before, too.) And while we are imagining possible scenarios here's another: the world's established democracies rise to the challenges of our global age, successfully managing to defuse the growing discontent of their own citizens and to present themselves, again, as models of success to people now under authoritarian rule. It is an interesting exercise to try to imagine which of these futures is more—or less—likely.

Democratization has never been just about a particular set of institutions, because the institutions of democracy have been subject to change, because the unending struggles of people for political influence are never altogether containable within institutions, and because hopes for something better and fears of something worse will continue to energize social movements that will surprise us. When governments first began to insist that they ruled on behalf of the people, and the disgruntled claimed that, as part of the people, they had certain rights, a debate began. It has never ended. And it won't.

APPENDIX

THE GEOGRAPHY OF DEMOCRATIZATION

Maps can clarify and suggest new questions. The following maps illustrate some of the themes of this book. A glance at these maps reminds us that democracy involves many different things that have had their own history and geography.

The first map shows that almost every country on this planet today was making some democratic claims by the late twentieth century. Few indeed were the places that did not claim to have "universal suffrage" in the 1990s. But why, one may then wonder, did this particular group of countries not make such claims?

Maps 2, 3, and 4 remind us how recently women attained full voting rights in Europe. The overall picture is of advance, particularly in the period around and immediately after World War I and then again after World War II. An exception: Spanish women gained the vote in the republic of the 1930s, lost it under Francisco Franco, and did not again have it until the 1970s. Map 5 shows which places in the United States took the lead in giving women the vote. What should we make of their locations? Some of these places—Wyoming, Utah, and Alaska—were not even states when women first attained suffrage.

Maps 6, 7, and 8 show something of the spread of constitution writing outside Europe. Why were so many constitutions written in the two decades after World War II?

Finally, maps 9 through 12 show the ebb and flow of democratization over six decades of South American history, a region famous for its pendulum swings, at twenty-year intervals.

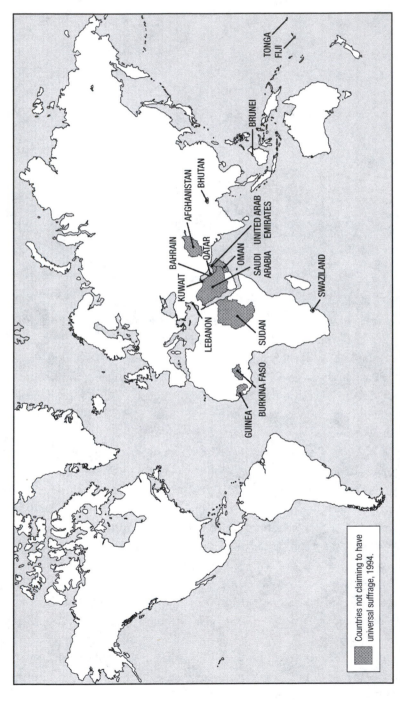

Map 1   Countries Not Claiming to Have Universal Suffrage, 1994

Map 2 Europe: Countries with Full Voting Rights for Women, 1910

Map 3 Europe: Countries with Full Voting Rights for Women, 1925

Map 4   Europe: Countries with Full Voting Rights for Women, 1950

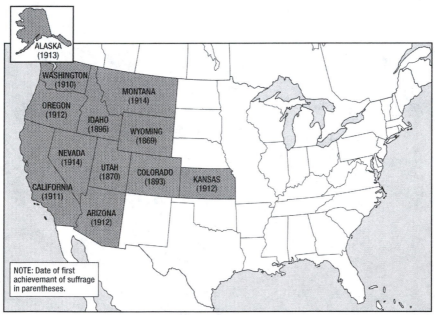

**Map 5   United States: Territories and States
with Full Voting Rights for Women, 1914**

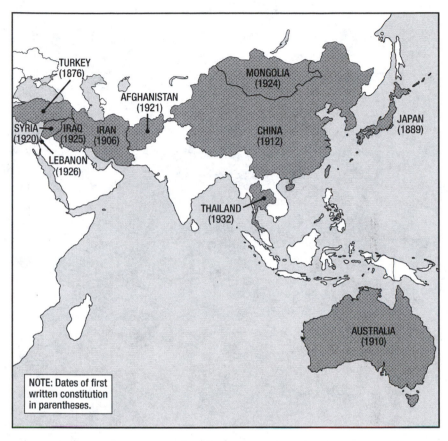

NOTE: Dates of first written constitution in parentheses.

Map 6 Asia: Countries with Written Constitutions before World War II

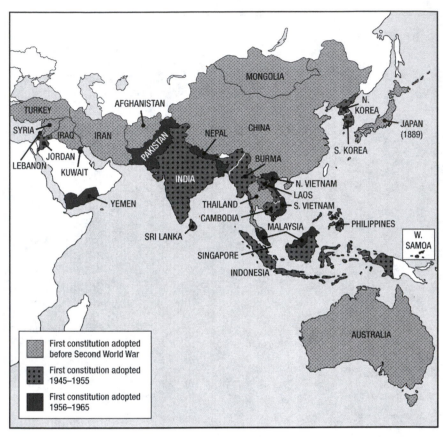

Map 7   Asia: Countries with Written Constitutions by 1965

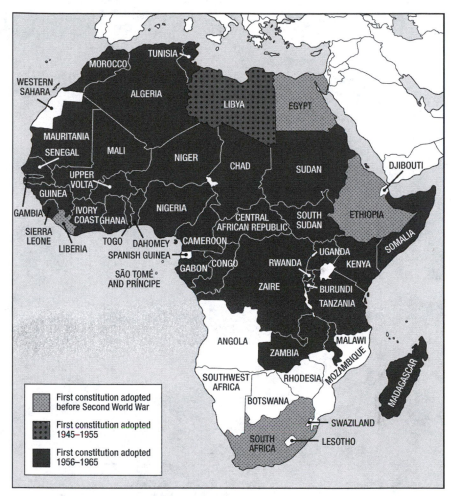

Map 8   Africa: Countries with Written Constitutions by 1965

**Map 9   South America: Elected Civilian Rule
with Credible Vote Counts, 1940**

BRITISH GUIANA
DUTCH GUIANA
FRENCH GUIANA
VENEZUELA
COLOMBIA
ECUADOR
PERU
BRAZIL
BOLIVIA
CHILE
PARAGUAY
URUGUAY
ARGENTINA

Military rule or dominance, incredible vote counts, major parties barred from competing, or suspension of constitution

Government based on credible elections, all major parties able to compete, not subordinate to military, and not suspending constitution

Under European rule

**Map 10   South America: Elected Civilian Rule
with Credible Vote Counts, 1960**

**Map 11   South America: Elected Civilian Rule
with Credible Vote Counts, 1980**

GUYANA
VENEZUELA
SURINAME
FRENCH GUIANA
COLOMBIA
ECUADOR
PERU
BRAZIL
BOLIVIA
CHILE
PARAGUAY
URUGUAY
ARGENTINA

Military rule or dominance, incredible vote counts, major parties barred from competing, or suspension of constitution

Government based on credible elections, all major parties able to compete, not subordinate to military, and not suspending constitution

Under European rule

Map 12 South America: Elected Civilian Rule with Credible Vote Counts, 2000

Sources for Maps

Albert J. Blaustein and Gisbert H. Flanz, *Constitutions of the Countries of the World* (Dobbs Ferry, NY: Oceana Publications, continually updated).

Caroline Daley and Melanie Nolan, eds., *Suffrage and Beyond: International Feminist Perspectives* (New York: New York University Press, 1994), pp. 349–352.

Samuel P. Huntington, *The Third Wave: Democratization in the Late Twentieth Century* (Norman: University of Oklahoma Press, 1991).

Thomas T. Mackie and Richard Rose, eds., *The International Almanac of Electoral History* (Washington, DC: Congressional Quarterly, 1991).

Paul Robert Magosci, *Historical Atlas of East Central Europe* (Seattle and London: University of Washington Press, 1993).

Barbara J. Nelson and Najma Chowdhury, *Women and Politics Worldwide* (New Haven and London: Yale University Press, 1994), pp. 774–775.

Amos J. Peaslee, *Constitutions of Nations* (The Hague: Martinus Nijhoff, 1965–1970).

Thomas E. Skidmore and Peter H. Smith, *Modern Latin America* (New York: Oxford University Press, 1983).

Arnold Whittick, *Woman into Citizen* (Santa Barbara, CA: ABC-Clio, 1979), pp. 303–311.

Howard J. Wiarda, *The Democratic Revolution in Latin America: History, Politics and U.S. Policy* (New York: Holmes and Meier, 1990).

World Factbook, www.cia.gov.library/publications/the-world-factbook/index .html.

Freedom House, annual surveys of *Freedom in the World*, various years, www .freedomhouse.org/reports#.U1K6qFcVC8A.

NOTES

Chapter 2

1. John Markoff and Daniel Regan, "Religion, the State, and Political Legitimacy in the World's Constitutions," in Thomas Robbins and Roland Robertson, eds., *Church-State Relations: Tensions and Transitions* (New Brunswick, NJ: Transaction Books, 1987), pp. 161–182.

2. "Declaration of the Rights of Man and Citizen," in Georges Lefebvre, *The Coming of the French Revolution* (Princeton, NJ: Princeton University Press, 1947), pp. 221–223.

3. Timothy Garton Ash, *We the People: The Revolution of '89 Witnessed in Warsaw, Budapest, Berlin, and Prague* (Cambridge, MA: Granta Books, 1990), p. 136.

4. Göran Therborn, "The Rule of Capital and the Rise of Democracy," *New Left Review*, no. 103 (1977), p. 11.

5. John Thornton, *Africa and Africans in the Making of the Atlantic World, 1400–1680* (Cambridge, MA: Cambridge University Press, 1992), p. 1.

6. David Brion Davis, *The Problem of Slavery in the Age of Revolution, 1770–1873* (Ithaca, NY: Cornell University Press, 1975), pp. 213, 218, 221.

7. Ibid., p. 68.

8. Arturo Valenzuela, "The Origins of Democracy: Theoretical Reflections on the Chilean Case," Working Paper no. 129 (Washington, DC: Woodrow Wilson Center, 1982), pp. 5, 19.

9. Sidney Tarrow, *Power in Movement: Social Movements, Collective Action, and Politics* (New York: Cambridge University Press, 1994), pp. 48–61.

10. Benedict Anderson, *Imagined Communities: Reflections on the Origin and Spread of Nationalism* (London: Verso, 1991).

11. Leopold H. Haimson, *The Russian Marxists and the Origins of Bolshevism* (Boston: Beacon Press, 1955).

12. Maurice Meisner, *Li Ta-Chao and the Origins of Chinese Marxism* (Cambridge, MA: Cambridge University Press, 1967).

13. I am indebted to Marcus Rediker for this information.

14. Aldon Morris, "The Black Southern Student Sit-in Movement: An Analysis of Internal Organization," *American Sociological Review* 46 (1981), pp. 744–767.

15. Aldon D. Morris, *The Origins of the Civil Rights Movement: Black Communities Organizing for Change* (New York: Free Press, 1984), pp. 157–166; Richard Gregg, *The Power of Nonviolence* (New York: Schocken Books, 1966), p. 10.

16. Jeffrey A. Wasserstrom, review of *Power in Movement,* by Sidney Tarrow, *American Historical Review* 100 (1995), p. 474.

17. Giovanni Arrighi and Beverly Silver, "Labor Movements and Capital Migration: The U.S. and Western Europe in World-Historical Perspective," in Charles Bergquist, ed., *Labor in the Capitalist World-Economy* (Beverly Hills, CA: Sage, 1984), pp. 183–216.

18. Tarrow, *Power in Movement,* pp. 31–47.

19. Marcus Rediker, *Between the Devil and the Deep Blue Sea: Merchant Seaman, Pirates, and the Anglo-American Maritime World, 1700–1750* (New York: Cambridge University Press, 1987).

20. John W. Meyer and Brian Rowan, "Institutionalized Organizations: Formal Structure as Myth and Ceremony," *American Journal of Sociology* 83 (1977), pp. 340–363.

21. Paul J. DiMaggio and Walter W. Powell, "The Iron Cage Revisited: Institutional Isomorphism and Collective Rationality in Organizational Fields," *American Sociological Review* 48 (1983), pp. 147–160.

22. Sasha R. Weitman, "National Flags: A Sociological Overview," *Semiotica 9* (1973), pp. 328–367.

23. John E. Boli-Bennett, "The Expansion of Nation-States, 1870–1970," Ph.D. dissertation (Ann Arbor: University Microfilms, 1976).

Chapter 3

1. Germán Arciniegas, *America in Europe: A History of the New World in Reverse* (New York: Harcourt Brace Jovanovich, 1986), pp. 49–71.

2. Quoted in William Brandon, *New Worlds for Old: Reports from the New*

World and Their Effect on the Development of Social Thought in Europe, 1500–1800 (Athens: Ohio State University Press, 1986), pp. 13–14.

3. Bruce E. Johansen, *Forgotten Founders: How the American Indians Helped Shape Democracy* (Boston: The Harvard Common Press, 1982); Anthony Grafton, *New Worlds, Ancient Texts: The Power of Tradition and the Shock of Discovery* (Cambridge, MA: Belknap Press, 1992).

4. Antoine Furetière, *Dictionnaire universel, contenant généralement tous les mots français, tant vieux que modernes, et les termes de toutes les sciences et des arts* (Geneva: Slatkine Reprints, 1970 [1690]).

5. Steven Muhlberger and Phil Paine, "Democracy's Place in World History," *Journal of World History* 4 (1993), pp. 23–45.

6. John Dunn, *Setting the People Free: The Story of Democracy* (London: Atlantic Books, 2005), p. 211.

7. Benedict Anderson, *Imagined Communities: Reflections on the Origins and Spread of Nationalism* (London: Verso, 1991).

8. George Rudé, *Wilkes and Liberty: A Social Study of 1763 to 1774* (Oxford: Oxford University Press, 1962); Sidney Tarrow, *Power in Movement: Social Movements, Collective Action, and Politics* (New York: Cambridge University Press, 1994), pp. 67–68.

9. Robert R. Palmer, *The Age of the Democratic Revolution: A Political History of Europe and America, 1760–1800,* vol. 1 (Princeton, NJ: Princeton University Press, 1959), p. 18.

10. Friedrich Donath and Walter Markov, eds., *Kampf um Freiheit: Dokumente zur Zeit der nationalen Erhebung, 1789–1815* (Berlin: Verlag der Nation, 1954), p. 47.

11. Timothy E. Anna, *The Mexican Empire of Iturbide* (Lincoln: University of Nebraska Press, 1991), p. 76.

12. Neill Macaulay, *Dom Pedro: The Struggle for Liberty in Brazil and Portugal, 1798–1834* (Durham, NC: Duke University Press, 1986), p. 132.

13. John Cannon, *Parliamentary Reform, 1640–1832* (Cambridge, MA: Cambridge University Press, 1973), p. 30.

14. T. B. Macaulay, speech of March 2, 1831, in J. B. Conacher, *The Emergence of British Parliamentary Democracy in the Nineteenth Century: The Passing of the Reforms Acts of 1832, 1867, and 1884–5* (New York: Wiley, 1971), p. 25.

15. Quoted in Michael Brock, *The Great Reform Act* (London: Hutchison University Library, 1973), p. 187.

16. Quoted in ibid., p. 255.

17. Walter Bagehot, *The English Constitution* (London: Collins, 1867).

18. Quoted in Gordon S. Wood, *The Creation of the American Republic, 1776–1787* (New York: Norton, 1969), p. 168.

19. Marchette Chute, *The First Liberty: A History of the Right to Vote in America, 1619–1850* (New York: Dutton, 1969), pp. 308–310.

20. Merrill D. Peterson, ed., *Democracy, Liberty, and Property: The State Constitutional Conventions of the 1820s* (Indianapolis: Bobbs-Merrill, 1966), p. 137.

21. Alexis de Tocqueville, *Democracy in America,* vol. 1 (New York: Knopf, 1945), p. 359.

22. Robert J. Dinkin, *Voting in Revolutionary America: A Study of Elections in the Original Thirteen States, 1776–1789* (Westport, CT: Greenwood Press, 1982), p. 42.

23. Garry Wills, *Inventing America: Jefferson's Declaration of Independence* (Garden City, NY: Doubleday, 1978).

24. Karol Lutostański, *Les Partages de la Pologne et la lutte pour l'indépendance* (Lausanne and Paris: Payot, 1918), pp. 139–140.

25. Paul Drake, *Between Tyranny and Anarchy. A History of Democracy in Latin America, 1800–2006* (Stanford, CA: Stanford University Press, 2009), p. 65.

26. Gordon Wood, *The Radicalism of the American Revolution* (New York: Knopf, 1992).

27. Leon F. Litwack, *North of Slavery: The Negro in the Free States, 1790–1860* (Chicago: University of Chicago Press, 1961), p. 75.

28. Quoted in Chilton Williamson, *American Suffrage from Property to Democracy* (Princeton, NJ: Princeton University Press, 1960), p. 232.

29. Ibid., pp. 242–259.

30. Benjamin Quarles, "Frederick Douglass and the Women's Rights Movement," *Journal of Negro History* 25 (1940), pp. 35–44.

31. Elizabeth Cady Stanton, Susan B. Anthony, and Matilda Joslyn Gage, eds., *History of Woman Suffrage,* vol. 2: *1861–76* (New York: Arno Press, 1969), p. 267.

32. Quoted in Richard J. Evans, *The Feminists: Women's Emancipation Movements in Europe, America, and Australasia, 1840–1920* (New York: Barnes and Noble Books, 1977), p. 49.

33. Ibid., pp. 48–49.

34. Arturo Valenzuela, "The Origins of Democracy: Theoretical Reflections on the Chilean Case," Working Paper no. 129 (Washington, DC: Woodrow Wilson Center, 1982), p. 5.

35. Paul Drake, *Between Tyranny and Anarchy. A History of Democracy in Latin America, 1800–2006* (Stanford: Stanford University Press, 2009).

36. Robert A. Scalapino, *Democracy and the Party System in Pre-War Japan: The Failure of the First Attempt* (Berkeley: University of California Press, 1953), pp. 45, 50, 56.

37. Marc Szeftel, *The Russian Constitution of April 23, 1906: Political Institutions*

of the Duma Monarchy (Brussels: Editions de la Librairie Encyclopédique, 1976), p. 396.

38. Evans, *Feminists,* p. 19.

39. Gordon S. Wood, *The Radicalism of the American Revolution* (New York: Knopf, 1992), pp. 229–270.

40. Philip S. Foner, *The Life and Writings of Frederick Douglass,* vol. 2: *Pre–Civil War Decade 1850–1860* (New York: International Publishers, 1950), p. 192.

41. Paul Finkelman, *Garrison's Constitution: The Covenant with Death and How It Was Made,* www.archives.gov/publications/prologue/2000/winter/garrisons-constitution-1.html (accessed February 23, 2013).

42. James Bryce, *The American Commonwealth,* vol. 2 (London and New York: Macmillan, 1889), p. 863.

43. Walt Whitman, "Election Day, November, 1884," in *Leaves of Grass: Comprehensive Reader's Edition,* ed. Harold W. Blodgett and Sculley Bradley (New York: New York University Press, 1965 [1892]), p. 517.

44. Nader Sohrabi, "Historicizing Revolutions: Constitutional Revolutions in the Ottoman Empire, Iran, and Russia, 1905–1908," *American Journal of Sociology* 100 (1995), pp. 1383–1447; Charles Kurzman, *Democracy Denied, 1905–1915: Intellectuals and the Fate of Democracy* (Cambridge, MA: Harvard University Press, 2008).

Chapter 4

1. Katherine Bowie, "Women's Suffrage in Thailand: A Southeast Asian Historiographical Challenge," *Comparative Studies in Society and History* 52, no. 4 (2010), pp. 708–741.

2. John Fitzmaurice, *The Politics of Belgium: Crisis and Compromise in a Plural Society* (New York: St. Martin's Press, 1983), p. 28.

3. Frederick E. Hoxie, *A Final Promise: The Campaign to Assimilate the Indians, 1880–1920* (Lincoln: University of Nebraska Press, 1984), pp. 231–233.

4. Samuel Huntington, *The Third Wave: Democratization in the Late Twentieth Century* (Norman: University of Oklahoma Press, 1991), p. 26.

5. Ithiel de Sola Pool, *Symbols of Democracy* (Stanford, CA: Stanford University Press, 1952), p. 67.

6. Jarbas Medeiros, "Introducão ao Estudo do Pensamento Político Autoritário Brasileiro, 1914/1945.1: Francisco Campos," *Revista de Ciência Política* 17, no. 1 (1974), p. 73.

7. Julian Go, "Modeling the State: Postcolonial Constitutions in Asia and Africa," *Southeast Asian Studies* 39, no. 4 (2002), pp. 557–584.

8. Thomas Paine, *The Complete Writings of Thomas Paine,* vol. 1 (New York: Citadel Press, 1969), p. 378.

9. Robert Craig Brown and Ramsay Cook, *Canada, 1896–1921: A Nation Transformed* (Toronto: McClelland and Stewart, 1974), pp. 271, 298.

10. Gary C. Stein, "The Indian Citizenship Act of 1924," *New Mexico Historical Review* 47 (1972), p. 264.

11. Caroline E. Daley and Melanie Nolan, *Suffrage and Beyond: International Feminist Perspectives* (New York: New York University Press, 1994), pp. 349–350.

12. Beverly Silver, "World-Scale Patterns of Labor-Capital Conflict: Labor Unrest, Long Waves, and Cycles of World Hegemony," *Review* 18 (1995), pp. 162–169.

13. Alfred Stepan, *The Military in Politics: Changing Patterns in Brazil* (Princeton, NJ: Princeton University Press, 1971), pp. 123–133.

14. Arturo Valenzuela, *The Breakdown of Democratic Regimes: Chile* (Baltimore: Johns Hopkins University Press, 1978), pp. 48–49, 56–57, 120.

15. Miklós Haraszti, *A Worker in a Worker's State* (New York: Universe Books, 1978).

16. Huntington, *Third Wave,* p. 33.

17. Susan George and Fabrizio Sabelli, *Faith and Credit: The World Bank's Secular Empire* (Boulder, CO: Westview Press, 1994).

18. "Closing the Book on One-Man Rule," *New York Times,* June 21, 1994, p. A9.

19. Quoted in Mark Tessler and David Garnham, "Introduction," in David Tessler and Mark Garnham, eds., *Democracy, War, and Peace in the Middle East* (Bloomington: Indiana University Press, 1995), p. ix.

20. Quoted in Shukri B. Abed, "Islam and Democracy," in David Tessler and Mark Garnham, eds., *Democracy, War, and Peace in the Middle East* (Bloomington: Indiana University Press, 1995), p. 127.

Chapter 5

1. Mario Solorzano, "Centroamerica: Democracia de fachada," *Polemica* 12 (1983).

2. "'Motor Voter' Program Works, Especially for Third-Party Rolls," *New York Times,* March 27, 1995, p. A8; Frances Fox Piven and Richard A. Cloward, *Why Americans Still Don't Vote and Why Politicians Want It That Way* (Boston: Beacon Press, 2000).

3. Paul F. Bourke and Donald A. DeBats, "Identifiable Voting in Nineteenth-Century America: Toward a Comparison of Britain and the United States before the Secret Ballot," *Perspectives in American History* 11 (1977–1978), pp. 269–270.

4. Alain Rouquié, "Clientelist Control and Authoritarian Contexts," in Guy Hermet, Richard Rose, and Alain Rouquié, eds., *Elections without Choice* (New York: Wiley, 1978), p. 19.

5. Juan J. Linz, "Non-Competitive Elections in Europe," in Guy Hermet, Richard Rose, and Alain Rouquié, eds., *Elections without Choice* (New York: Wiley, 1978), p. 60.

6. www.opensecrets.org/news/2013/01/new-congress-new-and-more-wealth .html (accessed January 27, 2013).

7. http://elections.nytimes.com/2012/campaign-finance (accessed January 27, 2013).

8. Max Farrand, ed., *The Records of the Federal Convention of 1787,* vol. 1 (New Haven, CT: Yale University Press, 1966), p. 134.

9. For example, James Madison, "Federalist No. 10," in Jacob E. Cooke, ed., *The Federalist* (Middletown, CT: Wesleyan University Press, 1961), p. 61.

10. Antifederalist quotes from Gordon S. Wood, *The Creation of the American Republic, 1776–1787* (New York: Norton, 1972), pp. 513–514.

11. John Tagliabue, "A Bitter Debate over Italy's Fininvest," *New York Times,* May 3, 1994, p. Dl.

12. It is for this reason that students of Central America have been especially fond of speaking of facade democracy: the democratic procedures of selecting officials may be real enough, but power has often not been in their hands.

13. Charles C. Cumberland, *Mexican Revolution: Genesis under Madero* (Austin: University of Texas Press, 1952), pp. 47–48.

14. Samuel Huntington, *The Third Wave: Democratization in the Late Twentieth Century* (Norman: University of Oklahoma Press, 1991).

15. Gordon S. Wood, *The Radicalism of the American Revolution* (New York: Vintage Books, 1993).

16. Carl J. Friedrich, *Constitutional Government and Democracy* (New York: Blaisdell, 1950), p. 387.

17. Andrew Abbot, *The System of Professions: An Essay on the Division of Expert Labor* (Chicago: University of Chicago Press, 1988).

18. Leszek Balcerowicz, "The Political Economy of Economic Reform: Poland, 1989–1992," paper presented at the Political Economy of Policy Reform Conference (Washington, DC, 1993).

19. Martin Gilens, *Affluence and Influence: Economic Inequality and Political Power in America* (New York: Russell Sage Foundation and Princeton: Princeton University Press, 2012).

20. Joanna Innes and Mark Philp, eds. *Re-imagining Democracy in the Age of Revolutions. America, France, Britain, Ireland 1750–1850* (Oxford: Oxford University Press, 2013).

21. Quoted in Michael Wallace, "Changing Concepts of Party in the United States: New York, 1815–1828," *American Historical Review* 74 (1968), p. 473.

22. Madison, "Federalist No. 10," pp. 56–57.

23. Quoted in Wallace, "Changing Concepts of Party," p. 487.

24. Thomas Paine, *The Complete Writings of Thomas Paine,* vol. 1 (New York: Citadel Press, 1969), pp. 370–371.

25. Madison, "Federalist No. 10," pp. 61–62.

26. Wood, *Creation of the American Republic,* pp. 593–615.

27. Richard Warren, "The Will of the Nation: Political Participation in Mexico, 1808–1836," paper presented to the Latin American Studies Association (Los Angeles, 1992).

28. Eduardo Posada-Carbó, "Electoral Juggling: A Comparative History of the Corruption of Suffrage in Latin America, 1830–1930," *Journal of Latin American Studies* 32 (2000), pp. 611–644.

Chapter 6

1. Larry Rohter, "In Rural Haiti, 'Section Chief' Rules Despite U.S. Presence," *New York Times,* October 31, 1994, pp. A1, A7.

2. Larry Rohter, "Among Haiti's Poorest, a Lawless Land Rush," *New York Times,* February 19, 1995, p. A8.

3. Laurent Dubois, *Haiti: The Aftershocks of History* (New York: Henry Holt, 2012).

4. Francis Fukuyama, "The End of History?" *The National Interest* 16 (1989), pp. 3–18; and *The End of History and the Last Man* (New York: Free Press, 1992).

5. Larry Diamond, "Why Democracies Survive," *Journal of Democracy* 22, no. 1 (2011), pp. 17–30.

6. www.ted.com/talks/michael_anti_behind_the_great_firewall_of_china.

7. Vincent Boudreau, *Resisting Dictatorship: Repression and Protest in Southeast Asia* (Cambridge: Cambridge University Press, 2004), pp. 84–102; Min Zin and Brian Joseph, "The Democrats' Opportunity," and Mary Callahan, "The Generals Loosen Their Grip," *Journal of Democracy* 23, no. 4 (2012), pp. 104–119 and 120–131.

8. Valerie J. Bunce and Sharon L. Wolchik, *Defeating Authoritarian Leaders in Postcommunist Countries* (Cambridge: Cambridge University Press, 2011).

9. Larry Diamond and Marc F. Plattner, eds., *Democratization in Africa: Progress and Retreat* (Baltimore: Johns Hopkins University Press, 2010).

10. Kathleen Fallon, *Democracy and the Rise of Women's Movements in Sub-Saharan Africa* (Baltimore: Johns Hopkins University Press, 2008).

11. Aili Mari Tripp, Isabel Casimiro, Joy Kweisiga, and Alice Mungwa, *African Women's Movements: Changing Political Landscapes* (Cambridge: Cambridge University Press, 2009), p. 75.

12. Michael Bratton and Nicolas van de Walle, *Democratic Experiments in Africa: Regime Transitions in Comparative Perspective* (Cambridge: Cambridge University Press, 1997); Larry Diamond, *The Spirit of Democracy: The Struggle to Build Free Societies throughout the World* (New York: Henry Holt, 2008), pp. 238–262; Steven Radelet, "Success Stories from 'Emerging Africa,'" *Journal of Democracy* 21, no. 4 (2010), pp. 87–101.

13. Diamond, *Spirit of Democracy*, p. 256.

14. Daniel N. Posner and Daniel J. Young, "The Institutionalization of Political Power in Africa," *Journal of Democracy* 18, no. 3 (2007), p. 128; Staffan I. Lindberg, *Democracy and Elections in Africa* (Baltimore: Johns Hopkins University Press, 2006).

15. Diamond and Plattner, *Democratization in Africa*.

16. "Hungary's Illiberal Turn," special section of *Journal of Democracy* 23, no. 2 (2012), pp. 132–155.

17. Cory Molzahn, Viridiana Ríos, and David Shirk, "Drug Violence in Mexico: Data and Analysis through 2011," Trans-Border Institute, Joan B. Kroc School of Peace Studies, University of San Diego, March 2010, justiceinmexico.files.wordpress.com/2012/03/2012-tbi-drug-violence.pdf (accessed June 12, 2013).

18. Marcelo Bergman and Laurence Whitehead, eds., *Criminality, Public Security, and the Challenge to Democracy in Latin America* (Notre Dame, IN: University of Notre Dame Press, 2009).

19. John Markoff with Amy White, "The Global Wave of Democratization," in Christian Haerpfer et al., eds., *Democratization* (New York: Oxford University Press, 2009), p. 57.

Chapter 7

1. Miguel Carter, "The Landless Rural Workers Movement and Democracy in Brazil," *Latin American Research Review* 45, Special Issue (2010), pp. 186–217.

2. Craig Calhoun, *Neither Gods nor Emperors: Students and the Struggle for Democracy in China* (Berkeley: University of California Press, 1994), p. 243.

3. Charlie Savage and Edward Wyatt, "Verizon Case Offers Glimpse of Vast N.S.A. Surveillance," *New York Times,* June 6, 2013.

4. Thanks to Małgorzata Markoff for these observations.

5. Mitchell A. Seligson and John T. Passé-Smith, eds., *Development and Underdevelopment: The Political Economy of Global Inequality* (Boulder: Lynne Rienner, 2008).

6. Paul Kennedy, *Preparing for the Twenty-First Century* (New York: Vintage Books, 1994), p. 24.

7. Parts of this section appeared in different form as John Markoff, "Democracy's Past Transformations, Present Challenges and Future Prospects," in *International Journal of Sociology* 43, no. 2 (2013), pp. 13–40.

8. Larry Bartels, *Unequal Democracy: The Political Economy of the New Gilded Age* (New York: Russell Sage Foundation, 2008), pp. 11–13.

9. Martin Gilens, *Affluence and Influence: Economic Inequality and Political Power in America* (New York: Russell Sage Foundation and Princeton: Princeton University Press, 2012).

10. William Wheeler, "Europe's New Fascists," *New York Times,* November 17, 2012.

11. Susan George and Fabrizio Sabelli, *Faith and Credit: The World Bank's Secular Empire* (Boulder, CO: Westview Press, 1994), pp. 207, 214.

12. Ibid., p. 159.

13. Noga Tarnopolsky, "Better Than Torture," *New York Times,* May 18, 1995, p. A17.

14. Donna Lee Van Cott, "Latin America's Indigenous Peoples," *Journal of Democracy* 18, no. 4 (2007), pp. 127–142.

15. Jackie Smith, Scott Byrd, Ellen Reese, and Elizabeth Smythe, *Handbook on World Social Forum Activism* (Boulder and London: Paradigm Publishers, 2011).

16. www.soc.umn.edu/~uggen/FD_summary.htm (accessed June 14, 2013).

17. Robert M. Hayden, "Constitutional Nationalism in the Formerly Yugoslav Republics," *Slavic Review* 51 (1992), pp. 657, 659.

18. Jon Henley and Lizzy Davies, "Greece's Far-Right Golden Dawn Party Maintains Share of Vote," *The Guardian,* June 18, 2012, www.theguardian.com /world/2012/jun/18/greece-far-right-golden-dawn (accessed August 11, 2013).

19. Denny Roy, "Singapore, China, and the 'Soft Authoritarian' Challenge," *Asian Survey* 34 (1994), pp. 231–242.

20. Ahmed Rashid, "Why, and What, You Should Know about Central Asia," *New York Review of Books* 60, no. 13 (August 15, 2013), pp. 76–81.

21. Pamela Paxton, Melanie M. Hughes, and Matthew Painter II, "Growth in Women's Political Representation: A Longitudinal Exploration of Democracy,

Electoral System and Gender Quotas," *European Journal of Political Research* 49 (2010), pp. 25–52; Inter-Parliamentary Union (2013), www.ipu.org/wmn-e/world .htm.

22. Graham Smith, *Democratic Innovations: Designing Institutions for Citizen Participation* (Cambridge: Cambridge University Press, 2009).

Index

About the Author

John Markoff is Distinguished University Professor at the University of Pittsburgh. He has published extensively in sociological, historical, and political science journals. His books include *The Abolition of Feudalism: Peasants, Lords, and Legislators in the French Revolution* (1996); *Revolutionary Demands: A Content Analysis of the Cahiers de Doléances* (with Gilbert Shapiro, 1998); and *Economists in the Americas* (with Verónica Montecinos, 2009). His work has appeared in eight languages. He has won awards from the American Sociological Association, the Social Science History Association, and the Society for French Historical Studies.